Violence against Women in Families and Relationships

Violence against Women in Families and Relationships

Volume 2
The Family Context

Edited by
EVAN STARK AND EVE S. BUZAWA

Praeger Perspectives

PRAEGER
An Imprint of ABC-CLIO, LLC

A B C ☷ C L I O

Santa Barbara, California • Denver, Colorado • Oxford, England

Library of Congress Cataloging-in-Publication Data
Violence against women in families and relationships /
edited by Evan Stark and Eve S. Buzawa.
    v. ; cm.
  Includes index.
  Contents: vol. 1. Victimization and the community response —
vol. 2. The family context — vol. 3. Criminal justice and the law —
vol. 4. The media and cultural attitudes.
    ISBN 978-0-275-99846-2 (set : alk. paper) — ISBN 978-0-275-99848-6
(vol. 1) — ISBN 978-0-275-99850-9 (vol. 2) — ISBN 978-0-275-99852-3
(vol. 3) — ISBN 978-0-275-99854-7 (vol. 4) — ISBN 978-0-275-99847-9 (ebook)
    1. Abused women. 2. Family violence. I. Stark, Evan.
II. Buzawa, Eva Schlesinger.
  HV6626.V56   2009
  362.82'92—dc22   2009006262

13   12   11   10   9   1   2   3   4   5

This book is also available on the World Wide Web as an eBook.
Visit www.abc-clio.com for details.

ABC-CLIO, LLC
130 Cremona Drive, P.O. Box 1911
Santa Barbara, California 93116-1911

This book is printed on acid-free paper ∞

Manufactured in the United States of America

Contents

Set Introduction

Evan Stark and Eve S. Buzawa

The first call for shelter in the United States was made to Women's Advocates in St. Paul, Minnesota one afternoon in May 1972. The story of this group of courageous women opens *Violence against Women in Families and Relationships*. As recalled by Sharon Vaughan, a founder of the program and a pioneer in the battered-women's movement:

> The call was … from Emergency Social Services. A worker said a woman was at the St. Paul Greyhound bus station with a two-year-old child. To get a job, she had traveled 150 miles from Superior, Wisconsin, with two dollars in her pocket. What were we expected to do? Where would they stay after two days at the Grand Hotel? One of the advocates borrowed a high chair and stroller and we took them to the apartment that was our office. These were the first residents we sheltered. The two-year-old destroyed the office in one night because all the papers were stacked on low shelves held up by bricks. His mother didn't talk about being battered; she said she wanted to go to secretarial school to make a life for her and her son. She tried to get a place to live, but no one would rent to her without a deposit, which she didn't have…. After a couple of weeks, she went back to Superior, and every Christmas for several years sent a card thanking Women's Advocates for being there and enclosed $2.00, the amount she had when she came to town.

This recollection captures several major themes highlighted in volume 1: the importance of women reaching out to other women, the reinforcing effects of poverty and domestic violence, and the extent to which those who escape abuse are intent on reconnecting with their hopes and dreams for a better life.

The shelter started in St. Paul was one stimulus for a domestic violence revolution that quickly circled the globe, stirring women from all walks of life, of all races, religions, and ages, and in thousands of neighborhoods, to challenge men's age-old prerogative to do with them as they willed. Even as these grassroots movements offered victims options for safety and empowerment that were never before available, they called on their governments to do the same. Importantly, these calls elicited an unprecedented response, almost certainly because women had become a formidable political and economic force. In its scope and significance, the domestic violence revolution is a watershed event in our lifetime.

On the ground, the domestic violence revolution consists of four critical components: the proliferation of community-based services for battered women; a growing sensitivity to how domestic violence affects families and particularly the children who are exposed to this violence; the criminalization of domestic violence and the corresponding mobilization of a range of state resources to protect abused women and their children and to arrest, sanction, or counsel perpetrators; and challenges to the normative values that have allowed men to exercise illegitimate forms of power and control in relationships and families. Although huge obstacles remain to changing cultural mores, these challenges now extend to the popular media, which shape how tens of millions of children and adults interpret the world around them.

Violence against Women in Families and Relationships takes stock of the seismic changes instigated by the domestic violence revolution, devoting separate volumes to its major components: community-based services (Volume 1), the family (Volume 2), the criminal justice response (Volume 3), and popular culture and the media (Volume 4). In addition to describing what happened, two overriding questions link these volumes. How is our world different today than when the domestic violence revolution began? Are abused women and their children better off because of these changes? We also identify the remaining obstacles to eliminating sexual injustice in relationships and families, ask what can be done to remove these obstacles, and identify a host of innovative programs designed to do this. The major conceptual contribution of these volumes is to provide an understanding of abuse that extends far beyond physical violence to the broad range of tactics actually used to coerce and control women and children in relationships.

THE DOMESTIC VIOLENCE REVOLUTION

Our goal is to provide a map of the scope and significance of the domestic violence revolution.

Since the opening and diffusion of shelters, the policies and the legal landscape affecting victims of partner abuse have changed dramatically. Reforms include billions of dollars in federal support for intervention, removing discretion in deciding whether to arrest those who assault their partners, a range of new protections for victims, the burgeoning of a vast network of researchers, specialized and integrated domestic violence courts and prosecutorial approaches (called "dedicated" or "evidence based"), one-stop justice centers, and putting partner abuse center stage in decisions about custody and visitation. In the past, battered women who retaliated against abusive partners hid their abuse, fearing it would provide a motive for their crimes. Today, women accused of crimes against abusive partners can use a "battered woman's defense" and call on a new class of experts to support their claims of victimization. The constitutional rationale for these reforms in the United States is straightforward: under the Equal Protection Clause of the Fourteenth Amendment, women assaulted by present or former partners are entitled to the same rights and protections as those who are assaulted by strangers. In other countries, domestic violence has been identified as violation of basic human rights.

The helping professions have also undergone radical changes in response to the domestic violence revolution. Medicine, nursing, public health, psychology, psychiatry, social work, and child welfare have introduced a range of innovative programs to identify and respond more appropriately to the adult and child victims of abuse. Forty years ago, when Anne Flitcraft asked the director of the emergency medical services at Yale–New Haven Hospital if she could study "battered women" for her medical school thesis, he was puzzled. "What's a battered woman?" he asked. Today, in part as a result of pioneering research by Dr. Flitcraft and hundreds of other scholars, training in the health, mental health, legal, and social service professions would be remiss if it did not include specialized units on domestic violence. Every major health care organization has made domestic violence a priority. Hundreds of hospitals in the United States have protocols requiring that medical personnel identify and refer victims of abuse. In hundreds of communities, once perpetrators are arrested, they are offered counseling as an alternative to jail through "batterer intervention programs." Moreover, several thousand localities now host collaborative efforts to reduce or prevent abuse in which community-based services such as shelters join with courts, law enforcement, local businesses, child protection agencies, and a range of health, education, and service organizations. In dozens of communities, small and large businesses alike have taken initiatives to extend protections from abusive partners to employees or supported broader community-based initiatives.

Never before has such an array of resources and interventions been brought to bear on abuse or oppression in relationships and families. By any conventional standard, the domestic violence revolution has been an incredible success. Politicians across a broad spectrum have embraced its core imagery of male violence and female victimization. As telling is an increasing sensitivity to the portrayal of abused women by the mass media and a growing awareness of how mainstream messages conveyed by sports, popular music, and other cultural media contribute to abusive behavior by males.

Hundreds of thousands of men, women, and children owe the fact that they are alive to the availability of shelters, to criminal justice and legal reforms, and to equally important shifts in research, health services, and popular culture. Just recently, historically speaking, a man's use of coercion to chastise or discipline his female partner or his children was widely considered a right inherited with his sex. This is no longer so.

In 1977, during one of the many incidents when Mickey Hughes assaulted his wife Francine, their 12-year-old daughter Christy called police. He threatened to kill Francine with police present. This seemed like "idle talk," an officer testified at Francine's trial for murder. "He hadn't killed her before; he wouldn't do so now." A few hours after they left, Francine set fire to the bed in which her husband was sleeping and he was fatally burned.

Things have changed dramatically since 1977. Mickey was never arrested, though he had raped Francine on several occasions and assaulted her dozens of times. Not until 1979, as the result of lawsuits in Oakland, California, and New York, were police required to replace their "arrest-avoidance" strategy, respond quickly to domestic violence calls, and presumptively arrest whenever they had probable cause to believe a felonious assault had occurred or when a misdemeanor assault was committed in their presence. Marital rape was still not a crime in 1977, and in New York and a number of other states was not even considered grounds for divorce. In several states, Francine could have gotten an injunction, though police had no role in enforcing these orders, and only if she was married, and only pursuant to a divorce.

Farrah Fawcett portrayed Francine in a TV film version of this story, *The Burning Bed*. In the mid-1990s, when her boyfriend slammed Fawcett to the ground and choked her after an argument at a restaurant, he was arrested, tried, and convicted. By this time, the marriage-rape exemption was largely abolished, police in most areas were mandated to arrest perpetrators whom they believed had committed a domestic violence crime, and courts in most countries were routinely providing a range of protections for abuse victims. On the two occasions that Francine left Mickey to return to her parents, he stalked and harassed her without consequence. Today, stalking is a crime and harassment is widely recognized as a facet of abuse. Aside from her family, Francine had no recourse, no shelter to enter, and no support services. A woman faced with a burning-bed situation today would mount a "battered woman's defense" rather than plead "temporary insanity," as Francine did. The forces of law and order that protected a man's right to "physically correct" his wife in 1977 now target this bastion of male authority for destruction.

Perhaps the most significant change that resulted from the domestic violence revolution involves the portrayal of male violence against women in the media, particularly in film and on TV, the ultimate family medium. As women made unprecedented gains in economic, political, and cultural status after 1960, the hazards that men pose to their wives and girlfriends became a moral compass for the integrity of relationships generally. From Johannesburg to Caracas, from Jerusalem to Dayton, Ohio, young girls understand that no male has the right to lay his hands on them if they do not want him to do so. Well into the 1980s, violence continued to be glamorized as the penultimate test of manhood (the ultimate test remains sexual conquest), as illustrated by the popularity of gangsta rap and *James Bond* and *Rambo* films. But male violence has increasingly been forced to share the stage with images of women as equally capable of using force and of abusive men as purposeful, obsessive, and cruel rather than romantic. Julia Roberts' portrayal of a housewife who kills an abusive husband who is stalking her in *Sleeping with the Enemy* (1991) contrasts sharply with Eleanor Parker's role in the 1955 film *The Man with the Golden Arm* as a wife who sets out to heal her husband (played by Frank Sinatra) while enduring his physical abuse, betrayal, heroin addiction, and mental torment.

Partner violence against women is no longer "just life." And yet, anyone with reasonable sympathies and a passing acquaintance with abuse or current interventions will have a range of questions about the impact of even the most dramatic reforms.

VICTIMIZATION AND THE COMMUNITY RESPONSE

Volume 1 reviews the development, operations, and effectiveness of battered women's programs; the progress of intervention in health; and the interplay of domestic violence with race, poverty, sexual identity, and the changing economic landscape of communities caused by globalization. The core questions addressed in this volume are as follows: what do battered women's programs actually do? Has the "success" of the shelter movement led it to compromise its original ideals? Is the support that advocates provide sufficient to help victims regain their footing? To what extent does help "help"? Or does it actually make things worse by blaming victims for their abuse? Does the medical system need to look beyond physical violence to improve its response? What special problems face lesbian victims of abuse? What unique dynamics are put into play in the experience of abuse by the disadvantages associated with poverty, racism, or deindustrialization? How must intervention change to accommodate these dynamics? Where do we go from here?

THE FAMILY CONTEXT

Volume 2 looks at the ways in which domestic violence shapes family dynamics in general and affects children in particular and at the two major systems responsible for managing these effects: the child welfare system and the family court. How are children threatened by domestic violence and coercive control? Domestic violence is the most common background factor for child abuse and neglect, and it is typically the same man who is abusing the mother who is the source of harm to children. After much prodding, the child welfare system began to address domestic violence. But its first steps were missteps. Instead of protecting mothers and their children, the child welfare system punished them for being beaten. Why did this happen, and what can be done to correct this problem? Family courts have also been pressured to consider domestic violence in custody and divorce cases. But are they doing so? How can the family court reconcile concerns for the safety of women and their children in abusive relationships with the widespread belief that children must have access to both parents after divorce? To what extent are each of the systems confronted by victims of battering and their children sending contradictory messages that do as much to confuse and further entrap them as to provide for their safety? What reforms are needed to set child welfare and family court systems on the right track? And what about the offending fathers? How do they extend their abusive strategies during custody disputes? And what about the movement for "father's rights"? Is it a positive or negative force in this process? Can offending men learn to father more appropriately? How does working with them on fathering affect how they understand and treat the women in their lives? What is at the root of the problems with these systems? Are we dealing primarily with individual bias or something more systemic? How would broadening our understanding of abuse to include the multiple ways in which men subjugate their partners enhance the child welfare or family court response?

CRIMINAL JUSTICE AND THE LAW

From the start, the domestic violence revolution in the United States called on the state to mobilize its justice resources to protect victims and hold offenders accountable for their acts, usually through some combination of arrest, incarceration, and/or reeducation. Volume 3 reviews the revolutionary changes in policy, criminal law, and policing affected by the domestic violence revolution. Severe violence against wives had been against the law for centuries. But it was only in the 1980s, as states passed domestic violence laws and made arrest mandatory in abuse cases, that police, prosecutors, and the criminal courts treated it as a crime. How are these reforms working? Has the domestic violence revolution relied too heavily on criminal justice? Have the changes in policing, prosecution, and criminal law gone too far or not far enough? Are abusive men changed by arrest? Does counseling for batterers work, and, if so, with what kinds of men? How should we understand and respond to partner violence by women or to families in which both partners are abusive?

THE MEDIA AND CULTURAL ATTITUDES

However much the domestic violence revolution may have reformed the helping and justice professions, these changes are unlikely to endure unless the underlying cultural supports for domestic violence are displaced. Prevailing cultural norms reproduce the sex stereotypes that underlie sexual inequality even as women win formal legal equality and make unprecedented gains in education, income, and political participation. Volume 4 maps how these stereotypes are represented and challenged in a range of cultural media, including newspapers, film, women's magazines, video games, and rap. After explaining how the core narratives in a culture shape experience, the chapters in this volume consider what the stories told about sexual violence in these media suggest about how and why violence against women happens; who or what causes it; whether it is the by-product of specific social factors, malevolence, or just "bad luck" for instance; and how it can be ended. How these stories are constructed is as important as what they say. This volume considers the transformative potential of the media, including theater, as well as the role they play in reinforcing the status quo. The closing chapter considers whether community values have, in fact, changed over the course of the domestic violence revolution.

WHAT YOU'LL FIND HERE

An estimated 13,000 books and monographs about domestic violence have appeared since the early 1970s. Digesting and translating this published material are obviously beyond our capacity. Nevertheless, we started this project by scouring this literature for the major trends and cutting-edge ideas about abuse. Next, we reached out to both established scholars as well as to younger researchers doing cutting-edge work. We asked these writers to do three things: tell us *what* has changed; tell us *how* these changes have affected families, particularly the women, children, and men most immediately involved; and speculate about *what is next*. Where are we likely to go, and where *should* we go from here? We welcomed criticism of existing approaches. We are not pushing a particular cause. But if there are new approaches, innovative practices, or changes in policy that would help set things right, we wanted readers to know about them. And we insisted they write for educated readers who have little or no prior knowledge of the subject, not always an easy thing for scholars whose main audiences tend to consist of academics like themselves. The model we suggested was a feature article for the Sunday newspaper. Think of yourself as the expert you are, we told them. This meant limiting notes to direct quotations and controversial statistics. We gave the contributors the option of directing readers to further information likely to be available on the Web or at a public library. Frankly, this charge posed an editorial challenge we had not anticipated.

One might think that summarizing the wealth of research on violence in families would be sufficient. Not so. One of the most insidious characteristics of the type of oppression we address in personal life is that it typically occurs "behind closed doors" and proceeds in ways that are often hidden from outsiders, often including close friends, neighbors, coworkers, and helping professionals. Researchers too have little direct access to victims or offenders and typically meet them or hear their stories only after they call police, come to court, or enter a shelter. Since whether victims report what is happening to them is largely a function of the opportunity to do so as well as the fear of possible consequences, millions of battered women and their children have no contact with police, shelters, courts, hospitals, or child welfare and so never appear in the public spaces where data are collected. Telephone surveys pick up some of this hidden abuse. But the questions asked on surveys are too broad to capture its meaning, contexts, dynamics, or far-reaching consequences. We were less interested in generalities about abuse than in the nuances, the particulars. We are not after sensationalism. But we wanted readers to know battered women as people, to walk in their shoes to some extent, as well as read *about* them. Another problem is that researchers can ask questions only about things they already know are present. A key theme in these volumes is that the images of violence and physical injury that have dominated our understanding of abuse miss an underlying reality of coercion and control in these relationships that can be as devastating as assault and is almost always more salient for victims. The harms caused by these coercive and controlling tactics are rarely recognized, let alone documented, even among those who are able to get help. The fact that so many of those affected are poor or from disadvantaged groups also contributes to their invisibility.

To unlock the knowledge contained in what Yale University political scientist James Scott calls the "hidden transcripts" of these lives, it is necessary to listen directly to the voices of women and children who experience battering as well as to their abusive partners. This means allowing them to tell their stories as they were lived rather than as filtered through the preconceptions we all bring to the field, ourselves included. In addition to chapters that summarize what is known about particular aspects of interpersonal violence, therefore, we have called on practitioners who work or have worked directly with victims, perpetrators, and their children in a variety of settings. A number of the practitioners herein have helped to design or implement imaginative programs. We include authors who have started or worked in shelters, facilitated batterer intervention programs, trained child welfare workers, and directed a state coalition for battered women. We have several chapters by lawyers who have represented battered women and their children in family and criminal courts and other chapters by forensic psychologists and social workers. Several of our authors have translated their research into practice. In a chapter in volume 4, anthropology professor Elaine J. Lawless describes a theater project she started with a colleague and some students at the University of Missouri. Professor Lawless had conducted fieldwork for a book at a battered women's shelter in her community. Feeling dissatisfied with a purely academic presentation of her "findings," she helped students perform the stories she had collected as monologues to stimulate a broad, community-wide discussion about abuse. The presentations not only gave audiences a picture of the abuse going on around them but also opened up a space in which student actors and audience members could tell their own stories about abuse, some of which became part of subsequent "performances," creating a community of witnesses that enhanced the overall safety of women and children in that neighborhood.

A basic premise of the shelter movement is that those who are battered by their partners are the only real "experts" on their experience and that their expertise is the centerpiece of any real knowledge about how abuse unfolds. We have tried to respect this view by interspersing the informational chapters with chapters that rely heavily on women's stories or explain why "storying" domestic violence is so important. If we have succeeded, the topical chapters should dovetail with lived experiences of abuse. Like the Missouri theater project, we hope these volumes help stimulate a broad-ranging conversation and new ways of seeing, listening to, and interpreting what is happening in our midst.

These volumes also have an international dimension, though it is unfortunately limited to English-speaking countries. We include writers from England, Canada, Scotland, and Australia. The authors of these chapters have done groundbreaking work in their particular areas for which there was often no parallel in the United States. For example, the report on child homicides prepared by Hilary Saunders on behalf of Women's Aid Federation England (WAFE) is a stunning model of advocacy that has elicited family court reforms that are long overdue in the United States. But the international focus also reflects the fact that both the grassroots women's movements in these countries and the systemic changes they elicited have grown from a continuing interchange between researchers and practitioners in these nations.

In each of the respects outlined above, this set of volumes is unique—in its breadth, its mix of researchers and practitioners, the emphasis on victim voices, the attempt to weigh changes in popular culture, its international scope, and its focus on what lies ahead.

But our approach will not satisfy everyone.

Most of us initially got involved in the domestic violence field because we hoped to call attention to and ameliorate the injustices suffered by millions of women and children who were being subjugated in their relationships, mainly (but not only) by male partners, and because we found the response to this suffering by the courts, police, hospitals, and other institutions woefully inadequate. From this vantage, behavior is seen as abusive and as meriting public concern if it involves coercive and/or controlling behavior whose primary intent and/or consequence is to hurt, threaten, frighten, or control a partner. Notice the broad understanding of abuse.

From the day we welcomed the first victims to our shelters, our strongest feelings of sympathy and anger were elicited by the physical scars caused by their partner's violence. Even though many women insisted that the "violence wasn't the worst part," hinting at a yet-to-be-identified range of tactics used by their partners that they found even more hurtful than physical abuse, it was the woman's bruised face or broken bones that held our attention as well as the media's.

We now know that abuse is limited to physical and psychological abuse in only a minority of cases, somewhere between 20 and 40 percent. In the rest, the vast majority, forms of coercion such as violence, threats, or stalking are combined with a pattern of control that can include tactics to isolate victims; restrict their access to money, food, transportation, medical care, or other basic necessities; and microregulate their everyday activities, such as how they dress, cook, clean, talk on the phone or relate to their children. This pattern, known as coercive control, is referred to repeatedly throughout the volumes and is the major focus of chapters by Stark (volume 2), Lischick (volume 2), and Turkheimer (volume 3). Because the aim of coercive control is to limit a victim's resources as well as their opportunities to escape, it greatly heightens women's risk of being seriously injured or killed as well as of developing a range of medical, behavioral, and mental health problems. But the major consequence of being subjected to this strategy over time is that victims become entrapped. Their autonomy is compromised, and their basic liberties protected by the U.S. Constitution are abrogated, such as the right to free speech, their freedom of movement, and their right to make decisions about their bodies. Many of the rights that are violated by coercive control are so tightly woven into the fabric of everyday life that they are rarely protected explicitly (such as the right to cook, clean, dress, or toilet as they wish) and have to be inferred as rights by our general right to pursue our lives as we please. While women frequently assault male and female partners, coercive control appears to be largely committed by men against female partners. Of the estimated 15 million U.S. women who are battered, somewhere between 8 and 12 million are victims of coercive control.

If our major focus is on the use of violence in these relationships despite our broad definition and on the provision of safety, this is because of the appalling consequence of violence for the women who seek help and because most research and almost all interventions are designed in response to domestic violence, not coercive control. But even here, it is not violence per se that concerns us, but coercion used in the context of inequality, coercion that exploits and strengthens existing disadvantages.

Our framework will make at least two groups unhappy. A significant minority of researchers in the domestic violence field morally opposes the use of violence in any form in families or relationships and believe that trying to distinguish the use of force by its motive, context, or consequence or by the relative standing of its victims expresses a personal bias. To this group, couples who use force during fights among relative equals are as wrong to do so as is the man whose violence is unilaterally designed to quash his partner's autonomy. So committed are many in this group to a vision of families and intimate relationships as nonviolent spaces of cooperation that they oppose a vigorous police response in any but the most extreme cases, favoring couples counseling and other forms of conflict resolution instead. This group also holds that women's use of force with their partners is as significant a matter of public concern as men's use of force, even though the probability of injury is far greater to victimized women in these situations; women are far more likely to report being threatened or controlled by abuse than men and they are far more likely to seek or require outside help. Another group will also be unhappy with us. This group opposes vigorous state intervention in abuse less because of its devotion to the family than because they worry that inviting the state into people's personal lives will ultimately do more harm than good, no matter the rationale. This group is willing to accept a wide range of controlling and physically hurtful behavior in relationships to preserve privacy.

We are concerned with preserving and protecting physical integrity at all levels of relationships. But we hope this set helps shift attention from the sheer physical violations caused by abuse to the ways in which coercion and control are used to deny persons their rights and liberties in personal life. However imperfectly they may do so, we believe that governments have an obligation to address these harms and with the same commitment they bring to stemming harms in public life.

Many of those who pick up these volumes will undoubtedly do so because they have experienced abuse in their own lives or known someone who has. As several of the authors eloquently report, the forms of violence, intimidation, isolation, humiliation, and "control" that excite much of the help sought by women who have been battered by partners are closer in their dynamic to hostage taking than to what we normally think of as assault. Except, of course, these victims are "hostages at home"; they have been prisoners in their personal lives. It is easy to be depressed by the statistics and descriptions presented in these pages or to become cynical about the willingness of humans to inflict cruelty even on those they supposedly care for.

But we ask readers to also consider this: that the women who populate these pages have survived to tell their own stories. And many women and children subjected to abuse have done more than merely survive, as Hilary Abrahams illustrates in volume 1 in her record of women who have left shelter: "I sometimes feel like a spring flower." Some elements of women's stories may elicit pity; other details we provide about abuse may provoke anger, even outrage, as they should. Clearly, no community can be truly whole or free so long as one group is allowed to use the means of coercion and control to subjugate others, whether sex or some other factor is the basis for this practice. Once we know such crimes are occurring in our midst, we cannot turn away. But in addition to our protection and concern, the women in these volumes deserve our respect and admiration because of the courage, strength of character, and resolve required to survive the forms of oppression they faced.

We have recently completed a presidential race in which one of the candidates was justly celebrated for his ordeal as a POW (prisoner of war) during the Vietnam War. To those of us who have worked in this field, it is absolutely clear that resisting, standing up to, or even just surviving coercive control is often comparable to the heroism exhibited by returning POWs. If only as a token, we offer these volumes in lieu of a public monument to those who have survived the horrors of personal life. And there is a larger lesson too. Once we appreciate what the women here have accomplished, we see that each of us may be capable of remaking the world we are given, even against what may seem at first impossible odds.

The final justification for this set is that our society has invested billions of dollars and hundreds of millions of human service hours in managing the domestic violence in our midst. Apart from the unprecedented commitment of resources to protect women and children and hold perpetrators accountable are the enormous costs of not effectively addressing abuse in families and relationships. We have made a huge investment in ending an age-old form of injustice. Readers deserve an accounting.

Introduction to Volume 2

Evan Stark

Volume 2 looks at domestic violence in the context of families, high-lighting how children are harmed; at the response of the two major institutions responsible for addressing these harms, the child welfare system and the family court; and at the positive and negative ways in which fathering and so-called fathers' rights have been brought to bear on partner violence. Three convergent developments underlie the con-cerns here: the substantial body of research on the effects of domestic violence on children's well-being; political pressure from the advocacy movement for the agencies responsible for protecting children to respond; and a growing body of evidence that the current responses of the child welfare and family court systems in particular are woefully inadequate and leave millions of women and children at risk.

Debate continues about exactly how many children witness domestic violence, how many become implicated as victim or participant in its physical dynamics, and which factors shape whether and how children will be harmed. There is no disagreement about the underlying reality, however. All children in homes where domestic violence occurs are affected to some extent, even when their parents believe they are not. The challenge is how to protect children in these situations without increasing the risk to their primary parent or violating parental rights.

In chapter 1, Judy Postmus estimates that between 3.3 million and 10 million children are exposed to domestic violence annually in the United States. Given the extent of children's exposure and the risks it poses, it is hardly surprising that partner abuse is a major issue in cus-tody disputes as well as for child protection. Somewhere between one-third and one-half of the cases seen by the family court and child wel-fare systems involve domestic violence. What *is* remarkable, however, is that domestic violence was virtually invisible in these systems when the shelter movement began. Things changed gradually, largely in response to political pressure. By the late 1990s, domestic violence training for child welfare and family court personnel had become commonplace and most jurisdictions had adopted special procedures or protocols to respond to cases where domestic violence was an issue.

The outstanding question is whether reforms have gone far enough or even, in some instances, may have made matters worse for victims and their children. In several well-publicized cases in the U.S. and England (see, for instance, the discussion of the British cases in Chapter 3) children were shown to have been hurt or killed by abusive dads whose domestic violence had been overlooked by the family court or child welfare system. In the end, our assessment of progress is mixed, with a number of obstacles to safety remaining despite the emergence of important and innovative programs.

Interestingly, child welfare and the family court systems have responded to the news about domestic violence in almost diametrically opposing ways.

The child welfare response to domestic violence was dramatically illustrated in *Nicholson v. Williams*, a landmark class action suit against the Administration for Children's Services (ACS) in New York City, the nation's largest child protection agency. The case was brought by mothers who had been charged with "neglect" and had their children placed in foster care solely because they were victims of domestic violence. The basic facts in Ms. Nicholson's case are instructive.

In 1999, a man from whom Sharwline Nicholson had been separated for some time returned to New York City from South Carolina to visit his infant daughter. He had never been physically violent before. But on this occasion, they argued; he beat Ms. Nicholson badly, breaking her arm, and then left. She managed to call 911 and to arrange for a neighbor to care for her infant, who had been asleep in her bedroom during the assault, and to pick up her son from school. She cooperated fully with the police. No matter. They arrived at the neighbor's apartment and, with guns drawn, took custody of her children. She was informed by ACS that the children were in their care and that she would have to go to court to get them back. When she appeared in court five days later, she was informed that she had been charged with "child neglect" for "engaging in domestic violence." During the nine months it took to get the charges against Ms. Nicholson dismissed, numerous other survivors of domestic violence came forward with identical stories, all of whose children had been removed and who had faced identical charges simply because a partner had beaten them.

Importantly, none of the children was shown to have actually witnessed or suffered the consequences of domestic violence. Instead, the agency was proceeding under the assumption that the simple presence of domestic violence in the home created so significant a risk that an emergency removal was justified. One irony of this was that the evidence for this belief was based on research by Evan Stark and other academics who had been closely identified with the battered women's movement.

After a lengthy trial during which dozens of witnesses and experts testified, the federal judge, Jack Weinstein, found for the plaintiff mothers on every count, ruling that the removal of children and allegations of neglect against mothers solely because of domestic violence were unconstitutional violations of their rights and had to stop immediately. Judge Weinstein's decision was supported by a similar ruling in New York State's highest court. Both the federal and state courts recognized that domestic violence can harm children. But they insisted that placement in foster care also carries risk. As a result, they reasoned, no removal should occur unless it is clearly shown that the harms to a child occasioned by removal are significantly less than the harms that would result if children remained with their primary parent. Since there was no evidence of harm of any kind to the children in the *Nicholson* class action suit, none of their removals could be justified. Instead of interventions that revictimized mothers and children, programs were required that reduced or eliminated the risk to mothers as well as their children.

In chapter 1, Judy Postmus reviews what we know about the probable physical, psychological, and behavioral consequences of children's exposure to domestic violence, including the probability that they will be abused or neglected. Importantly, she also identifies factors that protect or moderate the effects of these harms, information that is often lacking in such reviews. Finally, she describes a number of promising initiatives to reverse the practices revealed by *Nicholson*.

Postmus also identifies a number of myths that contribute to overly punitive reactions by child welfare workers, including the belief that children exposed to violence by their parents will grow up to become violent adults. What is known as the "intergenerational transmission" thesis is critically examined by Alison Cares in chapter 2. In its classic formulation, the thesis leaves little room for the nuanced paths through which social learning actually proceeds. In fact, Cares argues, whether as well as how violence is transmitted may depend on the type of violence to which children are exposed, its severity or frequency for instance, the gender of the person exposed, a range of vulnerability and resiliency factors, and, perhaps most importantly, the positive reinforcement afforded if the adult's use of violence is perceived to be a "success." This suggests that sanctions for current abusive behavior can influence whether children replicate it later in life as well as the current behavior of abusive men. Cares also suggests the need for research to focus on what children learn from observing parental abuse about gender behavior and the probity of controlling women.

In marked contrast to the overreaction by child welfare, the family courts have been far more reluctant to take domestic violence seriously, let alone to identify it as a child protection issue, even in the presence of credible evidence of abuse in custody disputes and even when state laws require judges to prioritize children's safety concerns in their decision making. In part, this difference reflects the relatively privileged clientele who engage in custody disputes compared to the child welfare system. Moreover, where fathers have been historically invisible in the child welfare system, in the family court their financial resources are often at stake.

Among the many reforms in divorce during the 1960s was the replacement of the primary parent doctrine, which had generally resulted in mothers being awarded custody and some form of child support, by a preference for joint custody and liberal visitation. The prevailing wisdom was that the child's best interest was served by having continued access to both parents, even if they had irreconcilable differences. This change was accompanied by a sharp increase in custody disputes, particularly where domestic violence was an issue, and in the involvement of clinically trained evaluators charged with assessing the relative fitness of contesting parties to parent. This change also created a number of dilemmas for victims of abuse, not the least of which arose from the continued risks women and children faced if courts sanctioned an abusive father's unregulated access to his former family. Women who refused such access were often deemed "unfriendly" by the court, even if they acted from a genuine fear for themselves or their children, and many lost custody or were sent to jail.

A dramatic consequence of granting custody or visitation to an abusive father is the death of a child. In chapter 3, Hilary Saunders summarizes a remarkable report she compiled on 29 cases where children in England and Wales were killed as a result of contact or residence arrangements. The significance of the report lies not merely in its contents but also in its role in eliciting a response from the highest levels of the judiciary in England.

In one of the cases, despite a long history of violence against the mother and serious mental health problems that included at least one suicide attempt, the father was given primary residential custody of two of three children and unsupervised contact with the third, the child he killed. In addition to documenting the circumstances under which these children died and whether and how court involvement can be implicated in the death, Saunders looked at how the court's response was evaluated by investigators. In this case, for instance, although the father left a note saying that he intended to kill all three children as revenge for his wife's leaving him, the investigators found no reason to identify a child protection issue or to criticize the court's response. She concludes the chapter with a series of recommendations that are applicable to family courts in the United States as well as in

Britain and describes how the British government responded to the report.

Chapter 4 also begins with the death of a child by his mother's partner. When David Mandel was asked to train child welfare workers in Connecticut about domestic violence after such an incident, he quickly realized that men are largely invisible to the child welfare system and almost never assessed as fathers. Mandel describes the multiple and contradictory meanings that surround abusive fathers who are expected to be protectors, providers, and role models as well as to accept responsibility for their role as "enemies" and for betraying basic trust. Ironically, he observes, their invisibility as fathers means that they are almost never held accountable for the harms they may have caused to their children. Nor do programs for batterers often build fathering skills. Importantly, even if they want little or no contact with abusive partners, many battered women may want their children to know their fathers, a point of contention in the advocacy movement. Mandel deals with the problems these interactions create, the challenges and dilemmas posed by batterers having legal access to their children, the double standard we use to evaluate mothers and fathers as parents, and our ambivalence about batterers as parents. He also considers some positive aspects of parenting by batterers, identifies public education campaigns that promote fathering, and suggests the possibility that some men may be able to stop their abuse for the sake of their children.

Despite the prevalence of domestic violence in custody cases, English family courts limit contact in only 1 percent of all cases. The proportion is only slightly higher in the United States. In response to this practice, the U.S. Congress passed the Morella resolution in 1997 recommending that state courts give presumptive custody to victims of domestic violence. Most states have adopted a version of this approach. But has family court practice changed?

I begin the discussion of domestic violence in custody cases in chapter 5 by reviewing the evidence on how domestic violence harms children, the types of domestic violence seen in custody cases, and the probability that violence will continue post separation or divorce. Fathers' rights organizations claim that concerns about domestic violence have been greatly exaggerated by women's groups. To the contrary, current assessments underestimate children's risk. This is because they are based on a narrow equation of domestic violence with severe physical abuse and the false belief that the domestic violence seen in custody disputes is less serious than the abuse identified in the general population. In reality, the most common and most devastating form of parental abuse involves coercive control, a strategy that falls beneath the radar in family court. The dynamics of harm in these cases include "child abuse as tangential spouse abuse," when a father uses children to extend control over his former wife, a strategy with which evaluators and family courts often unwittingly collude. Research documents that family courts place few restrictions on visitation in domestic violence cases. Indeed, compelling evidence from several states shows that abused mothers may actually be less likely to get custody if domestic violence is an issue than if it is not. The entire system of therapeutic jurisprudence appears geared toward minimizing or denying the importance of abuse in pursuit of resolutions that satisfy a joint custody standard and leave victimized women and their children at continued risk.

In chapter 6, Marianne Hester, one of England's leading researchers on sexual violence, maps the court systems developed to deal with domestic violence crimes, child protection, and child visitation as three separate planets with their own histories, culture, laws, and populations. On each of these planets, abuse is explained in a different way and the practices that follow from these different explanations are often contradictory, exacerbating the dilemmas faced by mothers. The same abused woman who may be seen as a cooperative witness when she testifies against her partner in criminal court will be defined as a neglectful mother by the child welfare system because she "engaged" in domestic violence or was "colluding" in her partner's abuse. If she presses the issue of domestic violence in custodial proceedings, meanwhile, she risks being defined as uncooperative and losing custody. The criminal court readily gives her an order of protection, while the child welfare court orders her not to allow the abusive partner to have contact with her children. Contradicting these positions, she is required to facilitate the father's access in the custody case. Hester not only details life on each of these planets, but also shows how each of these worlds, in its own way, promotes a certain image of gender that reinforces sexual inequality. To address the dilemmas that living on all three planets at once creates for women who are battered requires not only reconciling the contradictory cultures, but also confronting the ways in which they reinforce gender stereotypes.

PARENTAL ALIENATION AND FATHERS' RIGHTS

Among the studies I review in Chapter 5 is Seattle research showing that, in approximately three-fourths of the cases where there is documented evidence of domestic violence (usually because the husband has been arrested or issued a restraining order), either there is no mention of it in the family court file or it is mentioned only as an unsupported allegation. Because abuse often happens behind closed doors, skilled lawyers and expert witnesses are often needed to make a persuasive case. The expense of such a presentation is often increased dramatically by a common response from fathers alleged to have committed domestic violence, that their spouse is fabricating the charges to deliberately turn the children against them, a pattern that has been called "parental alienation syndrome" (PAS). PAS has been alleged almost exclusively against mothers, mainly victims of domestic violence, and has resulted in many women losing custody to abusive partners.

In chapter 7 about PAS, Joan Meier, one of the foremost family law advocates in the United States, traces the history of PAS from its initial description by psychiatrist Richard Gardner to its dissemination by fathers' rights activists, compares its assessment as "junk science" by leading researchers and professional organizations to its positive reception by the family courts, and considers whether its reformulation as "parental alienation" significantly strengthens its application. Women confronted with allegations of PAS face a dilemma: whether to persist in claims of abuse and possibly lose custody altogether, or drop their claims and risk further harm to themselves and their children. The presentation of PAS replicates the same dilemmas that batterers frequently pose to their victims, forcing them to choose between their own safety and the safety of their children, for instance, by pressuring them to use forms of harsh discipline or "I'll show you how to really do it." Meier considers a range of strategies to neutralize the use of PAS in custody cases.

The promotion of PAS has been largely spearheaded by a range of advocacy groups collected under the heading of fathers' rights. In chapter 8, journalist Joan Dawson tracks the history, politics, financing, and evolution of these groups, contrasting their development to that of the movement to reexamine manhood and male parenting roles in the 1970s. While one wing of the men's movement remained committed to social justice issues and provided strong support for the battered women's movement, another wing turned against feminism, forging ahead with its own agenda for "equal rights," a demand that resonated with disgruntled fathers whose access to their children had been curtailed by family courts. Dawson examines the relationship of the fathers' rights movement to the far right, their recruiting strategies, the ways in which they have aligned with religious conservatives to make divorce more difficult, their propensity to put their rights of access ahead of child safety, and their insistence that most allegations of domestic violence in the family courts are fabricated to deprive men of what is justly theirs.

REFRAMING DOMESTIC VIOLENCE AS COERCIVE CONTROL

In chapter 9, Cynthia Lischick melds all of the themes in this volume, emphasizing her original research showing the importance of coercive control and then applying this framework to illuminate the dynamics in a disputed custody case. The chapter opens with a puzzle:

Kelly, a woman with four children, has signed agreements giving up her right to assets to which she is clearly entitled and that could be vital to her parenting. The question is whether she signed under "duress." But the evidence of physical coercion appears minimal. So, if violence hasn't made her afraid to oppose her husband's wishes, what has?

Lischick begins to reconstruct this case by reviewing the coercive control model, including the tactics used to intimidate, isolate, and control female partners, as well the psychological dimension, the emergence of a "survival self" developed to accommodate these tactics. She summarizes research showing how coercive control can effectively annihilate a person's sense of self even in the absence of physical assault. She then fills in the details of the case, following the progression of isolation, intimidation, and degradation as it escalates into full-blown coercive control. She shows how the children were gradually brought into the pattern of control and how, as Kelly's husband extended his control to the money in the household, first employing his wife to manage his business but then depriving her of even the most basic information or resources needed to make simple financial decisions, Kelly became entrapped in the network of dependence reflected in the decision to give up everything. Throughout her analysis, Lischick shows that the behavior of the husband and wife were the by-product of gendered assumptions as well as of malevolent decisions by the abusive man. Coercive control continued after the couple separated, but with the implicit collusion of the family court. In the court's eyes, Kelly's choice was prompted not by external constraint and threats, but by the self-sacrificing nature we associate with womanhood. If her husband oppressed Kelly by enforcing stereotypic gender-role behavior, her abuse remained invisible because it seemed so natural for her to be dependent.

Chapter 1

Domestic Violence and Children's Well-Being

Judy L. Postmus

Concern about how domestic violence affects children is long-standing. Yet, numerous researchers, child advocates, battered women advocates, and policy makers still grapple with how best to keep families safe. The different and sometimes conflicting orientations that domestic violence and child welfare professionals bring to their work make it difficult to agree on a single strategy, frustrating families who need help. One outstanding question is who should be held accountable for the exposure to domestic violence. Should it be the mother, the usual caretaker, who has supposedly "failed" to protect her children from abuse, or the father or father surrogate, most often the abuser, who may be invisible to the child welfare system? And how should the child welfare system respond to families experiencing domestic violence? Do the harms children suffer from domestic violence constitute child maltreatment? Should child welfare remove children so exposed for their own protection and to break the cycle of violence?

This chapter will answer these questions by first describing the extent, nature, and consequences of children's exposure to domestic violence. The very different philosophies with which the child welfare system and domestic violence service providers approach the problems created by children's exposure to domestic violence will be reviewed. The third section describes state and local initiatives that address this issue. The final section discusses practice, policy, and research implications of the earlier analysis.[1] Please note that female victims and male perpetrators are referred to in this chapter because this is the most common domestic violence scenario where intervention is required.

However, domestic violence may also be initiated by women against male or female partners, or by men against male partners.

CHILDREN EXPOSED TO DOMESTIC VIOLENCE

Exposure to domestic violence can be both direct or indirect and can include being a co-victim during an abusive episode; watching or hearing violent events; suffering the consequences when a primary parent is partially or fully disabled by abuse or by adaptations to abuse, such as depression; or experiencing the aftermath of the events, such as watching a father being arrested. Exposure also includes being manipulated by the batterer to help him to gain further control over his partner. This may include being used to spy on a mother before or after separation, being made to watch abuse, or being used as a pawn during a custody dispute. (Please see chapter 5 by Stark in this volume.)

The following sections review how many children are exposed to or witness domestic violence and describe the consequences of that exposure. In truth, however, the term "exposure" only begins to capture the nuanced and multifaceted nature of their experience.

PREVALENCE

The most commonly cited estimates are that somewhere between 3.3 million and 10 million children witness domestic violence each year.[2] These estimates are problematic, however. For one thing, they are based primarily on reports from adult victims who are asked about their children's exposure or about whether they themselves were exposed to domestic violence as children. Thus, they reflect the limits associated with recall, particularly if the events recounted happened long ago or in the midst of a crisis. Another problem with these estimates is the fact that parents often believe that their children are not exposed to or even aware of domestic violence in the home. In fact, children consistently report witnessing domestic violence even when their parents insist they have not.[3]

It is also hard to interpret these statistics because the actual nature of exposure is rarely detailed. Researchers tend to pose the issue of exposure as a "yes" or "no" dichotomy and so fail to capture the coincidence of exposure with actual harm to the child; the severity, type, frequency, or duration of violence to which children are exposed; the developmental age of the child at the time of exposure; and the child's reaction. All of these factors tend to be significant in shaping how children are affected. Even with these caveats, the estimates of children exposed directly or indirectly to domestic violence make this a significant social problem.

As we've suggested, children can be inadvertently injured during domestic violence incidents. But data gathered at the scene of domestic violence incidents suggest this may occur in fewer than 3 percent of the incidents in which police make an arrest, presumably those at the higher end of severity. This percentage merits concern, particularly when we consider the frequency and duration of domestic violence. Still, while it is slightly higher than the estimated incidence of child abuse in the general population (3 versus 2.5 percent), it is probably lower than the percentage of children estimated to be abused by foster families (5 percent).[4]

CONSEQUENCES

Children may be deliberately abused during an attack on their mother, inadvertently hurt (e.g., if the mother is holding a baby when she is assaulted), or hurt because they try to stop the abuse or otherwise intervene when their mother is attacked. But in addition to becoming involved in the conflict, children may also distance themselves from it, either physically (by going somewhere else in the house to hide) or psychologically. Among the psychological consequences of exposure are the behaviors children use to cope. These include both "internalizing" behaviors, where children defend against their fear by disguising it in other problems, such as withdrawal, anxiety, sleep disturbances, somatic problems, and posttraumatic stress disorder, and "externalizing" behaviors such as exhibiting aggression against others (including their mother) and delinquency. Exposure may also lead to problems with school, including difficulties with forming peer relationships, acting out in classrooms, diminished concentration and memory, challenges with organizational or language abilities, and perfectionist tendencies. Indirectly, children may be affected by the lack of consistent parenting, secondary consequences of abuse of their primary parent such as alcohol or drug abuse, or the high levels of irritability and tension typical in violent homes. They may also be affected by the threat of violence toward the mother, rigid or authoritarian parenting styles of the batterer, being used to undermine the mother's authority, and the fear of abduction. Violence against a mother may escalate during a separation or after a divorce, and children may be harmed during visitation exchanges or be used in a range of ways by the abuser who seeks to control his former partner but cannot do so directly. Finally, although most harm to children in these families is the direct result of the perpetrator's abusive behavior, abused women are also more likely to abuse their children than nonabused women.

Although domestic violence can directly or indirectly influence children in any of the ways already described, the extent of these effects differs depending on the type, duration, and severity of domestic violence to which children are exposed. Another determinant of how children are affected is their developmental age and the developmental tasks associated with their age. Infants and toddlers appear to react differently to being exposed to domestic violence than school-age children or teenagers, for instance. Since attachment and bonding are critical tasks for younger children, an abuse-related separation or fear of separation induced by witnessing an assault against a primary parent is likely to be more traumatic for a younger child than a teen who may have some experience with getting by on his or her own. A child's sex may also influence how he or she is affected. Some research suggests that boys are more likely to become aggressive as a result of witnessing domestic violence, whereas girls are more likely to exhibit passive adaptations such as withdrawal. Not all researchers agree on this, however. Other important factors include the nature of institutional interventions and whether these were perceived as helpful or not. Importantly, the stress levels—and hence the probability of behavioral adaptations—appear to be cumulative rather than incident specific, with those children exposed to abuse for a longer period reacting more strongly than those exposed to only a few incidents.

Aspects of children's lives may protect them from the effects of exposure as well as increase their risk. These protective factors include the characteristics of the child, the quality of family support, and the quality of extrafamilial support. We know, for example, that poverty, divorce, exposure to violence in the community, and other stressors may have many of the same effects on children as exposure to domestic violence. When child psychologists Emmy Werner and Ruth Smith followed 700 children in Hawaii into adulthood, they found that children exhibited extraordinary resilience even in the face of extreme poverty, neglect, and abuse, particularly if there was a caring and supportive adult present. They report:

> One of the most striking findings of our two follow-ups in adulthood, at ages thirty-two and forty, was that most of the high-risk youths who did develop serious coping problems in adolescence had staged a recovery by the time they reached midlife.... They were in stable marriages and jobs, were satisfied with their relationships with their spouses and teenage children, and were responsible citizens in their community.[5]

In fact, only one out of six of the adult subjects at either age 32 or 40 was doing poorly, "struggling with chronic financial problems, domestic conflict, violence, substance abuse, serious mental health problems, and/or low self-esteem."[6] Thus, only by knowing the protective and risk factors in a particular case can we predict how any given child will be affected by exposure to domestic violence.

Like estimates about the prevalence of child witnessing, generalizations from research on child exposure can also be questioned. First, many of the studies of children's behaviors are based on reports by their mothers while residing in domestic violence shelters. These women have typically experienced abuse that is more severe and long lasting than the violence experienced by other victims. In addition, because of their education about domestic violence, they may be prone to interpret their children's behavior differently from other adults and from the children themselves. Additionally, children's behavior may be influenced by the disruption of their normal routine by going to a shelter, by the experience of shelter itself, or by their emotional reaction to leaving home and possibly a father figure whom they love. Research may also not have considered or given adequate weight to demographic factors, including age, gender, intellectual functioning, socioeconomic status, race, unemployment, age of parents, as well as other family factors known to affect children, such as substance abuse by parents, paternal or maternal physical or mental health, pathology, stress, parenting ability, and stability of the home environment.

THE PHILOSOPHICAL CONFLICTS

Even if we cannot predict exactly how a child will be harmed by exposure to domestic violence, or whether he or she will be harmed at all, there can be no question that children so exposed are at an increased risk of suffering some adverse short- or long-term reaction. The challenge, then, is how to best intervene with families experiencing domestic violence while keeping children and their mothers safe from further abuse. Apart from the police, the two systems that are most directly responsible for family members in these cases are child welfare and domestic violence services. So, it is worth considering how these services approach families experiencing domestic violence.

Tension and sometimes open conflict are common features of the relationship between child protective services (CPS) and domestic violence service providers. Much of this tension stems from a difference in philosophy and the preferred approach to dealing with violence in the home. The public mandate of CPS is to protect children. The preferred approach is to keep children in their homes by providing services or support that strengthens their family's capacity to keep them safe. Temporary removal is an option if services are deemed to have failed or the risk to the child is deemed emergent. Permanent placement and termination of parental rights are the most extreme interventions if efforts to reunify the family fail. Once a case is referred, CPS workers investigate reports of child maltreatment to determine if the report is substantiated, assess the risk of harm to the child, and determine what combination of services, support, or other interventions is needed.

In contrast, the first priority of battered women advocates is the safety of the adult victim. This, they believe, is best accomplished through a collaborative approach known as "empowerment" whereby victims and advocates work together to identify the victims' goals, which often include keeping themselves and their children safe. In this view, safety is a time-consuming and frustrating process that may involve victims struggling with life-changing decisions about leaving their partners and becoming economically and emotionally independent. Hence, while child safety is important and most shelter programs today also provide services and support for children, the physical, emotional, or financial needs of the victim as she perceives them are paramount. Advocates also emphasize "accountability" for violence, usually by encouraging the arrest of an abusive partner.

Both CPS and domestic violence programs want women and children to be safe. But there are a number of barriers that make it difficult for them to address this goal without conflict. On a practical level, there may be an adversarial relationship because CPS and domestic violence services compete for funding from the same general pool. CPS practices often include opening child abuse cases in the name of the primary caregiver, who is usually the mother, and who may or may not be the perpetrator of the abuse. Moreover, CPS workers typically develop a service plan that focuses on the mother's ability to protect her children, regardless of whether she herself remains at risk. If she continues to remain in an abusive home, CPS workers will often try to force a mother to leave an abuser or charge her with "neglect" or with "failure to protect" her own children. One result is that many mothers fear and distrust CPS workers, feel powerlessness to resist CPS mandates, and overtly resist any interventions.

Early on, in an attempt to work together, many battered women advocates supported laws equating exposure to domestic violence with child abuse because they believed charges would be filed against the partner responsible for the abuse, usually the man. Many also believed that highlighting harms to children could help courts respond more forcefully in domestic violence cases. But their support of such laws turned into opposition when it became clear that abused women were often being charged with failing to protect the children even if they themselves had been victimized. They were also worried that such laws would lead to mandatory reporting of child abuse in domestic violence cases, as it did in several states.

By contrast, CPS workers often become frustrated with the long process needed for victims to achieve safety and struggle with advocating for a mother when her decisions, or lack thereof, appear to jeopardize her children. Indeed, as time passes, CPS workers become more critical and controlling of a victim's decisions and may identify her as the person solely responsible for protecting the children. Additionally,

CPS workers may think they lack the authority to legally pursue the batterer. CPS workers may also feel more comfortable—and more optimistic about possibilities for change—when they concentrate on the parenting deficits of mothers than if they confront a male they regard as violent. Even so, by not focusing on holding the abuser accountable and keeping the mother as well as her children safe, CPS workers may unknowingly increase the problems faced by domestic violence victims and their children.

Both the CPS and domestic violence service approaches assume that the needs and goals of abused women and their children are in conflict. Unfortunately, in the midst of this conflict, little attention is paid to the abuser. If the abuser is neither the legal guardian nor the biological parent, he is often missing from the case file and is not officially a party to the service plan or any court decisions. This may make him largely inaccessible to the child welfare system. One response is for CPS workers to hold a victimized mother responsible for seeking a restraining order to remove her partner, even if this is not the safest option for her, or, worse, to demand she leave him regardless of the risks she perceives this may pose. When she fails to meet these requirements, a removal proceeding may be initiated.

The ideal situation is for CPS and domestic violence services to work jointly and collaboratively on protecting *all* victimized parties in the family and to clearly target the partner responsible for any violence in the home. Unfortunately, the conflicts between the two fields are largely a function of the assumptions made by child welfare workers and other helping professionals about domestic violence. These assumptions frame policy, the mandates that constrain the discretion of case workers, the services offered to mothers and their children, and how the efficacy of these services is evaluated. This section explores three of the core assumptions about children exposed to domestic violence that have historically guided the practices and policies of the child welfare system.

Assumption #1: Children Who Witness Domestic Violence Are More Likely to Become Abusers or Victims as Adults

Deciding whether exposure to domestic violence is a form of maltreatment may depend on the theoretical perspectives one holds on what causes domestic violence. To policy makers and child welfare workers who believe in the social learning model, where children learn behaviors from their parents and transmit them intergenerationally, it seems obvious that any child exposed to domestic violence is at risk of becoming an abusive adult regardless of any mediating factors (this issue is also addressed in chapter 2 in this volume by Cares).

However, if one starts with the feminist theory that domestic violence is not a personal problem, but a political one, and is rooted in sexism, sexual inequality, and a patriarchal culture that tolerates and even encourages male domination over females, then understanding the impact of being exposed to domestic violence lies with assuming that each child exposed to domestic violence should be assessed individually based on the type, amount, and severity of the exposure. Hence, one's belief about what causes domestic violence and the corresponding impact on children exposed to such violence will influence decisions about when and how to intervene with families experiencing domestic violence.

Research conducted from a social learning theory perspective concludes that being exposed to domestic violence as a child is positively correlated to involvement in a domestic violent relationship as an adult and that children learn how to use violence to control others from observing a parent doing so. Stith and her colleagues conducted a meta-analysis of 39 studies and concluded that when children grow up in families experiencing domestic violence, they are more likely to be involved in violent marital relationships as adults.[7] Another study found that children who had witnessed domestic violence were more likely than children who had not witnessed domestic violence to respond violently when they felt excluded or personally rejected.[8] Unfortunately, most research in this area fails to consider other risk factors that might predispose children to violence, including the media, schools, or communities.

Clearly, though exposure as a child increases the risk of violence as an adult, this is not automatic. Studies have estimated that anywhere from 70 to 90 percent of exposed children do not become abusive adults. One problem with research on this issue lies in the samples studied. For example, despite the self-interest persons have in justifying their current situation by finding a cause in their childhood, much of the evidence to support the intergenerational thesis comes from interviews with adult batterers and victims. In the comparison between children who did or did not witness domestic violence, for instance, Ballif-Spanvill et al. found that neither group used violence involving limited resources, intimidation, or jealousy. They concluded that "finding so many children with prosocial responses emphasizes the importance of assessing a range of positive social behaviors and exploring adaptive abilities in all children, even those who have been exposed to family violence."[9]

Thus, while exposure is a risk factor, other mediating factors exist, including protective or resiliency factors that may influence the outcomes for children. Studies have found such factors to include (1) having a strong relationship with a caring parent or other significant adult; (2) having safe and supportive locations, whether located in schools, community centers, or religious havens; (3) developing athletic, scholastic, or artistic talents; (4) being able to avoid self-blame; and (5) having strong positive peer relationships.

Much of the discussion about CPS intervention in domestic violence cases highlights the need to "break the cycle of violence." As we've seen, however, a range of protective or resiliency factors mediate any connection between exposure as a child and adult abuse. CPS workers who fail to assess for these factors on a case-by-case basis may unwittingly make decisions that negatively impact the children and their mothers.

Assumption #2: Victimized Mothers Often Abuse or Neglect Their Children

While we know there is often an overlap between domestic violence and child abuse, the challenge is to determine who the abuser of the children is, particularly if this means that children will be protected if the abusive partner is removed. A number of explanations have been offered for why battered women may abuse their children, including controlling the children to prevent both the mother and children from being abused by the batterer, using the children as an outlet for their frustration from being abused themselves, or blaming the children for their abuse. One widespread belief is that abuse leads mothers to be emotionally unavailable to their children, for instance, or that they are more likely to use corporal punishment than nonabused mothers. To test this belief, psychologist Cris Sullivan and her colleagues examined how women's victimization related to their parenting stress and, in turn, how their parenting affected their children's adjustment. Despite the fact that mothers had experienced substantial levels of physical abuse, they continued to be emotionally available to their children and enjoyed their role as a parent. Moreover, the battered women were more likely than nonbattered women to use nonviolent forms of discipline including using time-outs, removing privileges, or grounding their children. All of these results were confirmed by the children.[10]

Batterers also abuse their children as a means of controlling or hurting their adult partners or may use the children to spy on the mother's movements and relationships. While mothers are more often cited for child abuse than fathers, men are most often the perpetrators in the most severe forms of child abuse.

Finally, children can be hurt accidentally by getting in the middle of a violent episode either intentionally, in an attempt to protect their mother, or unintentionally because they happen to be in the same room. In one study of battered women in shelter, 44 percent of the children surveyed reported that they had attempted to protect their mothers on at least one occasion and 37 percent reported being hit in the process.[11]

Can battered women become abusers themselves? Absolutely. Even in these instances, however, it is important to understand the role of the batterer. For example, one dynamic may involve the batterer's use of violence and control to enforce traditional sex roles. "If violence is evoked by struggles around traditional sex roles," Stark and Flitcraft report, "the practical result ... may be to restrict a woman's perceived options, increase her vulnerability to violence, decrease her capacity to protect her children from violence, exacerbate her own frustration and anger, and increase the probability that she will be destructive to self and others, including her children."[12] In other situations, abused women make the shameful choice to use inappropriate physical discipline with their children because the abusive partner has warned he will hurt the children more seriously if she doesn't.

Assumption #3: Battered Women Must Leave the Abusive Relationship in Order to Keep Themselves and Their Children Safe

The common reaction of most service providers, including child welfare and many domestic violence providers, is to protect women and children from harm by urging them to separate from the abuser. Since child welfare uses removal as a means to protect children, it seems logical to some that the same tactic can be effective in protecting children from domestic violence. Even if we set aside the concerns raised by the *Nicholson v. Williams* (2001) case (see below), this approach raises a number of problems.

First, removing children from their home and placing them in foster care do not necessarily protect children from physical or psychological harm. We know that removal and long-term separation can be even more traumatic for children than the initial maltreatment, an important reason why courts increasingly require CPS to make their case for removal by weighing the harms this would cause against the harms of not removing. Additionally, longitudinal research has shown that living in multiple homes (often in foster care) is more predictive of poor outcomes in adulthood than is the original maltreatment. In any case, their limited resources make it impossible for child welfare agencies in most states to provide protective services for any but those children and families who have suffered the greatest harm.

Second, removing women and their children from the home does not automatically mean they are safe from further harm. Women may actually be more likely to be seriously injured or killed by their abusive partners when they leave the relationship than if they stay. And, for those who leave, their perpetrators continue to harass or hurt them during a separation or after a divorce. So even where leaving is encouraged, it is not a stand-alone solution. Meanwhile, a growing body of work suggests that a mother's efforts to protect children can significantly reduce the danger posed by a batterer. Hence, we must identify ways in which mothers keep themselves and their children safe whether in the relationship or not.

Instead of removing the children and the mother, an alternative is to remove the perpetrator by having him arrested or getting a restraining order—strategies the domestic violence movement frequently uses. Child welfare agencies may lack the authority to remove the adult per-petrator, particularly if he is unrelated to the child, and, in some cases, use "no contact" orders as part of a service contract to avoid placement in a shelter.

Unfortunately, the remedies used to keep women and children safe have not always been effective in protecting battered mothers and their children. For instance, in my own research I've found restraining orders are inconsistently enforced and have varying effects on stopping abuse for women.[13] Research finds the efficacy of mandatory arrest, dedicated prosecution, and other criminal justice approaches mixed at best. Finally, while women generally rate their experience at shelters positively, there is little evidence that a shelter stay ends violence in most cases.

UNINTENDED CONSEQUENCES

Although these assumptions have a weak empirical foundation at best, they have exerted a powerful ideological force on public policy and the institutional response. One result of these assumptions was pressure on states to require professionals to report children who wit-nessed domestic violence to the state's abuse hotlines and to include exposure to domestic violence as a form of child abuse or neglect. Both child welfare and battered women advocates initially supported the enactment of these laws; unfortunately, several unintended consequen-ces resulted.

For example, when Massachusetts and Minnesota enacted policies that required that all cases of domestic violence be reported to child welfare, their already overburdened and underfunded CPS systems were quickly overwhelmed, reducing their capacity to respond appro-priately to cases where abuse or neglect were clearly identified. Addi-tionally, battered women may be less willing to disclose domestic violence to professionals who are mandated reporters because they fear CPS involvement may lead to losing their children.

Other states left their reporting policies ambiguous, leaving the deci-sion to report up to the individual professional. States also use ambigu-ous protocols for investigations and assessments, giving the worker broad discretion on whether to assess for and include domestic violence in his or her findings and whether to substantiate a finding of neglect in domestic violence cases. Faced with ambiguous policies, a wide range of discretion, frustrations or fear of working with batterers, and pressures to resolve the report in a timely fashion, workers may fall back on their mandate to protect children from harm and place the blame on the mother for not protecting her children from exposure to domestic violence. Or they may not officially "see" domestic violence at all.

Another unintended consequence of the questionable assumptions is that CPS workers are citing victimized mothers with "neglect" and removing children for witnessing domestic violence. In a study of children labeled as abused or neglected, Stark and Flitcraft reported that the children of battered women were more likely to be removed from the home than children from nonbattered mothers even when the level of harm to the child was the same. Using data from the National Survey of Child and Adolescent Well-Being, another study reported that more than half (52 percent) of families *currently* experiencing domestic violence had abuse reports substantiated compared to only 29 percent of families with a *history* of domestic violence or 22 percent of families with *no* domestic violence.[14] Most of the substantiated cases fell under the neglect category, with mothers typically assigned blame or held responsible. Child welfare workers rarely identified past or current domestic violence as the critical factor in their decision making unless other risk factors (e.g., substance abuse and/or mental health issues) were also present. The researchers concluded by discussing the importance of having consistent risk assessment protocols that differentiate between past and present domestic violence along with appropriate training on the multiple challenges that plague families.

To get an even fuller picture of the child welfare response to domestic violence, English and her colleagues examined 2,000 randomly selected child welfare cases. Their results indicate that fewer than half of the cases reported to CPS were accepted for investigation; of those accepted, most were viewed as "high standard of investigation," that is, requiring a face-to-face interview with a CPS worker. Domestic violence was listed as a risk factor in 40 percent of the cases investigated (20 percent of all referrals). In cases where domestic violence was indicated, classified as moderate to high risk after investigation and opened for services, four out of five children were removed from their homes, a far higher proportion than in other cases.[15]

The practice of charging battered mothers with neglect and removing their children to foster care either because of the domestic violence or because they had refused services mandated due to domestic violence led to the federal class action lawsuit in 2001 in New York City, *Nicholson v. Williams*. After a trial that included dozens of caseworkers, administrators, researchers, and mothers as experts, Judge Jack

Weinstein ruled that the removal policies and practices were unconstitutional and that "government may not penalize a mother, not otherwise unfit, who is battered by her partner, by separating her from her children; nor may children be separated from the mother, in effect visiting upon them the sins of their mother's batterer."[16] The judge further stated that reasonable efforts, a term not unfamiliar to child welfare agencies, must be made to separate the batterer from the victim and her children while providing reasonable, adequate protection such as assisting in helping the family find shelter or other safe accommodations and filing a protective order against the batterer. Additionally, the judge stated that mothers are to be informed of their rights and those of their children prior to child welfare systems taking any actions to remove children and that these rights be provided in both English and Spanish. Finally, the judge ordered that training and supervision be given to child welfare workers and contractors, a domestic violence specialist be hired as part of a clinical consultant team, and a review committee be established to enforce the terms of the findings, which shall provide the court and all other interested parties with monthly reports. The agency targeted by the lawsuit, the Administration for Children's Services (ACS) in New York City, appealed Judge Weinstein's decision. The case was finally resolved when the New York Court of Appeals, to whom the case had been referred by the federal court, concurred with Judge Weinstein and added the stipulation that in its petitions for removal, ACS had to weigh the harms of leaving a child in his or her home against the trauma of removal. After three years of operation, the Nicholson Review Committee (NRC), representing all the parties to the lawsuit, concluded that the practice of removing children solely because of domestic violence had largely ended in New York City.

CURRENT PRACTICES

Nicholson had a ripple effect across the country. Child welfare agencies began examining their strategies when intervening with families experiencing domestic violence. Some states had already established practices, while others are still examining how to best serve families that experience domestic violence. The following section reviews the current practices of local and state agencies.

The response of state agencies, domestic violence programs, and communities has not kept pace with research on the overlap of domestic violence and child maltreatment. Few states have developed strategies to address the overlap, and few of those who initiated policies have evaluated their programs to see if their strategies are working.

Twenty-one states and Puerto Rico address the challenge of children witnessing domestic violence in their state statutes.[17] Many other states have attempted to include screening and services for children exposed to domestic violence as part of the child welfare system. In general, most of these efforts involve collaborating with other agencies and/or training for child welfare workers to screen and intervene with families experiencing domestic violence. The review of these efforts includes those with promising ideas as well as those that are empirically evaluated and found promising.

Massachusetts

Massachusetts has a long history of addressing the challenges when children are exposed to domestic violence. In a review of their case files, the Department of Social Services (DSS) discovered that 70 percent of referrals for intensive services included domestic violence but that the investigative worker identified domestic violence in less than half of these cases. In response to these findings, DSS piloted a project that required professionals to report child abuse and initiate an investigation if a child was exposed to domestic violence. As a result of the project, reports of domestic violence increased dramatically, but without additional funds or staff to handle the reports. Additionally, they found that women were reluctant to disclose their abuse to professionals for fear of losing their children to DSS. Instead of continuing the pilot project, DSS created a domestic violence unit staffed by advocates or specialists from the domestic violence field. The purpose of this unit was to provide training and consultation to child protective staff; to offer education, training, and collaboration with other community agencies, including shelters; and to provide direct services to battered women who were identified by the child welfare system. A six-month follow-up showed that 70 percent of *all* child welfare cases were referred to the new DSS unit for domestic violence services, a dramatic increase compared to the proportion of cases in which domestic violence was identified prior to co-locating a battered women advocate with child welfare workers.[18]

Michigan

Similar to Massachusetts, Michigan has a long-standing history of addressing the challenges faced when CPS works with families experiencing domestic violence. In the mid-1990s, Michigan established the Domestic Violence Prevention and Treatment Board, a statewide coordinated effort to end domestic violence. The mandate of the board included CPS collaborating with family preservation services and domestic violence programs. The collaboration resulted in the establishment of Families First, a program that recognized that safety for children can best be accomplished by ensuring the safety and

self-sufficiency of their mothers. The focus of Families First was to provide cross training on domestic violence for all program managers,
supervisors, and workers as well as battered women advocates and
domestic violence shelter staff. The biggest change in services occurred
when shelter staff was allowed to make direct referrals to the Families
First program. In the past, cases could only be referred to the CPS hotline and child welfare would decide if a domestic violence referral was
appropriate.

Through a collaboration of battered women advocates with Families
First staff, mandated training is provided for all child welfare workers
in Michigan. These training sessions focus on batterers, the criminal
and civil laws pertaining to domestic violence, community resources,
and such related topics as substance abuse, sexual abuse, parenting, and
child development. An evaluation found that, as a result of their training, workers decreased their blame of holding victims responsible for
their children's safety from 54 to 40 percent and decreased their referrals
to couples counseling from 74 to 46 percent. The proportion of child
welfare workers empathizing with battered women increased, and less
emphasis was placed on ending the relationship.[19]

Oregon

In a review of case files prior to the introduction of specific domestic
violence training or assessment, Oregon found that 26 percent of families with children entering foster care were exposed to domestic violence. They also found that domestic violence was an important factor
that distinguished severe physical abuse cases from those of moderate
or mild abuse; unfortunately, only 2 percent of all families were offered
domestic violence services.[20] Following this review, several Oregon
communities were funded to develop training, encourage collaboration
among community organizations, and implement a pilot project in
which a battered women advocate would be co-located in a CPS office.

San Diego, California

San Diego also has a proven track record of addressing the problem
of domestic violence in their community. But the link between domestic violence and child protection was not addressed until the early
1990s, when a mother and her child were murdered by her boyfriend
who had been on probation. The mother had been referred to the
Children's Services Bureau (CSB) for voluntary services, and the case
worker was not aware of the boyfriend's probationary status. After
running a cross-check on other cases, CSB saw a large overlap between
the child protection and the justice systems and decided that changes
were needed. The Family Violence Project was created to better protect

victims of domestic violence by coordinating case management activities between probation staff and the CSB staff. This project provides an administrative and technological bridge between the two agencies with the intent of holding batterers accountable and increasing awareness of staff about domestic violence and child abuse from both agencies.

Hawaii

In Hawaii, the primary linkage between domestic violence and child welfare services lies with the criminal justice system. Child welfare workers have access to the criminal histories of batterers as well as any restraining orders, permanent or temporary. Additionally, the family court judge presides over all child abuse and neglect cases as well as all petitions for restraining orders; hence, the judge can cross-reference restraining order cases, directly question families about the safety of their children, and make referrals to CPS. While this ability to cross-reference cases in the criminal justice and child welfare systems is helpful, there still is a lack of available services from which to make referrals for families experiencing domestic violence.

The Greenbook Initiative

A committee designated by the National Council of Juvenile and Family Court Judges to develop recommendations for how to best work with families with children who are exposed to domestic violence produced a report, formally called *Effective Intervention in Domestic Violence and Child Maltreatment Cases: Guidelines for Policy and Practice*, commonly known as the Greenbook.[21] In early 1991, the U.S. Department of Justice and the Health and Human Services funded six sites across the United States to implement the Greenbook's recommendations and focus on coordinating efforts between the courts, child welfare agencies, domestic violence shelters, and other professional groups involved with families experiencing domestic violence, such as law enforcement, medical providers, and schools, in a "seamless service delivery system." Evaluators have identified several barriers to the success of these collaborative efforts, including a lack of trust among participating organizations, a limited willingness to work together to overcome ideological differences, inadequate resources, and members who compromised the ability of the organizations to work collaboratively.

Family to Family (F2F)

The F2F initiative, funded by the Annie E. Casey Foundation in the early 1990s and later expanded to 60 cities in 17 states, encourages child welfare systems to keep children who are removed from their homes in their own neighborhoods and keep families involved. The F2F grantees realized that failing to address domestic violence could significantly interfere with their ability to reach their stated outcomes, but lacked the resources or knowledge needed to adequately respond to these cases. A more recent assessment noted the wisdom of these fears, citing the philosophical differences between CPS staff and battered women advocates and their reluctance to frankly discuss these differences as major barriers. The participating sites also noted how difficult it was to gather information about domestic violence with children and their families, foster families, or adoptive families and the lack of screening for domestic violence in foster families or support for victims in these families. The sites were also frustrated with the lack of knowledge and training on domestic violence for all involved, including community representatives.

Safe Start Demonstration Projects

As a result of a national summit in 1999 to create "a multidisciplinary continuum of prevention, intervention, and accountability," the U.S. Departments of Justice and Health and Human Services created the Safe Start Demonstration Project, piloted in 11 sites throughout the United States between 2000 and 2005. The idea was similar to the Greenbook Initiative—developing partnerships and collaborations between service providers, law enforcement, and the courts with the intent to create a comprehensive and coordinated system of care for families experiencing domestic violence. The major achievement of this initiative involves the materials and information produced, including policies, protocols, and a judicial checklist. Unfortunately, neither the initiative nor the materials it has produced has been evaluated.

Other Communities

Other local communities have also taken initiatives to address the overlap of domestic violence and child abuse. For example, a pilot project developed in New Haven and Hartford, Connecticut, by the Yale Child Study Center deploys mental health specialists on call 24 hours a day to support police responding to cases of homicide or domestic violence where children are present. The on-call therapist may either go to the scene or provide mental health services or referrals within 72 hours of the incident.

In the late 1980s, battered women advocates and medical professionals in the Children's Hospital in Boston created Advocacy for Women and Kids in Emergencies (AWAKE). The goal is to colocate an advocate at the hospital who provides services, including safety planning, with families experiencing domestic violence. AWAKE advocates also provide training and consultation to hospital staff and the surrounding community.

A program in Los Angeles, California, brings together elementary school teachers, mental health specialists, law enforcement, the district attorney's office, and probation departments to work with children exposed to domestic violence. Therapy, mentoring, and educational programs, all intended to help children cope with the violence they witnessed, provide opportunities for children to interact with professionals from different backgrounds who may be involved with their families.

In Boston, New Orleans, and other cities, programs focus on training law enforcement and teachers about child development and the impact of witnessing domestic violence; setting up 24-hour hotlines for information, education, and referrals for children; and providing education and information for physicians, especially pediatricians, to better inform them about the impact of domestic violence on children and the best way to screen for such impact.

IMPLICATIONS AND CONCLUSION

Does exposure to domestic violence indicate child maltreatment? How should child welfare and service providers respond to families with domestic violence? This chapter attempted to answer these complicated questions by reviewing the research on the number of children impacted by domestic violence and the consequences faced when exposed, and then discussing the philosophical challenges between the child welfare system and domestic violence shelters. State and local initiatives were then presented as a review of the attempts of these systems to collaborate together. What can we learn from this review? This concluding section outlines the implications for collaboration, training, practice, and policy for those working with or encountering families experiencing domestic violence.

Implications for Collaboration

Collaboration among all interested organizations and agencies is crucial when working with these families. The Greenbook and Safe Start Initiatives are solid first steps in encouraging communities to work together to keep families safe, but much more work and evaluation are needed.

It is common for service-providing organizations in the community to work together either voluntarily or as a mandate from federal, state, and local governments. Indeed, as discussed earlier, many communities have developed collaborative efforts between CPS, domestic violence service providers, and other entities. Unfortunately, there is little empirical evidence that suggests that successful interagency collaboration leads to improved client outcomes.

Past research on interagency collaboration "suggests that organizations whose cultures support teamwork, flexibility and participation in decisions, with an open flow of communication and a shared vision, tend to be better able to deliver positive outcomes for clients."[22] Johnson also cautions that there will be problems with collaborations when evidence-based practices are vague or when there are different philosophical views—such as the differences discussed earlier between CPS and domestic violence agencies.

As such, workers must take the initiative to learn about domestic violence and work closely with different professionals with a common commitment to keep families safe without blaming the mother and leaving the abuser unaccountable for his actions. Workers must also be patient; system change, community change, and individual change do not occur overnight. Nonjudgmental support is key to working with others, whether professionals or battered women and their children.

Implications for Training

While training has been helpful for child welfare workers, it is not the panacea to deal with the complex issues faced by families experiencing domestic violence. The issues raised by battered women and their children are often complex and cannot be solved through training alone. Issues such as poverty, substance abuse, and mental health may complicate plans to keep women and children safe from further abuse. Additionally, the attitudes and beliefs of child welfare workers may also impact the decisions they make with regard to assessing for and intervening with domestic violence. Finally, training can be a fruitless endeavor if not coupled with changes at the organizational and supervisory levels. A CPS, judicial, medical, or domestic violence worker may have the best knowledge on how to serve families experiencing domestic violence but may be thwarted by policies or protocols established by his or her respective organization.

Practice Implications

The key ingredients to successfully working with families experiencing domestic violence, as suggested in the literature, include the goals of holding the batterer accountable, supporting battered women and their children, and keeping the family safe from further harm. Both CPS and domestic violence service providers must come to an agreement on how to help families and keep everyone safe from harm. Some suggested elements for a common practice framework include the following: (1) all members of the family need to be safe; (2) children need to experience warm, supportive, nurturing relationships with parents; (3) all members of the family should have their basic needs met; (4) service providers need to be welcoming, supportive, and culturally competent; and (5) services should include strengths-based interventions that avoid unintended consequences.

Other principles outlined by experts in the field include (1) a willingness to work together across disciplines in a coordinated and collaborative manner; (2) a focus on prevention and supportive services to families at risk; (3) the importance to think developmentally about prevention and intervention services; (4) the emphasis on keeping mothers safe who, in turn, will keep children safe; (5) the enforcement of the law, holding perpetrators accountable; (6) the provision of adequate resources; (7) relying on sound and evidence-based practices; and (8) creating a culture of nonviolence at the individual, family, and community levels.

Policy Implications

Child welfare agencies and domestic violence service providers must evaluate the current policies and practices to determine what works and what does not work when it comes to keeping women and children safe from abuse. Without statewide policy shifts, reallocation of resources, changes in agency philosophy, and the development of standard procedures or protocols for screening, protective investigations, and case management, workers will be left frustrated not only in their dealings with battered women but also with their place of employment.

For example, during a recent training I conducted on domestic violence, child welfare supervisors expressed their frustrations of wanting to give women time to go through the process of leaving an abusive relationship yet were forced to maintain the deadlines dictated by the Adoption and Safe Families Act (ASFA). ASFA requires that permanency be achieved for every family involved with CPS in a specific time period; hence, the clock is ticking once a family becomes part of a CPS caseload. Even if a CPS worker was sensitive to the challenges faced by survivors, the worker's hands are tied regarding the amount of time allowed for families to become safe.

Additionally, supervisors expressed frustrations with local law enforcement's inability to hold batterers accountable—especially those who violated restraining orders. While their frustrations were anecdotal, more work is needed to examine how child welfare policies and other criminal justice policies may hinder child welfare workers as they attempt to be supportive of battered women.

Additionally, policy makers should establish minimum competency standards that include training for staff at all levels from all service providers that might encounter families experiencing violence. Protocols should also be established that clearly provide direction to CPS workers and supervisors when encountering the overlap of child abuse and domestic violence *and* to advocates and administrators working in the domestic violence field. These standards and protocols should include information about and guidance on working with any family, including those with different cultural, ethnic, or immigrant backgrounds. Additionally, it is imperative that staff from CPS and domestic violence service providers be involved in the development and implementation of these standards and protocols and be responsible for providing training and consultation when necessary to their peers in their respective fields.

In conclusion, the future lies with service providers from different fields being able to set aside their differences, work together, learn from each other, and create meaningful policies in order to meet the needs of families experiencing domestic violence. Without such collaboration, we will continue to punish families by removing children, blaming mothers, and not holding abusers accountable.

NOTES

1. Please note that an earlier version of this chapter appeared in G. P. Mallon and P. McCartt-Hess, *Child Welfare for the 21st Century: A Handbook of Children, Youth, and Family Services: Practices, Policies, and Programs* (New York: Columbia University Press, 2005). Courtesy of Columbia University Press.

2. B. E. Carlson, "Children's Observations of Interparental Violence," in *Battered Women and Their Families*, ed. A. R. Roberts (New York: Springer, 1984); and M. A. Straus, "Children as Witness to Marital Violence: A Risk Factor for Life Long Problems among a Nationally Representative Sample of American Men and Women" (paper read at Ross Roundtable on Children and Violence, Washington, D.C., 1991).

3. M. O'Brien, R. S. John, G. Margolin, and O. Erel, "Reliability and Diagnostic Efficacy of Parents' Reports Regarding Children's Exposure to Marital Aggression," *Violence & Victims* 9 (1994): 45–62.

4. E. Stark, "The Battered Mother in Child Protective Service Caseload: Developing an Appropriate Response," *Women's Rights Law Reporter* 23, no. 2 (2002): 107–31.

5. E. Werner and R. Smith, *Journeys of Childhood to Midlife: Risk, Resiliency and Recovery* (New York: Cornell University Press, 2001), 167.

6. Werner and Smith, *Journeys of Childhood to Midlife*, 37.

7. S. M. Stith, K. H. Rosen, K. A. Middleton, A. L. Busch, K. Lundeberg, and R. P. Carlton, "The Intergenerational Transmission of Spouse Abuse: A Meta-Analysis," *Journal of Marriage and the Family* 62, no. 3 (2000): 640–54.

8. B. Ballif-Spanvill, C. J. Clayton, and S. B. Hendrix, "Witness and Nonwitness Children's Violent and Peaceful Behavior in Different Types of Simulated

Conflict with Peers," *American Journal of Orthopsychiatry* 77, no. 2 (2007): 206–15.

9. Ballif-Spanvill, Clayton, and Hendrix, "Witness and Nonwitness Children's," 210.

10. C. M. Sullivan, H. Nguyen, N. E. Allen, D. I. Bybee, and J. Juras, "Beyond Searching for Deficits: Evidence That Physically and Emotionally Abused Women Are Nurturing Parents," *Journal of Emotional Abuse* 2, no. 1 (2000): 51–71.

11. A.D. Hazen, S. Miller, and J. Landsverk (1995), as reported in L. Mills, C. Friend, K. Conroy, A. Fleck-Henderson, S. Krug, R.H. Magen, R. L. Thomas, and J.H. Trudeau, "Child Protection and Domestic Violence: Training, Practice, and Policy Issues," *Child and Youth Services Review* 22, no. 5 (2000): 315–32.

12. E. Stark and A. H. Flitcraft, "Women and Children at Risk: A Feminist Perspective on Child Abuse," *International Journal of Health Services* 18, no. 1 (1988): 102.

13. J. L. Postmus, "Challenging the Negative Assumptions Surrounding Civil Protection Orders: A Guide for Advocates," *Affilia* 22, no. 4 (2007): 347–56.

14. P. L. Kohl, J. L. Edleson, D. J. English, and R. P. Barth, "Domestic Violence and Pathways into Child Welfare Services: Findings from the National Survey of Child and Adolescent Well-Being," *Children and Youth Services Review* 27 (2005): 1167–82.

15. D. J. English, J. L. Edleson, and M. E. Herrick, "Domestic Violence in One State's Child Protective Caseload: A Study of Differential Case Dispositions and Outcomes," *Children and Youth Services Review* 27 (2005): 1183–201.

16. Judge Weinstein's opinion is cited by Janet Carter, *Policy Talks* (Washington, D.C.: Family Violence Prevention Fund, 2002), 3.

17. Information about state statutes can be found at http://www.childwelfare.gov/systemwide/laws_policies/state.

18. Mills et al., "Child Protection and Domestic Violence."

19. D. G. Saunders and D. Anderson, "Evaluation of a Domestic Violence Training for Child Protection Workers and Supervisors: Initial Report," *Children and Youth Services Review* 22 (2000): 375–98.

20. Saunders and Anderson, "Evaluation of a Domestic Violence Training."

21. Author, *Effective intervention in domestic violence and child maltreatment cases: Guidelines for policy and practice.* (Reno, Nevada: National Council of Juvenile and Family Court Judges, 1999).

22. P. Johnson, G. Wistow, S. Rockwell, and B. Hardy, "Interagency and Interprofessional Collaboration in Community Care: The Interdependence of Structures and Values," *Journal of Interprofessional Care* 17, no. 1 (2003): 81.

Chapter 2

The "Transmission" of Intimate Partner Violence across Generations

Alison C. Cares

As readers are probably well aware, exposure to violence at home has a negative impact on children. It affects children both directly, because they may be victimized by coercion and control, and indirectly, because one or both of their parents are adversely impacted. These children may be arrested, driven from the home by violence, or suffer any of a number of violence-related physical, psychological, cognitive, or behavioral problems. Many of these problems also manifest in adulthood.

One of the most common beliefs about domestic violence (hereafter referred to as "intimate partner violence") is that a child who grows up in a violent household is bound to repeat that pattern as an adult. This belief is reflected in phrases such as the following: "The home is a breeding ground for violence," "Violence begets violence," and "The apple does not fall far from the tree." Researchers, criminal justice professionals, domestic violence service providers, and others refer to this pattern as the "cycle of violence" or the "intergenerational transmission of violence."

In fact, the intergenerational transmission belief is a myth both as an empirical claim and as a causal explanation for intimate partner violence. While children from violent homes are more likely to be involved in intimate partner violence as adults than children who grew up in nonviolent homes, most children from violent homes do not repeat a pattern of violence. Moreover, most abusive partners were not themselves abused or exposed to parental violence as children. Still, there is an important reality behind this myth. This chapter highlights what we know about the risks associated with childhood exposure and when and why the cycle is likely to be repeated. I also assess the major theoretical explanations for the intergenerational transmission. I close with questions about intervention suggested by our current knowledge about intergenerational transmission.

WHAT DO WE KNOW ABOUT THE INTERGENERATIONAL TRANSMISSION OF PARTNER VIOLENCE?

One of the most consistent predictors of adult intimate partner violence is violence in the family of origin. However, while that relationship has been documented repeatedly, it is probably small. The best estimate is that somewhere from 20 to 30 percent of current perpetrators were raised in violent families. Among those perpetrators responsible for more severe levels of violence, identified primarily in clinical populations, the percentage raised in a violent family is often higher—ranging between 50 and 60 percent.[1,2] Still, we can confidently say that *the majority of perpetrators did not grow up in a violent family*.

What is it about violent families and the children in them that matters? For whom is the pattern more likely to be repeated? There is contention over the answers to those questions. But it appears that gender matters.

For both males and females, growing up in a violent family increases the risk of being a perpetrator or victim of intimate partner violence in adulthood. However, the probability of later perpetration or victimization may differ by gender. Males who grow up in a violent home are more likely to become adult perpetrators than females, whereas females who grow up in a violent home are more likely to be victimized by adult partners. This pattern may be a continuation of the gendered patterns of reaction to family violence found in childhood, where boys tend to externalize and act out by hurting others and girls are more likely to internalize, often becoming depressed and withdrawn and engage in self-injurious behaviors.

Is adult partner violence perpetration only more likely if a child's same-gender parent was the perpetrator? Although there is not enough known on the topic to make definitive statements, the gender of the perpetrator and victim in the family of origin may also impact the cycle of violence. There is some support for same-gender transmission, with children who witnessed a same-gender parent perpetrating intimate partner violence being more likely to perpetrate intimate partner violence as an adult. To illustrate, a boy who witnessed his father abuse his mother would be more likely to commit intimate partner violence than a boy who witnessed his mother abuse his father. There is no similar evidence of same-gender transmission for victimization across generations.

It is also possible that the type of violence in the family of origin influences whether the gender of the perpetrator matters. Children experience violence in their family of origin in either or both of two ways: (1) they witness violence between their parents (referred to as interparental violence or parental domestic violence), and/or (2) they experience violence from one or both of their parents. Since these experiences can run the gamut in terms of severity and frequency, it is important not to equate all types of exposure with child abuse—it may or may not have risen to this level. (See the discussion of this issue by Postmus, chapter 1.) Some studies suggest that witnessing parental violence is a stronger predictor of later partner violence than experiencing parental violence. However, there is widespread disagreement on this claim.

WHY DO PATTERNS DIFFER BY GENDER?

So why are adults from violent families more likely to be involved in adult intimate partner violence? Why might the cycle of violence differ by gender? The most common explanation is provided by social learning theory, but there are competing explanations.

Social Learning Theory

Social learning theory builds off of the work of psychologist Albert Bandura and posits that humans learn behavior through patterns of observation, imitation, and reinforcement. Behaviors that children see or experience as successful or positively rewarded are more likely to be repeated, especially if that behavior was enacted by someone with whom the child closely identifies. Behaviors that do not achieve the desired outcome or result in something unpleasant are not likely to be repeated. Social learning theory argues that this is the basis for all human behavior, not just violent behavior. Regarding the cycle of violence, the concern is more specific: do violent families, especially those with intimate partner violence, teach children to be involved in later partner violence?

If social learning theory is applied to the intergenerational transmission of partner violence, there are a number of specific patterns that should follow. First, witnessing parental violence should be a better predictor of later partner violence than experiencing violence at the hand of a parent because it is a more direct form of learning and modeling behavior. As mentioned above, there is some evidence that this is so. Second, since children more closely identify with the parent who shares their sexual identity, we should see same-gender modeling. This would mean the relationship between witnessing and perpetrating should be stronger for boys who witnessed a father perpetrating than boys who witnessed a mother perpetrating, and for girls who witnessed a mother perpetrating than girls who witnessed a father perpetrating. It would also mean that the relationship between witnessing and later victimization would be stronger for boys who witnessed their fathers as victims versus boys who witnessed their mothers as victims, and it would be stronger for girls who witnessed their mothers as victims than girls who witnessed their fathers as victims. To date, evidence in support of same-gender modeling of intimate partner violence and victimization is mixed, as already suggested. However, if we assume that male-to-female violence is the more common pattern in families of origin, the gender-identity learning model could explain why exposed males are more likely to become perpetrators and exposed females are more likely to become victims.

Although more difficult to prove empirically, there are additional relationships suggested by social learning theory. Behavior is more likely to be repeated if it was successful or led to something positively valued. Thus, we might predict that children are more likely to repeat intimate partner violence that they witness if they perceive it as "successful." How should we determine if partner violence is "successful"? If a perpetrator's violence succeeds in gaining a partner's compliance to his or her demands, for example, would a child learn that this sort of behavior is advantageous and so should be repeated? If a child witnesses the victim changing behavior to try to avoid future incidents and anticipate the perpetrator's demands, would that be perceived by a child as the successful use of violence? Is violence less likely to be perceived as "successful" if a victim physically resists or fights back, or in situations where the distinction between the perpetrator and the victim is unclear? In other words, does someone have to "win" for imitation or learning to occur? Does the length of exposure contribute to the use of violence in the next generation? Specifically, if adults stay together amidst the violence, do children view this violence as a successful way to handle conflict in a relationship? If the perpetrator gains compliance in the immediate incident, but the victim then ends the relationship and leaves, does that mitigate the "success" of the violence and lead the child to conclude that, ultimately, violence is not successful? Answering these questions requires more knowledge about the nature and context of partner violence in the first generation and its impacts on children than we currently possess.

Thus, social learning theory offers a very inexact and partial account of the contexts in which violence and aggression are transmitted across generations or of its psychosocial dynamics or the degree to which learning explains current perpetration and victimization. This is true even of research that considers multiple dimensions of violence and differentiates by gender. It is becoming apparent that the relationship between violence in the family of origin and later partner violence is not as simple and direct as the basic explanation provided by social learning theory. Something else appears to intervene. So, a significant next question should be as follows: exactly what is being passed from generation to generation? What is being learned, and from whom? Answering this question may involve variations on social learning theory as well as abandoning the theory altogether in favor of other theoretical explanations.

An alternative application of social learning theory considers the possibility that something other than violence is being learned through witnessing parental abuse that is then later modeled. A plausible argument is that what children are learning in these situations are attitudes about the use of violence or attitudes about women and the role women play. Are children learning how to interpret the reactions of others? Are they learning models of how to handle conflict in intimate relationships? If they are learning these attitudes, do they have the same effect on later perpetration as on victimization? This raises the controversial and politically sensitive question: Do people *learn* to be victims?

Examples abound in popular culture suggesting that people have "learned" to be victims. But it is unclear what this means. Is it that victims have learned a pattern of social interaction and conflict management that is more likely to lead to violence? Have they learned to select aggressive partners or, at least, to tolerate violence as a part of a relationship? Have they failed to develop the psychological, social, and material resources needed to avoid being vulnerable to victimization? A quick review of accounts that advance these arguments suggests that social learning theory is better at explaining violence perpetration than victimization. Moreover, when it is used to advance these arguments without supportive empirical evidence, social learning theory can effectively "blame" the victim for the harms he or she experiences at the hands of others.

Social learning theory dominates explanations of the relationship between violence in the family of origin and later partner violence. But while a number of studies have supported its account, other studies have found it wanting. This suggests that we explore additional theoretical accounts of the intergenerational transmission of violence.

Attachment Theory

Social psychologists have explored the relationship between attachment style and the intergenerational transmission of violence. Attachment theory helps trace the path from infancy through adult romantic relationships to explain how violence passes between generations. At the core is a belief that certain attachment styles increase the likelihood of intimate partner violence. The intergenerational relationship is made possible by two, possibly related, mechanisms: (1) the replication of attachment styles between generations; and (2) violence in the family of origin increasing the likelihood of certain, problematic attachment styles.

According to attachment theory, infants develop a primary attachment to a caregiver, and the nature of that attachment becomes a model for that child's attachment in later relationships. Generally, there are two types of attachment: secure and insecure. Insecure attachment is typically examined by subtypes (with categories such as avoidant, anxious, and disorganized, or preoccupied, dismissing, and fearful) or, in recent work on adult attachment, along dimensions of anxiety and avoidance in relationships. Of concern in this case is how early attachment is related to attachment styles in adult romantic relationships, and how those adult attachment styles may be related to intimate partner violence.

In infancy and childhood, a home with marital conflict, which could include intimate partner violence, is more likely to elicit an insecure attachment style in children. Two intertwined paths are thought to produce this adaptation. First, whether parents are victims or perpetrators, marital conflict appears to increase the negativity of their interactions with their children, increasing the likelihood of an insecure attachment. Second, as a result of victimization in particular, parents may become emotionally unavailable or uninvolved with their children, increasing the likelihood of insecure attachment. When children perceive that one or both parents may become physically or psychologically unavailable, as in the case of separation or divorce, this creates fear and anxiety, leading to insecure attachment. In short, a child who does not have a parent he or she can depend on for stability, warmth, availability, and love cannot develop a secure attachment. Intimate partner violence negatively impacts parenting, thereby influencing a child's attachment.

Because childhood relationships with primary caregivers provide the model or training ground for how to function in later relationships, children who do not form secure attachments in childhood are less likely to be able to establish trusting and stable relationships as adolescents and adults. It is suspected that attachment styles extend over time, so that insecurely attached children are more likely to become insecurely attached adults, even in marriage. Indeed, an individual's attachment classification in infancy corresponds to his or her classification in adolescence or early adulthood in almost 75 percent of cases.[3,4] More to the point, adults who witnessed interparental violence in childhood are more likely to exhibit an insecure attachment style.

Insecure attachment styles are problematic for two reasons related to the intergenerational transmission of violence: (1) the link between attachment style and intimate partner violence; and (2) the link between attachment style and marital quality. Male intimate partner violence perpetrators are more likely to have an insecure attachment style than men who are not violent in their marriages or cohabiting relationships. Adults with insecure attachments also exhibit higher levels of relationship-related anxiety, avoidance, or both. In this context, anxiety is the degree to which a person has low self-worth and is concerned about abandonment and rejection. Avoidance is the degree to which a person seeks out physical or psychological closeness and his or her comfort level in being dependent on other people. What matters in terms of intimate partner violence is how these concerns become manifest in a relationship context to make violence more likely. For example, those high on the anxiety dimension may be excessively needy, constantly requiring reassurance from a partner, even on relatively small matters, thereby increasing tension in the relationship and the likelihood for conflict and, therefore, violence. This possibility is tapped by items often used to assess the anxiety dimension, such as "If I can't get my partner to show interest in me, I get upset or angry" (Experiences in Close Relationships Inventory [ECR]).[5] As another example, individuals high on avoidance may push away, figuratively and literally, if they feel a partner is getting too close for comfort. Manifestation of heightened levels of either or both dimensions can have significant negative implications for the health of an adult romantic relationship.

The health of an adult romantic relationship may be a key factor in the relationship of attachment style and intimate partner violence. It is well established that low-quality marriages are more likely to include violence as well as the converse, but which comes first is unclear. The first possibility is that insecure attachment styles lead to lower marital quality, which can increase the risk of intimate partner violence. Those with more secure attachment have higher marital quality. Since the level of marital quality is negatively related to risk of violence in a marriage, those with higher marital quality are less likely to experience marital violence. The second possibility is that insecure attachment increases the risk of violence in a romantic relationship, which lowers the relationship's quality. In either case, attachment style either directly or indirectly influences the presence of violence in an adult romantic relationship. If that relationship includes children, violence may be creating insecure attachment in the next generation, hence increasing the possibility of violence.

Attachment theory is a common explanation for the intergenerational transmission of intimate partner violence. Much greater specificity is required, however, before its utility is proved. There are four paths that the intergenerational cycle of intimate partner violence can follow. Two involve whether perpetration in the first generation influences perpetration or victimization in the second, and two involve the influence of victimization on subsequent perpetration or victimization.

In these cases, research would consider the victimization or perpetration status of the adult to whom the child is primarily attached, which is typically thought to be the mother, and their attachment style. There is some evidence of replication of maternal attachment style. Whether the same holds true for males is unknown. We need to know, therefore, whether a child who learns an insecure attachment style from a victimized mother is at greater risk for intimate partner violence perpetration, victimization, or both. Or would that depend on the type of insecure attachment? Perhaps those high on avoidance are at greater risk for perpetration when they feel a relationship is becoming too intense, and when other signals for their partner to back off are not heeded. Or, where insecure attachment is manifested in high anxiety, perhaps persons use violence out of frustration when their needs are not met. Unpopular as the suggestion may be, would those high in relationship anxiety be more likely to be intimate partner violence victims because they are too dependent on a partner, allowing a partner little room for autonomy?

A larger question is whether we should limit our examination to paths between individual parents and children or consider a gestalt that includes the attachment interactions of both partners in the family of origin and both partners in the adult romantic relationship. It may be that certain combinations of attachment patterns predict violence in physical relationships better than others. Violence may occur in one relationship involving someone high on avoidance, for instance, but not another, because of the partner's attachment style. Finally, is the relationship between attachment style and perpetration or victimization conditioned by gender either because attachment styles differ by gender or because their significance for transmission differs by gender? To answer this, we would have to correlate family-of-origin violence, sex identity, and attachment style. At least one study that linked violence in the family of origin to later partner violence perpetration failed to find that attachment style was a significant factor. In any case, attachment theory offers a viable and increasingly popular alternative to social learning theory, despite the popularity of the latter as an explanation for the intergenerational cycle of intimate partner violence.

Lifecourse or Developmental Theory

Lifecourse or developmental theory addresses a weakness of both social learning theory and attachment theory—the lack of attention to the years between childhood and adulthood. According to an application of lifecourse theory to the intergenerational transmission of violence, the effect of childhood experiences with violence in the family of origin may depend on the individual's stage of the lifecourse, and therefore, the nature of the relationship may vary over time at different developmental stages. The initial predictors of aggression may change over time in a relationship.

Developmental theory may also explain why the relationship between violence in the family of origin and violence in later intimate partner relationships varies across high school student, college student, and older community or couple samples. The effect of violence in the family of origin on later partner violence varies with age. An important developmental phenomenon appears to be the influence of peers. Higher quality of friendships in adolescence is related to reduced intimate partner violence, but that influence is stronger earlier in the transition to adulthood (early 20s) and seems to lose any influence later. This suggests that the influence of peers and of parents may wax and wane over time, with the influence of parents being important early in life, and again as children enter adult-like romantic relationships, and the prominence of peer influence being strongest during adolescence. Given research on the influence of peers on delinquency in the field of criminology, such findings should not be surprising. Peers are considered to be the strongest influence on delinquency in adolescence, but according to lifecourse theory, their influence wanes as individuals enter early adulthood and take on adult responsibilities such as a marriage and jobs.

If the influence of violence in the family of origin is not static, the relationship needs to be investigated further, considering a broader spectrum of the lifecourse beyond early adulthood. What is the relationship between violence in the family of origin and later partner violence for those beyond their 20s and early 30s or after the first few years of marriage? This may be especially important in light of the fact that adults exhibit lower levels of partner violence with increasing age and marital duration. Rates of desistence of partner violence within marriage tend to be quite high, ranging from 24 to 58 percent.[6] Do couples or marriages "age out" of intimate partner violence as they enter later developmental stages? Is there another explanation? For example, are violent relationships more likely to end than nonviolent relationships? And how does this relate to any ongoing influence of violence in the family of origin? As patterns in a marriage become established, does the influence of violence in the family of origin wane? What is the relationship of violence in the family of origin if there are multiple transitions in marital status?

The prospective or panel data needed to support lifecourse theory allow for the exploration of change at multiple points in time, but are considerably more difficult and expensive to collect than the evidence for attachment or learning theory. However, lifecourse theory offers a promising approach to explaining the variable influence of violence in the family of origin on later partner violence, although exploration of these patterns is still rare.

Behavioral Genetics

Any discussion of a relationship across generations would be remiss if it failed to consider a biological influence. A key question in any investigation of an intergenerational transmission is how much, if any, of the similarity between generations is due to nature (i.e., heredity) and how much is due to nurture. While social learning and attachment theories posit explanations for the influence of nurture, biological theories may explain the unique contribution of nature.

The application of genetically based research designs to the study of intimate partner violence remains in its infancy, as most pieces to date have been theoretical or otherwise nonempirical. Directly testing the effects of nature versus nurture typically utilizes a twins' sample. When comparing sets of twins, if the behavior of identical (monozygotic) twins is more alike than the behavior of same-gender fraternal (dizygotic) twins, that difference is attributed to genetic influence. There is new evidence of a genetic component to perpetration of and victimization by psychological and physical partner aggression, estimating that approximately 25 percent of the variability in psychological partner aggression and 15 percent of the variability in physical partner aggression are due to genetic influence.[7] This preliminary research did not find support for the influence of shared environment, which is the explanation given by social learning theory.

Even if inherited genetic material is partially responsible for passing intimate partner violence between generations, many questions have yet to be explored. For example, the same question applies here that we asked of social learning theory, namely, what exactly is being passed along? There are at least three possibilities. First, is it hormone levels? Research on general aggression has identified levels of androgen, the male sex hormone, often focusing on testosterone, as causally linked to levels of physical aggression. (Androgens are also present in females to a lesser degree.) Since intimate partner violence is a subtype of aggression, perhaps that same relationship between androgen levels and aggression may apply. That possibility would predict a stronger relationship between violence in the family of origin and later perpetration of partner violence for males than females, a finding for which there is some support, as we saw above.

A second possibility is that what is being inherited is the biological basis of antisocial behavior, which has frequently been highlighted as a risk factor for perpetration of family violence and child abuse, and as an outcome of violence in the family of origin. Thus, it may be spurious to identify a causal path from violence in the family of origin to later partner violence because both are due to a third factor. A genetic risk for antisocial behavior may lead antisocial parents to be more likely to abuse their children and partners *and* also pass along a predisposition to antisocial behavior through genetic material to their children that makes them more likely to be involved in family violence as adults.

A third possibility is that a type of genetic resilience is inherited. For example, maltreated male children with high monoamine oxidase A (MAOA) expression appear less likely than other maltreated children to develop antisocial behavior. Essentially, MAOA is functioning as a protective factor that may "break" the cycle of violence, and there may be more genetically driven protective factors that have yet to be uncovered.

Although still in the exploratory stage, behavioral genetics offers exciting new possibilities to help explain the intergenerational cycle of violence. However, it also requires a word of caution. Like the relationship between violence in the family of origin and later involvement in partner violence, heredity is not destiny. Instead, what is inherited is a predisposition, in this case to partner violence, that may or may not ever be realized based on countless environmental and contextual factors. As modern behavioral-genetic theories emphasize, the nature of what is inherited is probabilistic, not deterministic. There is no intimate partner violence gene.

Missing Pieces

None of the theories cited offer a conclusive explanation of how violence in the family of origin leads to later partner violence. That leaves two possibilities. The first is that prior theorizing is incorrect and that other causal mechanisms are at work. The second possibility is that the theorizing is not incorrect, but is incomplete. These "missing pieces" are potentially important factors that might intervene in or modify the relationship between violence in the family of origin and later partner violence. While there is an extensive list of possible missing pieces, this discussion will be limited to just a handful.

One set of "missing pieces" is exactly what is being transmitted between generations. As mentioned above, perhaps witnessing parental violence leads offspring to develop attitudes favorable to the use of violence and so makes them more likely to use violence or accept it. Although attitudes justifying dating or spousal violence may join violence in childhood and among adults, it is unclear what relationship there is between family-of-origin violence, attitudes condoning general violence, and intimate partner violence in adulthood. This may be particularly important because many perpetrators of family violence also perpetrate violence in nonfamily relationships, and both types of violence may have the same underlying cause.

A related gap is the extent to which attitudes influence the transmission of victimization across generations. Do children who experience violence in their family of origin develop attitudes condoning and accepting violence in their own adult relationships? This seems to be the case for younger females in dating couples.

Another missing piece concerns the acquisition of communication and conflict styles in violent families of origin that are more likely to lead to violence in adult intimate relationships. Certain styles of interaction may escalate conflict, rather than diffuse it, making physical violence more likely. For example, an aggressive conflict-response style partially explains the effect of family-of-origin violence on later physical violence for boys and girls in dating couples. Male perpetrators of intimate partner violence often exhibit more anger and hostility, a pattern that may be modeled on experiences in childhood with family violence.

Most discussion of the intergenerational transmission of violence centers on linking violence witnessed or experienced in childhood to experiences with partner violence in adulthood. Such an approach overlooks a number of intervening years and important aspects of human development that may alter the relationship between family-of-origin violence and later partner violence. Experiences with family violence in childhood may lead to the development of certain problematic personality types or conduct patterns that make violence in adult intimate relationships more likely. For perpetration, a conduct disorder may amplify the effect of witnessing parental violence on later perpetration, but not victimization. Experience with family violence in childhood may also be linked to the development of certain personality disorders known to be more common amongst partner violence perpetrators. These personality disorders include antisocial personality trait or disorder and borderline personality organization or disorder.

The course of later intimate partner relationships may be influenced by events or life experiences that occur in the years between childhood and adulthood as well as by problematic personality traits or behaviors. This builds on a developmental framework approach. In social learning theory, the relationship witnessed between parents in childhood is the main reference for how to behave in adult intimate partnerships. However, it appears likely that other relationships during childhood and adolescence are important to children and provide a training ground for adult intimate partnerships as well as an opportunity to modify the effect of childhood experiences on family violence. While adolescent romantic relationships are often not taken seriously by adults, they are taken very seriously by the adolescents involved. Since marriages and cohabitations arise from dating relationships, many of which originate in adolescence, it seems important to investigate the effect of family-of-origin violence on dating violence and the ability of dating violence experiences to predict later intimate partner violence. The young people from violent homes involved in dating relationships in high school and college appear more likely to perpetrate violence in their nascent relationships. How this links to violence in later relationships or even later in the same relationship is largely unknown. Is the combination of exposure to intimate partner violence in childhood and the perpetration of dating violence in adolescence most likely to elicit intimate partner violence in adult partners? Can a nonviolent dating relationship derail the "transmission" of violence across generations, perhaps by providing an alternative model?

Dating and interparental relationships may not provide the only contexts for learning how to behave in intimate relationships. Parent-child and sibling relationships as well as friendships may exert an influence on the quality of adolescent romantic relationships. For example, the violence in a friend's dating relationships has been found to be a better predictor of an adolescent's own perpetration of dating violence than witnessing interparental violence. Again, an important question is if types or qualities of these other relationships exert influence beyond the dating relationship or change the relationship between violence in the family of origin and later partner violence. It also may matter if the friend in the dating relationship is the same gender as the focal person, and if the friend is a victim, perpetrator, or both.

Finally, there exists the distinct possibility, which has been mentioned briefly above, that it is not the violence that is passed to the next generation, but the causes of the adults' aggression in the family of origin that are being transmitted. This could be due to heredity that results in a genetic disposition to violence. It is also possible that parents with poor social or communication skills, with personality disorders, or who demonstrate high levels of anger and hostility pass those attributes along to their children, and it is those attributes that make violence more likely in both generations.

WHAT MORE WE NEED TO KNOW

The exploration of the "transmission" of intimate partner violence is at a crossroads. From researching whether a relationship exists between violence across generations, we have progressed to consider factors that enhance or disrupt that relationship. There should be an examination of protective factors, as well as risk factors, in order to provide practitioners and policy makers with the knowledge needed to solve the problem. Questions asked also need to more comprehensively examine distinctions and expand to consider the role of race and culture in transmission.

Distinctions

Two key distinctions can be made regarding the relationship between intergenerational transmission of violence and intimate partner violence: distinctions among types of perpetrators and distinctions among types of intimate partner violence. Clearly, a "one-size-fits-all" approach to categorizing domestic violence perpetrators does not work, as evidenced by the perceived widespread failure of batterers' treatment programs. There is little research that distinguishes types of partner violence among females (see the chapters by Goodmark and by Swan and her colleagues in Volume 3 of this set). But there appear to be important differences amongst male perpetrators of intimate partner violence. These differences extend to experiences with violence in the family of origin, and therefore, there may be different causal processes linking violence between the generations for different types of perpetrators. For example, we have seen that men who use the severest forms of violence are more likely than other perpetrators to have witnessed domestic violence as a child. These perpetrators were also more aggressive earlier in a marital conflict, and were more likely to be antisocial. When looking at a wider cross section of perpetrators, differences remain. Those who limit their violence to the family witnessed less interparental violence than other groups of perpetrators. Additionally, it appears that batterers who employ more severe violence can also be distinguished by their attachment styles.

Also important is the ability to distinguish between types of partner violence in the family of origin and in the adult intimate relationship. Certain types of partner violence may be more likely than others to be repeated. Using information on control tactics and use of violence from both partners, it appears that there are two main types of intimate partner violence. These are referred to as "intimate terrorism" (or coercive control) and "situational couple violence." Intimate terrorism is what is traditionally portrayed as partner violence. It is disproportionately perpetrated by males against their female partners, linked to patriarchal norms and traditions, and part of a larger constellation of behaviors aimed at establishing power and control over a partner. The violence is more likely than other types to escalate over time, occur more frequently, be more severe, and cause fear and injury. The more common type of partner violence is situational couple violence. In such cases, one or both partners use violence in the context of an argument, but not as part of an attempt to gain more global power and control in the relationship. Although this violence can be serious, repeated, and even frequent, it tends to include more minor acts of violence, and be specific to the situation or conflict at hand. Another way to think of situational couple violence is that it occurs when arguments spin out of control, which helps explain why it is equally likely to be perpetrated by men and women (although it is still perpetrated by only one partner at least half of the time). Compared to intimate terrorism, it is less likely to escalate over time and is less serious.

It appears that witnessing parental violence is only related to perpetrating intimate terrorism among men. In other words, no relationship has yet been demonstrated between witnessing and perpetrating situational couple violence by men or between witnessing and female perpetration of intimate terrorism or situational couple violence. This suggests that what men "learn" from witnessing is not merely violence, but also the use of violence in a larger context of power and control (facilitated by patriarchy). This would also explain why population surveys (which pick up cases of primarily situational couple violence) often find only a weak relationship between violence in the family of origin and later partner violence.

Ideally, research on the intergenerational transmission of intimate partner violence would consider the combination of gender and type of intimate partner violence both in the family of origin and in adult intimate relationships. However, we currently lack the data needed for this kind of examination. We simply do not know enough about the context of intimate partner violence—its frequency, its severity, whether it is embedded in a larger pattern of power and control, who initiated it, if it was "successful" (see earlier discussion), and if the victim and perpetrator are biological parents of the child or not—to make the distinctions necessary to advance knowledge of the intergenerational transmission of violence and create programs to address it.

Diversity

However much we have learned about the intergenerational cycle of intimate partner violence, the accumulated knowledge is largely limited to Western, largely white populations of married heterosexual couples experiencing physical violence. Research today is largely confined to the United States, Canada, and Australia and New Zealand—samples that are predominantly white and use English as a first language. Exploration needs to be expanded to non-Western, non-English-speaking countries as well as to nonwhite and nonheterosexual relationships in Western countries. If violence is a result of a genetic predisposition, studies of the behavioral genetics of the intergenerational transmission of violence should uncover a similar strength of prediction in other countries and among nonwhites. Exploration also needs to be undertaken with same-gender couples. For example, if much of what is passed down has roots in patriarchy, how would that affect children of same-gender couples or in same-gender couples? Would it matter if the couple consisted of two males rather than two females? Finally, more attention needs to be paid to the diversity of abuse experiences in childhood and adulthood. The co-occurrence of other types of abuse (e.g., sexual abuse or psychological abuse) may be key in whether physical abuse is repeated, or it may be that psychological abuse is passed down and is not garnering sufficient attention or that abuse in the first generation may manifest in a different form in the second generation.

CONCLUSION

The good news is that although growing up in a violent home is by no means a positive experience, the negative impact in terms of repeating the action has been vastly overstated. Some have suggested that the intergenerational transmission of violence and cycle of violence are terms we should avoid, particularly given their victim-blaming potential and the weak nature of the actual relationship between violence in the family of origin and later partner violence. Still, violence in the family of origin remains one of the stronger predictors of later partner violence, but only in certain circumstances, some of which we have identified. None of the theories detailed here provides a complete explanation even of the relationship that has been uncovered. However frustrating this may be, it is hardly surprising given the complexity of the world and human nature, especially over the time spanned from childhood to adulthood.

So why does this all matter? For two reasons: growing up in a violent home can have a host of other negative effects for children, and for some, it does appear to increase the likelihood that they will be involved in intimate partner violence as adults. Those who have the opportunity to improve the lives of children need the best possible tools to support those exposed to violence at home. This is particularly important since we do know that exposure to violence does not set these children on an inevitable path toward further violence in their relationships. Conversely, most of the factors that appear to increase the probability that violence will be transmitted can be modified with thoughtful intervention, making it possible for even those at highest risk to get out of intimate relationships what most people are seeking: love, support, and companionship.

Researchers can contribute to this process by further delineating the pathways by which violence in childhood is replicated and, as importantly, by documenting the strengths and resiliencies in children and families that have kept them from replicating the violence to which they've been exposed. This includes making careful distinctions by gender, types of violence experienced, developmental stage, and the context of the violence, as well as considering issues of national and cultural diversity. Should we have gender-specific programs, or can programs be applied equally to men and women with different cultural or economic backgrounds? Will certain types of exposure require specially targeted interventions, while other types may respond to universal services? What programs do we need to help children transition from being in a violent home to cultivating a romantic relationship of their own? Should programs focus on talking about the violence in the home or addressing possible problematic intervening outcomes, such as therapeutic treatment of personality and behavioral disorders, and attachment styles? In sum, understanding that children exposed to partner violence are not fated to become violent or violence victims as adults should give us hope that we—and they—can help to shape the adults they will become.

NOTES

1. M. P. Johnson and K. J. Ferraro, "Research on Domestic Violence in the 1990s: Making Distinctions," *Journal of Marriage and the Family* 62 (2000): 948–63.

2. A. Holtzworth-Munroe, L. Bates, N. Smutzler, and E. Sandin, "A Brief Review of the Research on Husband Violence, Part I: Maritally Violent versus Nonviolent Men," *Aggression and Violent Behavior* 2, no. 1 (1997): 65–99.

3. E. Waters, S. Merrick, D. Treboux, J. Crowell, and L. Albersheim., "Attachment Security in Infancy and Early Adulthood: A Twenty-Year Longitudinal Study," *Child Development* 71, no. 3 (2000): 684–89.

4. C. E. Hamilton, "Continuity and Discontinuity of Attachment from Infancy through Adolescence," *Child Development* 71, no. 3 (2000): 690–94.

5. K. A. Brennan, C. L. Clark, and P. R. Shaver, "Self-Report Measurement of Adult Attachment: An Integrative Approach," in *Attachment Theory and Close Relationships*, ed. J. A. Simpson and W. S. Rhodes (New York: Guilford Press, 1998), 46–76.

6. A. C. Cares, *Marital Quality, Marital Violence, and Gender: A Longitudinal Analysis* (University Park: Pennsylvania State University, 2005).

7. D. A. Hines and K. J. Saudino, "Genetic and Environmental Influences on Intimate Partner Aggression: A Preliminary Study," *Violence and Victims* 19, no. 6 (New York: Springer Publishing Company, 2004): 701–18.

Chapter 3

Securing Safety for Abused Women and Children in the Family Courts

Hilary Saunders

For years, agencies working with victims of partner abuse such as the Women's Aid Federations have expressed concern that the family courts in England and Wales do not provide adequate protection when violent fathers apply for contact orders to see their children. However, it has been extremely difficult to convince the government, the judiciary, and the public that this is a problem that needs to be addressed. This chapter considers the reasons why the issue of safety for women and children became almost "invisible" in family cases, and it describes the findings of a report that challenged and helped to change family court practice. Whether these changes go far enough is debatable, but at least there is now much greater awareness of the risks to children associated with domestic violence.

A word on the terminology used in this chapter. In the United Kingdom, the terms "contact" and "residence" are used for "access" and "custody." Instead of "batterer," the term widely applied in the United States, we use the terms "domestic violence perpetrator" or "abuser." We also have a large network of "refuges" and "domestic violence organizations" for abused women and children as opposed to "shelters."

WHY DID SAFETY BECOME LESS IMPORTANT THAN CONTACT?

Numerous factors contributed to child contact being perceived as having the greatest importance: some are common in other countries, while others are specific to the legal system in England and Wales. Perhaps the most fundamental reason is the widespread belief, shared by many abused women, that children need to know both their parents. This belief is so deeply entrenched in our family justice system that judicial statistics for England and Wales show that contact orders were refused in less than 1 percent of private law family cases in 2005. Indeed, even in public law child protection cases, contact sometimes appears to be prioritized over safety. A recent study of 130 children removed from their families for their own safety found that 12 percent had been physically abused and 6 percent sexually abused again as a result of unsupervised contact visits, and it was suspected that a further 11 percent had been physically or sexually abused during contact.[1]

In England and Wales, the confidentiality rules in family proceedings involving children made it very difficult to protest cases in which children suffered harm as a result of contact orders being granted to violent parents. In the county courts, the media and the public were excluded from family proceedings involving children, and judgments were not made public. Litigants were warned that documents such as court welfare reports should not be shown to any third party. Although the confidentiality rules have recently been relaxed, it remains an offense to publish anything that might identify a child publicly as being involved in family court proceedings. This secrecy made it almost impossible to provide evidence that safety issues were not being dealt with appropriately. Agencies wishing to give examples of bad practice to government ministers could only provide anonymous details, whittled down to a bare minimum to ensure that the case was not identifiable. Inevitably such evidence was dismissed as "anecdotal."

The need to preserve anonymity also limited the possibility of obtaining media coverage. Abused women are wary of using the media to challenge contact decisions because of the risk of further violence from their ex-partner and fears of how the family courts might respond. This is not surprising; a survey of 178 domestic violence organizations in England and Wales found that the most common threat used to make an abused woman comply with a contact order was that the child could be ordered to live with the abuser.[2]

In contrast, fathers' groups used the media very effectively to put pressure on the government to reform the family courts, which they claimed were biased in favor of women. Through a series of publicity stunts such as "Superman" demonstrating on the façade of Buckingham Palace, they gained a huge amount of media coverage for their claims that loving fathers were being denied contact with their children by the family courts. Although Fathers for Justice (the highest profile group) eventually disbanded following an undercover television investigation, there was still considerable support within Parliament for their demands for legal reform to ensure "reasonable contact" and the rapid enforcement of contact orders.

In England and Wales, the Children Act 1989 provides the basic legal framework for contact and residence proceedings. The act states that the welfare of the child is paramount, and it contains a welfare checklist that requires the court to consider various factors including the ascertainable wishes and feelings of the child and any harm that the child has suffered or is at risk of suffering. There is no provision requiring the court to ensure that arrangements are safe for the child, and the grounds for appeal are very limited because the court has wide discretion to make whatever order it considers is in the best interests of the child. Proposals for safety amendments were rejected as unnecessary on the grounds that safety is clearly a crucial element of the child's welfare, which is already paramount.

Unfortunately, some case-law precedents have been very damaging in family court cases involving domestic violence or child abuse. In 1995 the Court of Appeal ruled that contact is "almost always in the interests of the child,"[3] a ruling that leaves hardly any room for exceptions. In 1996 the House of Lords (our highest court) ruled that a higher standard of proof than the simple balance of probabilities should be required in family court cases involving "more serious allegations"—a judgment that one dissenting law lord feared would "establish the law in an unworkable form to the detriment of many children at risk."[4] Both these cases undermined the principle that the welfare of the child is paramount by requiring the courts to focus on other issues, although new case law in 2008 finally reinstated the simple balance of probabilities as the standard of proof for family law cases. The Court of Appeal took this further by ruling that the welfare of the child is not paramount when the court considers committing a parent to prison for not complying with a contact order. In this case the mother was given a six-week sentence for refusing to comply with a contact order, although "the father had a history of violence, including a very serious assault on his former wife for which he was sent to prison."[5]

It had been hoped that a Court of Appeal ruling in four test cases would improve practice, because it required the courts to decide whether allegations of violence are proved or not and to ensure the safety of the child and the resident parent before, during, and after contact.[6] It also incorporated helpful advice on child contact and domestic violence from two eminent child psychiatrists. However, this judgment did not overrule the case-law precedents outlined above. Indeed, it reinforced the ruling that contact is almost always in the interests of the child. This means that judges have to find some way of reconciling conflicting instructions about "almost always" granting contact, while also ensuring the safety of the child and the resident parent.

Other attempts to improve safety included the introduction of very sound but nonmandatory good practice guidelines, the addition of questions about domestic violence to court application forms and the extension of the definition of "harm" to include witnessing domestic violence.

If all these measures had combined to improve safety, it would be reasonable to expect an increase in the number of cases where contact is refused. However, the judicial statistics for England and Wales show that the opposite happened between 2000 and 2005. Although the number of contact orders granted more than doubled, reaching 107,199 in 2005, the number of contact orders refused decreased by about a third from 1,276 in 2000 to only 848 in 2005. During this time Women's Aid reported that orders for unsupervised contact were still being granted to violent parents, who had been convicted of offenses against children or whose behavior had led to the child being placed on the Child Protection Register.[7]

However, believing that the issue of safety had been dealt with, the government announced their intention to introduce legislation and other practical measures to facilitate contact and to enforce contact orders more effectively. In doing so, they were seeking to meet the demands of the judiciary and the fathers' groups, who both insisted that "vindictive" or "unreasonable" mothers were refusing to comply with contact orders. (The government had not commissioned any research to find out why so many women were not complying with contact orders.)

The voices of children were rarely heard in this debate. However, on June 16, 2004, Women's Aid organized a Listening to Children event, where 50 children and young people from refuges put questions to a government minister. Several of their questions related directly to child contact and the family courts:

> Why do the courts force children to see their dads when they are frightened of them?

> My father was given unsupervised access after I had given my views to CAFCASS [Children and Family Court Advisory and Support Service] of why I didn't feel safe. I was asked my views and not listened to.... Can you do anything to change this for others?

> Why don't the courts make sure it is safe for mums and children when they know the dads are violent?

> Who tells the judge off when he doesn't listen to children?

Despite the concerns expressed by these children, the government pressed ahead with their contact enforcement reforms. It was in this context that Women's Aid decided to write a report on children who had been killed as a result of contact arrangements. The reasoning behind this decision was that (1) this evidence could not be dismissed as anecdotal; (2) publicizing these cases would be unlikely to put any-one at risk since the children had already been killed; and (3) hopefully the report might convince the government of the need for legislation requiring the courts to prioritize safety in cases involving allegations of domestic violence or child abuse.

THE TWENTY-NINE CHILD HOMICIDES REPORT

Over the years Women's Aid Federation of England had compiled details of 29 children in 13 families who had been killed as a result of contact or residence arrangements in England and Wales between 1994 and 2004. Ten of these children had been killed between 2002 and 2004. Because the government did not collect statistics on child contact homicides, the actual number could be higher. A letter from a govern-ment minister confirmed that with regard to five of the 13 families, contact had been ordered by the court.

In the report, Women's Aid considered the lessons that should have been learned in relation to these 29 child homicides. Although it was often claimed that there was no way in which these tragedies could have been prevented, Women's Aid did not accept this view. Instead, they insisted that there was a need for effective risk assessment and adequate legal protection for children involved in contact or residence proceedings with abusive parents. They also emphasized that contact must be safe *before* it is enforced.

In particular, Women's Aid sought answers to the following questions:

1. Did the court knowingly grant unsupervised contact or residence to a violent parent—and, if so, has anyone been held accountable?
2. Was domestic violence recognized as a serious child protection issue?
3. Did professionals understand the dynamics of domestic violence?
4. Were children listened to and taken seriously?
5. Did frontline staff recognize high-risk indicators?
6. Was government guidance followed?
7. Why was no Serious Case Review carried out with regard to seven of the children?

METHODOLOGY

Since 1991 government guidance has required statutory agencies to undertake Serious Case Reviews into child deaths, where child abuse is confirmed or suspected. The aim of such reviews is to improve mul-tiagency work on child protection and to ensure that any lessons from the events under review are acted upon promptly and effectively. The full report on a Serious Case Review is not made public, but since 1999 local authorities have been required to make an executive summary available to the public.

By contacting the local authorities in whose area the children were living when they were killed, Women's Aid was able to obtain executive summaries of the Serious Case Reviews. While some of the executive summaries were detailed and linked recommendations to particular aspects of the case, others did not comment on the case but simply provided a list of "learning points," and in three cases (involving seven children) there was no Serious Case Review. For these reasons the information available is incomplete, and there may have been examples of good practice that were not included in the executive summaries and perhaps also good (unexplained) reasons for some of the decisions that were taken or not taken.

The child homicide report was not long (only 32 pages), because it was largely based on the limited information provided by the executive summaries of the Serious Case Reviews. Other sources of information included newspaper reports of criminal court proceedings and hearings in the Coroner's Court. Telephone interviews were also conducted with two of the mothers whose children had been killed.

As Women's Aid had no wish to cause further distress to the mothers or relatives of children who had been killed, comments about individual cases were kept anonymous and local authorities were not named. For this reason, comments from Serious Case Reviews or media reports on court hearings were not referenced. Instead the report focused on the policy issues that need to be addressed if similar tragedies are to be prevented in the future. However, Women's Aid provided a list of the children's names and brief details of their deaths to the government and to the Family Division.

Throughout this report, statements made in quotation marks are taken directly from the executive summary of the relevant Serious Case Review.

EXTRACTS FROM THE TWENTY-NINE CHILD HOMICIDES REPORT

1. Did the court knowingly grant unsupervised contact or residence to a violent parent—and has anyone been held accountable for this?

It was not possible for Women's Aid to identify all of the five cases where contact was ordered by the court and the children were subsequently killed. This was because the executive summaries of the Serious Case Reviews did not always state whether contact or residence was ordered by the court or agreed to informally by the parents.

However, in three cases it was clear not only that the court had granted orders for unsupervised contact and residence to extremely violent fathers but also that these decisions had been made against professional advice, without waiting for professional advice or without requesting professional advice.

In one case a judge granted residence of two children to a very violent father without waiting for a mental health assessment of the father, although the Social Services report "outlined an expectation that [the father] would receive treatment for his mental health needs." He had apparently taken an overdose recently and declined hospital admission. The court also determined "detailed direct and indirect contact between each child and the noncustodial parent." The child, who chose to live with the mother, was subsequently killed by the father during an unsupervised contact visit. It was reported at the father's trial that he had also left a note indicating that he intended to kill all three children to take revenge on his wife for leaving him. The Serious Case Review stated that "with hindsight, it could be argued that the Court should have waited before making a final decision until all the recommended reports were placed before them." However, the executive summary did not contain any recommendations with regard to court practice.

In another case the father was on bail, awaiting trial for injuring the mother during a violent incident. The executive summary stated that "no significant risks of a child protection nature were identified. Nevertheless the Family Court Welfare Officers had recommended to the County Court that [the children's] contact with their father should not include overnight stays." In spite of this, the mother's lawyer "encouraged her to make a compromise" and the judge "made the decision on contact, contrary to the recommendations in the Family Court Welfare report." The children were killed during the first overnight stay. The local authority confirmed that they brought this case to the attention of the government. Neither the judge nor the solicitor was involved in the Serious Case Review. The local authority stated that they had been advised that this would not be possible.

In a third case two children were killed by their violent father after their mother was reluctantly persuaded at the door of the court to agree to a contact order by consent. The mother stated that she had asked in vain for reports from the police, the doctor, and a psychiatrist to be added to the court welfare report. After her children were killed, a member of her family wrote to inform the judge of what had happened, but she was appalled to discover subsequently that his secretary had concealed this letter from him because she was afraid that he would find it upsetting. Despite considerable involvement with the police and medical services, no Serious Case Review was carried out in this case.

These three cases raised serious questions about accountability within the family justice system. Indeed, with regard to these cases, it was not clear whether all the family court professionals involved had even discussed the case after the killing of the children.

In other professions where a person makes a decision that results directly or indirectly in the death of a child, there would normally be some means of holding that person to account. However, judges are immune from prosecution with regard to judicial decisions, and even after the death of a child, documents such as the court welfare report are still protected from scrutiny under the confidentiality rules in family court proceedings.

Women's Aid also emphasized that, until evidence was provided to the contrary, they believed that it would be wrong to assume that the pro-contact culture of the family justice system had no bearing on the other homicide cases, where contact was agreed to informally. This was because any solicitor or family court advisor providing realistic advice for an abused woman concerned about the safety of her child would normally point out that litigation is unlikely to be successful because contact is hardly ever refused. In the experience of Women's Aid, such advice often results in abused women reluctantly agreeing to unsafe informal contact arrangements.

One mother described the pressure that could be put on an abused woman in this position. She stated,

> "They tell you, if you don't agree to give him access, the judge will just put you both in the witness box, you'll do a character assassination on each other, and he'll grant overnight access to him anyway. Their remit is, all children should see mum and dad. They think, no matter how badly he's beaten me, and no matter what sort of role model he might be, and no matter whether he would go on to harm them, the children should still see their father."

If the courts are determined to grant contact even in high-risk cases, professionals working in statutory agencies may feel that there is very little they can do to protect the child. This view was clearly expressed in one of the executive summaries, which stated,

> "Given the involvement of the court prior to [the child's] death in determining contact arrangements and the wishes [of the children] to see their father, there would seem to have been no opportunity nor grounds for any inter-agency intervention that could have prevented [the child's] death."

Women's Aid acknowledged such difficulties but did not accept this view, especially because the executive summary in this case did not mention any attempt to provide support for the nonviolent parent, as recommended in government guidance (see information under question 6, below).

2. Was domestic violence recognized as a serious child protection issue?

It was clear that domestic violence was involved in 11 out of the 13 families in which children were killed due to contact arrangements. In one of the two remaining cases the mother had spoken of her ex-partner's obsessively controlling behavior (a characteristic feature of domestic violence), and in the other case domestic violence was not mentioned but it was clear that there were concerns about the child's safety.

The cases already quoted show that domestic violence was not always recognized as a serious child protection issue by family court professionals dealing with private law contact or residence cases. However, the executive summaries showed that before the children were killed, statutory agencies were also involved in eight of the 10 cases, where Serious Case Reviews were subsequently carried out. Were these professionals aware of the risks to the children?

The central message of *Making an Impact*, a training pack launched in 1998 by the Department of Health, is that professionals working with children should be aware that domestic violence is an important indicator of risk of harm to children and that children are frequently abused physically, sexually, and emotionally by the same perpetrator who is abusing their mother.

These risks often continue after the parents have separated, and contact is a particular danger point. In 1999, a survey found that 76 percent of 148 children ordered by the courts to have contact with a violent parent were said to have been abused as a result of contact visits.[8] More recently, a survey involving 178 domestic violence organizations across England and Wales found that only 3 percent believed that appropriate measures were being taken to ensure the safety of the child and the resident parent in most contact cases involving domestic violence.[9]

The widespread prevalence of domestic violence clearly makes it difficult for hard-pressed statutory agencies, such as children's services and the police, to respond adequately to the needs of children in these families. However, in some of these cases there was considerable involvement with statutory agencies, which did not result in the children being protected. So what went wrong?

Several executive summaries make it clear that the children were not viewed as being at risk of "significant harm" (the threshold for intervention in child protection cases):

"It is known that [the father] had been violent to [the mother] on a number of occasions and all agencies had contact with the family. However, at no point did any agency ever believe there was a risk of 'significant harm' to the children or that they were in need of protection. As a result the children were never the subjects of a Child Protection investigation or Child Protection Committee."

The same executive summary continues,

"Particular attention should clearly have been given to the children's whereabouts when the violence took place; the timing of the violence, it was clearly occurring in the early hours of the morning; and the exact nature of the incident i.e. the fact that some incidents involved knives should have been treated very seriously."

In this case the police had been called to a number of violent incidents, and the mother had disclosed that she believed the father was capable of "taking a number of lives including his own."

In a second case, the police had been called out to three domestic incidents following the parents' separation, including an incident where the mother was injured, and the father was remanded on bail. Despite this, the executive summary states that "no significant risks of a child protection nature were identified."

In a third case, "[T]he police attended an incident following an argument when [the mother] alleged that [the father] had grabbed her around the neck. The children were present during this incident." Four days later, "[T]he police were called by neighbors who heard screaming"; the father was charged with actual bodily harm and released with stringent bail conditions, which he broke within two days. The following month, "[I]t was reported that [the mother] had fallen out of a first floor window and that there had been an argument with her boyfriend when he had tried to kill her." The executive summary concluded, "Social Services staff highlighted to [the mother and father] the dangers for the children of domestic violence. The case was seen as one of family support rather than child protection."

With regard to these cases it is tempting to ask just how much domestic violence needs to occur within a family before it is recognized as a serious child protection issue. It could also be argued that by focusing mainly on whether there was significant harm to the children, the statutory agencies failed to take sufficient account of the escalating violence that would soon engulf the children.

The key learning point here is that, if the child's primary caregiver is facing a potentially lethal level of violence, this should always be recognized as a serious child protection issue and efforts should be made to ensure the safety of both the nonabusing parent and the child(ren).

In one of the child homicide cases, the violence had been directed not only at the mother and child but also at professionals working within statutory agencies—and still this was not recognized as a dangerous situation for the children living in that family.

The executive summary stated, "When domestic violence was identified, it was not deemed relevant to child protection concerns." The police and social services made two joint visits to the family, one as a result of a domestic violence incident, and the other "an alleged incident of non-accidental injury" to the child whom the father subsequently killed. They concluded, "There was no evidence of any injuries to any of the children, or other concerns that would have warranted further action at the time." The executive summary also stated that the father

"had a criminal record which included offences of violence. In his contacts with professionals he was abusive both verbally and physically, and numerous occasions of this behaviour are recorded by all agencies. Legal advice was sought on at least two separate occasions about taking steps to prevent [the father] from entering local authority premises and to protect staff. If behaviour is so extreme as to warrant this type of action, questions about the safety of the children in the family should have been asked."

There was also a tendency noted in two cases for professionals to focus on the needs of the adults rather than the children.

A young child had remained at home with his violent father after the mother and an older child had fled to a refuge. The executive summary stated,

"It was known that [the father] had a history of violence towards his wife.... However, it appears that there was no mention of the history of domestic violence to the duty CMHT [Community Mental Health Team] when their involvement was requested. Neither had there apparently been any mention of the fact that [the mother] had left the family home and was living in a refuge with her older child.... It was perhaps the very fact [that the child] did appear well and generally unaffected by events that led some of the professional interventions to become adult, rather than child-focused."

Instead, concern shifted to the father's well-being and how difficult he would find life if the child was not there "to keep his father together." The duty social worker challenged the view that there was no risk to the child from his father, but the Review Group found that "there was a lack of a child-centered approach." The case was closed before the child was killed, although "no realistic assessment of risk to [the child] had been made."

Another executive summary stated, "All agencies appeared to overlook the links between domestic violence and the protection needs of children. Overall, they tended to focus on the adult's behaviour and needs."

Finally, in a case where there was no mention of domestic violence, the executive summary of the Serious Case Review included the following recommendation:

> "In every case referred to Psychiatry where the patient is a parent and there are issues of disputed custody, unsupervised contact etc, psychiatrists should be mindful of the broader family context and should consider consulting Social Services (Adult Services or Mental Health Services) and/or checking the Child Protection Register."

In this case it is not clear whether the family justice system was involved and, if so, whether the psychiatrist was an expert witness. However, the failure of a psychiatrist to make such a basic check is extremely serious in the context of child protection and disputes about contact, as a psychiatric report would usually be significant in determining the responses of statutory agencies and would also be influential in family proceedings.

DID PROFESSIONALS UNDERSTAND THE DYNAMICS OF DOMESTIC VIOLENCE?

It is widely acknowledged that domestic violence perpetrators have an obsessive need to exert power and control over their partners and also over their children. Indeed, perpetrators maintain control by seeking to ensure that their victims are too frightened or too ashamed to mention the abuse to anyone or to flee from the family home. Key tactics include making dire threats, isolating victims from their friends and relatives, and preventing them from having contact with helping agencies or sitting right beside them when they do. The following comments from the executive summaries showed that this was clearly a major problem in two cases:

> "[The father] appeared to be able to control the decision-making of professionals in his absence. There are also examples of the control [he] exerted over his family. He also refused routine pediatric surveillance and immunization of the children at times, and interfered with their normal medical care by frequent changes of GP and the refusal of consent for surgery for [the child whom he killed]."

> "[The child] was seen on two occasions by the duty social worker, once on a joint home visit with the Police after the failed attempt to return [the child] to the mother's care, and then a few days later when [the father] briefly attended the Social Service office with [the child]. On both these occasions [the father] was in control of the situation in terms of not allowing the professionals to have any meaningful contact with [the child]." (In this case, the father also refused to cooperate with professionals and did not accept the need for a mental health assessment.)

It is essential that statutory and voluntary agencies dealing with cases of domestic violence are able to recognize controlling behavior and to respond in a way that enables abused women and children to speak freely. More fundamentally, there is a need to build trust with children and with the nonabusing parent, so that they can feel confident enough to disclose abuse. This can be a slow and painful process, because most mothers who experience domestic violence say that their greatest fear is that their children will be taken into care (see chapter 3 by Abrahams in volume 1 of this set), and for this reason they are likely to distrust statutory agencies.

Frontline staff also need to be aware that abusers often monitor every interaction involving their partner, including phone calls and letters, so any attempt to communicate in this way could potentially endanger the nonviolent parent. One executive summary stated,

> "It is important in tackling violence against women that the women involved are encouraged and enabled to come forward to seek help and support. Contact therefore needs to be handled extremely sensitively to ensure the woman is not put at risk of further violence. It requires staff, particularly within statutory agencies, to develop a creative approach to making contact. For example using the school and staff there as a contact point and/or communication channel. This ensures that letters are not sent to the home where the perpetrator of violence can open them. Unfortunately letters were sent in this way in this case."

As perpetrators have such a strong need to maintain power and control over other family members, it is perhaps not surprising that they are often most dangerous when they can no longer control the situation (e.g., when the nonviolent parent has fled from the family home, taking the children). Indeed, women are at greatest risk of homicide at the point of separation or after leaving a violent partner.

For this reason, it is crucial for professionals to be aware of the high risk of postseparation violence. That awareness was clearly lacking in one case. The executive summary stated that

> "recent contact with the family did not indicate that circumstances had changed, apart from the recent separation of [the mother and father]. There was still no evidence of direct harm to the children."

In two of the contact homicide cases, violent fathers were facing the ultimate loss of power and control, as they were awaiting trial with the possibility of being sent to prison for violent offenses against their ex-partner. Instead, both of them chose to kill themselves and their children. In one of these cases, the court welfare report had recommended that there should be no overnight stays. However, on the basis of this evidence, Women's Aid recommended that when a parent is awaiting trial for a violent offense against a family member, unsupervised contact of any kind should not be granted.

Finally, it is important to note that violent parents sometimes kill their children as a means of taking revenge on their former partner for leaving them. It was very clear that five of these cases could be described as "revenge killings":

- In one case the coroner described the father as vindictive and commented, "He viewed the children as his possessions. If he personally could not have them, then no one else would."

- At the trial of another father, the prosecution described him as follows: "He was seething. He knew he could no longer control his wife. Apart from seething, he was wallowing in self-pity. 999 calls will show us the self-pity he was feeling and the anger he felt towards his wife. He then took what he saw as being the ultimate revenge by killing their two children. This was the most vicious way he could strike back at her, because she had left him. He wanted to teach her a lesson she would never forget."

- One mother stated that her ex-partner had phoned to tell her that he had killed their child, and when she asked him why, he replied. "If I can't have you, you can't have [the child]."

- Another mother stated that her ex-partner phoned to let her know that he had killed the children and commented, "You've hurt me. Now I'm going to hurt you."

- One father told his ex-partner over the phone what he was doing, so that she could listen in horror as her children were asphyxiated. This was his response to learning that she had found a new partner, by whom she was pregnant. Apparently he commented, "I hope you're happy. I hope you have a grudge against that baby for the rest of your life."

In the other cases the motivation for killing the children was not reported, but it could be argued that most of these child homicides were "revenge killings."

3. Were children listened to and taken seriously?

The welfare checklist in the Children Act 1989 requires the family courts to have regard to the "ascertainable wishes and feelings of the child concerned," taking account of the child's age and understanding. The executive summaries of the Serious Case Reviews often did not mention whether or not the wishes and feelings of the children had been considered, but in some cases it was clear that professionals did not even talk to the children.

This can be very difficult in domestic violence cases, because the perpetrator will usually make sure that there is no opportunity for the partner or the children to speak freely. Often they will also be too frightened to say anything even when the perpetrator is not there, as they may be scared of the consequences of speaking out. As already noted, two of the executive summaries expressed frustration that the father was able to control the situation in this way. It was likely that similar constraints had made it difficult for professionals to talk to the children in the other cases.

In one case, the Review Panel concluded that the welfare report on the children was "sufficiently child-focused." However, in the following cases it appeared that there had been no assessment of the children's needs:

> "The issue of the children's safety appears to have been lost in the concentration on the adults. It was noted by the Panel that the children appeared effectively hidden from view. It was apparent that no one ever asked the children directly about what they had witnessed and how it made them feel. In reality, no assessment of the children's needs really took place."

> "Another significant factor to emerge with the benefit of hindsight is the need to undertake full and holistic assessments of the needs of children and their carers. . . . This family was known to a number of agencies over a long period of time and in this situation there is the potential to respond and provide a service without taking full account of the presenting issues on each occasion. A sort of 'agency exhaustion' sets in. The additional fact with this family was the level of hostility and personal danger to professionals presented by [the father]."

One executive summary contained the following recommendation: "Where a service user describes a history of marital violence that a detailed history is taken to establish the risk to the service user and any children." Apparently in this case the children were doing very well at school, so there was "no indicator of need."

In some cases the fact that the children appeared to be healthy seemed to have convinced statutory agencies that they were unaffected by the domestic violence and therefore not at risk. In one case, where there was no mention of anyone talking to the children about the serious violence they had witnessed, the executive summary commented, "Both schools saw the [children] as normal healthy pupils who on the whole enjoyed the school experience and were very popular with other children. They did not disclose or indicate any distress to their teachers." Besides, "[T]here were no known instances where any physical harm had come to the children in the past."

In another case, there was a "very limited attempt" to ascertain the child's wishes and feelings, but it was noted that the child appeared physically well and "unaffected by events."

One executive summary, which hardly said anything about the case, included the following learning points:

- "Getting the concerns of professionals through to the Courts in cases where private law proceedings are involved.
- The importance of helping children to get their voice heard."

This suggested that there were court proceedings in this case and that the children had concerns about their situation, which had not been taken into account. However, due to the omission of case details, it was impossible to confirm this.

The psychiatrists' report used in the four test cases (*Re L, V, M & H*) had emphasised that emotional trauma can be deep-seated and persistent, and that children must be listened to and taken seriously if they do not want to see a violent parent. However, this did not appear to be happening in practice. The Women's Aid survey involving 178 domestic violence services in England and Wales found that only 6 percent believed that children who said they did not want contact with a violent parent were being listened to and taken seriously in most cases.[10]

Women's Aid recommended that this problem be urgently addressed by the family justice system, and that statutory workers with child protection responsibilities should all receive training to enable them to understand the dynamics of domestic violence.

There was a further consideration. If a child says that he or she wants to see or live with a violent parent, should a "child-centered" statutory agency always accede to the child's wishes? This issue was highlighted by the following comments in an executive summary:

"The result of the Court proceedings was to determine residence and detailed direct and indirect contact between each child and [the] non-custodial parent. It appears at this time that the wishes and feelings of the children were being listened to and acted upon." (In this case, there was a long-standing history of the father being violent to his wife and abusive to professionals.)

As very few children in England and Wales are granted separate representation in private law proceedings, it is vital that family court professionals assess risk carefully and are aware of the need to protect children, particularly in cases of domestic violence. Women's Aid pointed out that children should have a right to protection as well as a right to be heard, but that this often seemed to be overlooked in family court practice.

Women's Aid also recommended that, in cases where there are allegations of abuse but insufficient evidence to prove it, children should be assessed in a child-friendly environment, using child-friendly techniques over several weeks to establish the child's perspective and whether the child is at risk and to make appropriate recommendations for the child's welfare. This is necessary, because children are unlikely to disclose abuse during a one-off interview with a person whom they do not know and trust.

4. Did frontline staff recognize significant risk indicators?

One executive summary stated,

"Clearly, women need to feel empowered and engaged if they are to leave violent relationships. However, the dilemma for statutory agencies is when the level, frequency and impact of the violence becomes so significant that those agencies need to take action because of the 'likelihood of significant harm' to the children. In cases of domestic violence, staff require clear guidelines, protocols and, more importantly, risk assessment tools that guide them in deciding when this threshold has been reached.... It appeared to the Review Panel that the staff operating in this case had few of these 'tools' at their disposal and there was a lack of awareness about the link between domestic violence and risk to children."

Many frontline practitioners—including police officers and social workers—have low levels of knowledge and understanding about indicators of potential serious harm in domestic violence cases. Women's Aid commented that although some agencies had formal systems for assessing and managing risk in the context of domestic violence experienced by adults, others did not. Moreover, there appeared to be no risk assessment and management tools for identifying children who face a significant risk of being killed due to contact or residence arrangements with a violent parent.

This was despite a recent study of 40 Serious Case Reviews, which had found that 22 of the cases involved previously violent behavior.[11] An overview of the literature had also identified three antecedents to child homicide: prior history of child abuse, prior agency contact, and a history of domestic violence in the family. This study concluded that confronting domestic violence amongst adults may provide multiple points of proactive intervention against child deaths in the home.[12]

As it is essential that the family courts do not make orders that place children in danger, Women's Aid urged the government to commission research to identify significant risk indicators for children involved in contact or residence proceedings or arrangements with a violent parent.

Women's Aid also listed the following significant risk indicators, identified by the Cardiff Women's Safety Unit, the National Society for the Prevention of Cruelty to Children, and the South Wales Police as part of a coordinated multiagency response to domestic violence. These had been developed with reference to a review of 47 local domestic homicides, which identified the top 15 significant risk indicators. These questions now formed a checklist to be completed by the police whenever they attended a domestic violence incident. The process had been evaluated and found to be effective in identifying the level of risk faced by women and children in domestic violence cases.[13]

The significant risk indicators are as follows:

- Assailant's criminal record
- Use of weapons
- Injuries inflicted
- Financial problems
- Assailant's problems with alcohol, drugs, or mental illness
- Victim is pregnant
- Assailant expressing or behaving in a jealous or controlling way
- Has been or is going to be a separation between victim and assailant
- Conflict over child contact
- Threats made to kill
- Attempts made to strangle and/or choke
- Abuse becoming worse and/or happening more often
- Assailant threatens and/or attempts suicide
- Sexual abuse (e.g., rape, indecent assault)
- Victim's own assessment

Using the very limited information available about the 13 families featured in the child homicide report, Women's Aid counted the numbers of significant risk indicators in each case. In three cases, there were 10–12 significant risk indicators, in seven cases there were 5–8 significant risk indicators, in two cases there were four indicators, and in one case there were three indicators. However, in this last case the child was on the Child Protection Register, so a risk had already been clearly identified. With regard to most of the cases, the number of significant risk indicators counted was proportionate to the amount of information available. This suggested that anyone who was familiar with the case could probably have identified more.

It is important to note that any risk assessment tool based on checklist categories will provide only a limited picture of the nature, severity, and danger of a particular domestic violence situation. Previous assault is one of the most straightforward and robust risk indicators for domestic violence.

As acknowledged in the list of indicators, there is always likely to be some risk in contact disputes where the parents have separated due to domestic violence. For this reason, Women's Aid called for legislation to require the courts to assess risk and to prioritize the safety of the child in cases involving allegations of domestic violence.

It is important to note that there appeared to be a high coincidence of domestic violence and the perpetrators' involvement with mental health professionals in the child homicide cases. Nine of the 13 fathers who killed their children were described as mentally ill, unstable, or suffering from depression and anxiety, while six had already threatened or attempted suicide. Although domestic violence itself is not a form of mental illness, these cases suggest a need for further work on risk assessment and management protocols in the context of domestic violence and mental health.

The extent to which the perpetrator feels the need to control his or her partner is also a vital indicator of the possible level of risk. Two of the mothers whose children were killed described their ex-partner's controlling behavior:

> "It's hard to explain, but it comes on really slowly, really gradually. You'll hear lots of women say the same thing. I'm ashamed to say this now, but I had an allowance to get me to work and back, and to buy my magazines and my lunch. I had no control over things like that. The bank account was in both names but he kept the cards. Then you find that you haven't got a car, and you haven't got your own money, and that actually you are not in control at all. You suddenly realise that you have no power."

> "He was always watching me. He controlled where I went, who I was with, and what I wore. I had to be covered from head to toe, and if I wore a V neck top he would insist that I got f . . . ing changed before going to work. We had to have sex when he said. If a meal was late, he would be verbally abusive and would say he didn't want it—or sometimes he would throw the food at me. He demanded to know what I had bought and wanted to check receipts to make sure I had not spent money on anything else. He didn't like talking to my friends—when they came round, you could cut the air with a knife, so they stopped coming round. If I spoke to a man, it was even worse—he wanted to know who I was 'slagging around with'. It was like walking on eggshells, having to be so wary."

Jealousy was mentioned in half of the 13 child homicide cases. In two cases the children were killed after their parents had separated and the mother had started a new relationship. In a third case the parents had divorced two years previously and the mother had recently remarried without telling her ex-partner, who subsequently killed her and the children. This mother appeared to have been aware of the risk, but jealousy was not mentioned in the executive summary, although domestic violence training was listed as a learning point.

Another executive summary stated,

> "The context of domestic violence in this situation is critical to understanding how [the] children could be killed by their father. . . . Domestic violence can be an ongoing and long term feature of relationships and

often the severity of the abuse increases over time. It is important to identify patterns over the long term and to understand how possessiveness, jealousy and control can be manifested and concealed. Ensuring agencies are aware of serious incidents but also the need for universal services to remain vigilant when things are less obvious is equally important. The period following separation and particularly when a new relationship is formed by the victim is often the time when increased harassment and risk is present."

It is significant that, despite often suffering extreme violence themselves, only four of the 13 mothers had expressed concern that their ex-partner might kill the children. Most of them clearly found this inconceivable.

In two cases where threats to kill the children were made directly or reported to professionals, they also seemed to have viewed this as inconceivable, as no child protection investigation was instigated. One executive summary stated that the mother "who knew [the father] best was confident that he would not harm the children." In the other case, a local authority official explained that the mother "had always made sensible decisions to protect her children in the past," and when she decided that the father did not mean what he had said, the local authority "saw no reason to disbelieve her." While it is commendable that these local authorities respected the mother's decision making, it is also the role of frontline staff with child protection responsibilities to assess and manage risk and to offer appropriate information and advice. There was nothing in the executive summaries to indicate that anyone had told these mothers that a threat to kill is a significant risk indicator or that there were other significant risk indicators in their respective cases. If this had been pointed out, would these mothers have handed over their children for contact?

These cases indicated a clear need for independent domestic violence advocacy services to provide support for women, to explore the risks involved, and to identify safe options. Women's Aid recommended that domestic violence advocacy services be developed in every local area as part of a coordinated community response to domestic violence.

Women's Aid also recommended the following:

- All frontline staff responsible for the welfare of children should receive training to enable them to recognize significant risk indicators in domestic violence cases.
- Threats to kill or to commit suicide should always be recognized as significant risk indicators and taken seriously in cases of domestic violence, particularly during contact or residence disputes.

5. Was government guidance followed?

The Children Act 1989 requires the court to consider any risk of harm to the child when making decisions with regard to children. In April 2001 this was reinforced by Good Practice Guidelines, endorsed by the government, which stated that in cases of domestic violence the court should "only make an order for contact if it can be satisfied that the safety of the residential parent and the child can be secured before during and after contact."

Because the 29 child homicides all occurred when the children were having unsupervised contact—or, in one case, residence—with the perpetrator, Women's Aid concluded that in the five cases involving court orders, insufficient attention had been paid to ensuring the safety of the child(ren). Several of the homicides occurred during overnight stays.

With regard to statutory agencies, detailed guidance is provided in Working Together to Safeguard Children. This includes identifying the perpetrator, recognizing that there may be an increased risk of domestic violence toward the abused parent and/or the child after separation and especially during contact proceedings, helping women and children escape from violence, working separately with the parents so that abused women can speak freely, and supporting nonabusing parents in making safe choices for themselves and their children.

Women's Aid expressed concern that this guidance seemed to have been overlooked in some of the homicide cases, particularly with regard to supporting the nonviolent parent. In some cases there seemed to be a reluctance to identify the perpetrator, even when it was abundantly clear who was being violent. Two Review Panels used terms that suggested that both parents were responsible for the violence (e.g., stating that the parents had "an abusive relationship" or referring to "marital conflict" or "marital violence"). This kind of approach means not only that the perpetrator is not identified, held to account, and prosecuted, but also that there is no recognition of the need to provide support for the nonviolent parent.

6. Why were Serious Case Reviews not carried out in three cases?

In three cases involving a total of seven children there was no Serious Case Review, and the local authorities concerned could not give any reason for this. In one of these cases, where there had been considerable involvement with the police and medical services, the mother commented,

> "I cannot tell you how upset I am that a Serious Case Review was overlooked. Right from the beginning I felt badly let down by the court system.... Now, I find that a lot could have been done at the very beginning to learn lessons. I am absolutely furious and devastated to

realise that not only did the legal team not care about the children's safety when they were alive, but they don't care that they are dead. And they don't care about learning lessons."

Women's Aid recommended that Serious Case Reviews should always be done when children die in circumstances that suggest abuse, and that family court professionals should be required to take part whenever this is relevant.

SHARING INFORMATION SAFELY

Statements in some of the executive summaries emphasized the importance of agencies sharing information:

"In respect of this family no single agency had the full picture or identified the need to make a full assessment of the situation. The fact remains that within each agency there was considerable information available that could have been collated and analysed."

"There is no evidence that an approach based on examining the chronology of information available over time, even on a single agency basis, was taken by any of the agencies within this case."

"Any enquiry made from Social Services to the Police regarding concerns about a child or family, should lead to a full list of known incidents being provided, that reflects all the contact that has been made between the family and the Police, whatever its classification."

Women's Aid commented that the information-sharing databases (set up under the Children Act 2004) could provide a powerful means of collecting evidence of domestic violence and its adverse effects on children, and that such evidence should be made available to the family justice system. However, it is also important to ensure that the basic information recorded on the databases is not given to perpetrators because that could help them to track down their victims.

CONCLUSIONS

Women's Aid concluded that there is an urgent need for new legislation to require the family courts to prioritize safety in cases of abuse. They recommended the New Zealand legislation as a suitable model for the following reasons:

- It contains a clear, comprehensive, and gender-neutral definition of domestic violence, which includes abuse to children.
- If a parent is found to be violent within the family, the court must not grant an order for unsupervised contact or residence to that parent unless it is satisfied that the child will be safe.

- A mandatory risk assessment checklist is used in all family proceedings involving allegations of domestic violence or child abuse.
- Even if there is insufficient evidence to prove that a parent has been violent within the family, the court can make whatever order it considers necessary if it is satisfied that there is a genuine risk to the child.

These measures do not ban child contact in domestic violence cases but require the court to be satisfied that the child will be safe.

Women's Aid also raised the issue of accountability:

Mechanisms are required for holding family court professionals accountable for decisions that result in children being killed or seriously harmed. If found to be responsible, professionals (judges, magistrates, barristers, solicitors, expert witnesses or family court advisers) should lose their right to adjudicate, represent parties, provide evidence or report to the court in family proceedings.

THE RESPONSE TO THE CHILD HOMICIDE REPORT

After the homicide report was published in December 2004, Lord Justice Wall was asked to investigate the five homicide cases where contact had been ordered by the court. His report to the president of the Family Division, published in February 2006, acknowledged that 11 children in five families had been killed. He stated that he was satisfied that eight of these children "died as a result of parental actions which could not have been reasonably foreseen or prevented by the court, and in which no criticism can be made of the judges who made the respective contact orders." With regard to the remaining three children, he said that "it is arguable that the court should have taken a more proactive stance and refused to make a consent order for contact," but he firmly rejected the implication that the judges concerned should be held "responsible" for the deaths of the children.[14] However, his comments on the individual cases were not made available to the public.

Lord Justice Wall recommended that the Family Justice Council should be asked to prepare a report on the use of consent orders for contact in domestic violence cases. He expressed the view that it is "high time that the Family Justice System abandoned any reliance on the proposition that a man can have a history of violence to the mother of his children but, nonetheless, be a good father," and wanted this point to be reinforced "in a judgment or a lecture." He also recommended that no judge should sit in private law family proceedings without having training and multidisciplinary instruction on domestic violence—but he did not recommend legal reforms.

The Children and Adoption Act 2006, which was going through Parliament at the time, had already been amended to include a requirement to assess risk if there is reason to believe that a child may be at risk of harm. (This followed a highly critical inspection report on CAFCASS by Her Majesty's Inspectorate of Court Administration).[15] Although the government resisted demands for the frequency and length of contact visits to be determined legally according to the age of the child, they also rejected amendments seeking better safeguards for abused women and children.

However, in 2007 the Family Justice Council produced an excellent report, setting out how applications for contact orders by consent should be handled by the court in domestic violence cases. This stated that a cultural change is required with a move away from the assumption that "contact is always the appropriate way forward" to one that "contact that is safe and positive for the child is always the appropriate way forward."[16] The Family Justice Council recommended that a Practice Direction should be issued, that ensuring safety should be paramount, and that consideration should be given to including the family court process in Serious Case Reviews and establishing a system of feedback to judges if orders result in harm to the child.

The Practice Direction: Residence and Contact Orders: Domestic Violence and Harm was finally issued on May 9, 2008. It applies in both private and public family law cases and is to be followed in every case where domestic violence is alleged or suspected. Recognizing that abuse is not always disclosed initially, it requires the court at all stages of the proceedings to consider whether domestic violence is raised as an issue. It states that the court shall not make a consent order for residence or contact unless the parties are present in court and it is satisfied that there will be no harm to the child. It also requires the court to take account of factors such as the effect of domestic violence on the child and the perpetrator's motivation, likely behavior, and capacity to change. Most importantly, it states that the court should only make an order for contact if it can be satisfied that the physical and emotional safety of the child and the resident parent can, as far as possible, be secured before, during, and after contact.

We are still waiting to see what effect this Practice Direction has, but at least it is clear that safety is now firmly on the family justice agenda.

NOTES

1. J. Selwyn, *Costs and Outcomes of Non-Infant Adoptions* (London: BAAF, 2006).

2. H. Saunders and J. Barron, *Failure to Protect? Domestic Violence and the Experiences of Abused Women and Children in the Family Courts* (Bristol: Women's Aid Federation of England, 2003).

3. *Re O (Contact: Imposition of conditions)* [1995] 2 FLR 124 at 128.

4. *Re H & R (Child sexual abuse: Standard of proof)* [1996] 1 FLR 80–101.

5. *Re A v N (Committal: Refusal of contact)* [1997] 1 FLR 533–543.

6. *Re L, V, M & H (Contact: Domestic violence)* [2000] 2 FLR 334–371.

7. Saunders and Barron, *Failure to Protect?*

8. L. Radford, S. Sayer, and AMICA, *Unreasonable Fears? Child Contact in the Context of Domestic Violence: A Survey of Mothers' Perceptions of Harm* (Bristol, UK: Women's Aid Federation of England, 1999).

9. Saunders and Barron, *Failure to Protect?*

10. Ibid.

11. J. Sinclair and R. Bullock, *Learning from Past Experience: A Review of Serious Case Reviews* (London: Department of Health, 2002).

12. N. Websdale, *Understanding Domestic Homicide* (Boston: Northeastern University Press, 1999).

13. See http://www.crarg.org.uk for more information about significant risk indicators.

14. N. Wall (a Lord Justice of Appeal), *A Report to the President of the Family Division on the Publication by the Women's Aid Federation of England Entitled "Twenty-Nine Child Homicides: Lessons Still to Be Learnt on Domestic Violence and Child Protection" with Particular Reference to the Five Cases in Which There Was Judicial Involvement* (London, UK: Family Division, March 2006).

15. HM Inspectorate of Court Administration, *Domestic Violence, Safety and Family Proceedings* (Bristol, UK: HMICA, 2005).

16. Family Justice Council, *"Everyone's Business"—How Applications for Contact Orders by Consent Should Be Approached by the Court in Cases Involving Domestic Violence* (London: Family Justice Council, 2007).

Chapter 4

Batterers and the Lives of Their Children

David Mandel

It hurt me to see the pain across my mother's face
Every time my father's fist would put her in her place.

Christina Aguilera, "I'm Okay"

Protector. Provider. Mentor. Friend. Abuser. Abandoner. Betrayer. Enemy. Violent. Father. What if all these words described your father? How would you make sense of the contradictions? What if you only experienced your father as the "enemy," as someone who couldn't be trusted and with whom you never felt safe? How would you fill the space in your heart that should have been occupied by the father who was your protector, the provider and mentor? What lessons would you learn from the pain you felt about masculinity and relationships? And how would you want the police and other systems to respond to your father and his abuse of your mother?[1]

These and related questions about the intersection of domestic violence and fatherhood have preoccupied me. About 20 years ago, hoping to support victims of abuse, I started leading six-week classes for men arrested for violence against their partners. Seeing the need for a more comprehensive response to abusive men, two colleagues and I started an agency that has provided batterer intervention programming for a few thousand court-mandated and self-referred men. I was struck by the lack of knowledge about batterers among social workers, substance abuse counselors, police, and other professionals working with families. So, I began training these and other groups to integrate principles of batterer intervention into their work with families.

After a batterer killed his partner's child, the Connecticut Department of Children and Families (DCF) invited me to train child welfare workers to improve their interview and assessment skills with perpetrators. This work led to my current passion, improving the capacity of professionals and systems to respond to the needs of children exposed to batterers' behavior. My approach focuses on the needs of children to be safe and together with their mothers and interventions that address the harms created by violent fathers. My work has included research into batterers' perceptions of their children's exposure to their violence, speaking to different groups about batterers as fathers, and consulting to child welfare agencies around the country who are seeking to improve their response to domestic violence. I currently oversee a team of domestic violence consultants who work to help child welfare workers respond more appropriately to domestic violence.

As meaningful as my work is, many experiences reinforce how far we still have to go to make violent fathers "visible," and therefore accountable, in our response to domestic violence. I am still amazed by how many conversations I've participated in where nobody ever mentions the violent father—even when it's his actions that have led to the system's involvement with the family. These "invisible" batterers frequently find unwitting allies in systems that are intended to keep children and their mothers safe. For example, family court files often say little or nothing about an abuser's role as a father. Child welfare agencies typically open cases in the names of mothers, regardless of who perpetrated the abuse and/or neglect. Double standards are routinely applied, with mothers expected to assume virtually all household responsibilities from cleaning to getting children to doctor's appointments while fathers are praised if they change a diaper. Paradoxically, low cultural expectations of fathers and high expectations of mothers often work to batterers' advantage by reducing the probability they will be held accountable for violent behavior, let alone for the harms children suffer because of their domestic violence. A greater emphasis on the role of batterers as parents is critical if children in these families are to be kept safe.

When I began this work, fatherhood was ignored in the domestic violence field as well as in discussions about men and violence. The entire experience of parenthood, arguably one of the most important aspects of any person's life, was left out of the conversation about men and violence. It was a cultural and programmatic blind spot. The field has evolved since then thanks to the efforts of survivors, their advocates, batterer intervention providers, and family violence researchers. Despite advances in our understanding of how violent fathers impact their children, we are still in the youth of our understanding and the infancy of our ability to tackle with focus, energy, and sophistication the complexity of batterers in their role as parents and co-parents.

Children didn't ask to have a violent and abusive parent. But violent fathers are permanent fixtures in their lives. This fact doesn't change when their father is labeled a batterer, arrested, or ordered out of the house.

This chapter looks at batterers' interactions with their families in the role of parents, and the problems these interactions create, the challenges and dilemmas posed by batterers having legal access to their children, the double standard we use to evaluate mothers and fathers as parents, and our ambivalence about batterers as parents. Finally we consider some positive aspects of parenting by batterers, including looking at the possibility that some men may be able to stop their abuse for the sake of their children, and how to promote these transformations.

I will be using examples from my work to illustrate the complexity surrounding batterers as parents. The following sketch juxtaposes the real physical danger batterers can pose to their families with how children can motivate them to change.

Tom speaks of how his children stopped him from killing their mother. It was their screams that made him suddenly aware that he had his hands around her throat. He realized he had been moments from choking her to death. "They saved my life at the same time," he relates. Tom's children became the reason for changing his violent and abusive ways. "When they get old enough to understand, I want to be able to tell them honestly that it was because of my behavior that me and their mother are no longer together." Initially coming in on his own, Tom attended court-ordered counseling for his violence for five years. When he finally left counseling he and his wife had safely divorced, he was working on getting along with her partners, and he was beginning to see the sexism in his parenting.[2]

Batterers make choices that harm their children and the children of their partners. Tom made a series of choices that brought him to the brink of killing his wife. Through his choices, he terrorized her and the children. The near murder perpetrated by Tom that particular day was merely one event in a long history of physical, emotional, and financial abuse he had perpetrated against multiple women.

Patterns of coercive control like Tom's are the defining characteristic of battering and affect their children's lives at numerous points. Understanding the scope and subtlety of the impact that batterers have on children is essential if we are going to create meaningful expectations for change and healing.

A range of mental health problems in children have been linked to their being exposed to domestic violence, including posttraumatic stress disorder (PTSD). As we come to appreciate the broad nature of partner abuse, however, an entirely new range of harms come into view, like the financial and emotional tolls of losing the role model of an educated, engaged, and independent mother when she is prevented from working, completing a college degree, or carrying on a normal social life with family or friends. Even the "remedies" used to protect children from a batterer—removal from violent homes, going to a shelter, divorce, and incarceration of the batterer—can lead to jarring dislocations and disruptions of a child's normal development. Children often feel profound grief and loss when separated from a violent parent even if they also feel some relief from fear.

Like many batterers, Tom went through stages of denial and acceptance related to his violence. Initially, he admitted to some of the violence but struggled against accepting responsibility for the consequences of his actions. But as he faced criminal punishment, and received counseling and positive and constructive support from family and friends, he begun to understand his culpability. He began to appreciate not only his wife's fear and hurt, but also the damage to his children. His process of change included stopping his physical abuse and control, identifying and interrupting the pattern of feelings and thoughts that undergirded his behavior, and helping his children heal. Changes like these are reasonable to expect from coercive, controlling men who aspire to be better fathers.

BEFORE THE BEGINNING: FERTILITY, PREGNANCY, AND CHILDBIRTH

When we appreciate the extent to which "control" is the aim of battering as well as one of its principal means, it is easy to appreciate how conception, pregnancy, and each developmental stage of a child's life after they are born are fertile grounds for violence, psychological abuse, intimidation, isolation, sexual abuse, and financial exploitation. For some batterers, having a child with a woman is a way of tying her to him by making her more financially dependent and indicating to other men that "she's his property." Teenage girls report that their partner wanted them to have a child to stop them from working or completing school, a process referred to as "sabotage." Batterers may assume their partner will be less attractive to other men if she has children, will need to be home more often rather than with friends, or will embrace "family values" or redefine herself as a "mother," making it less likely she will leave him. Women often talk about how they didn't leave their batterer because they "wanted their child to have a father."

What do batterers do when they want to exercise control over a partner's fertility? Some batterers simply use physical force. They rape their partners to get them pregnant, or the pregnancy is a side effect of the unwanted sex. Other partners engage in manipulation, deceit, and emotional coercion. Some batterers will throw out birth control or replace it with placebos. Other batterers will threaten to get sex somewhere else or pressure someone into not using a condom because "they love them." They may insist on "makeup" sex after being abusive to their partner.

Once their partner is pregnant, a batterer may use violence and abuse to control her behavior during pregnancy. Unfortunately, because medical providers are often unaware of the abusive dynamics in these cases, they may inadvertently collude with the batterer in exploiting an apparent concern for a woman's well-being as a pretext to extend his control. In this example, a partner's smoking during pregnancy becomes the justification for one man's violence.

> Alan was in recovery for alcoholism and drug abuse. He and Alicia were about to be first-time parents. Both he and Alicia were smokers. She said she would quit while she was pregnant. One afternoon he smelled smoke in the house and angrily confronted her, accusing her of smoking and endangering their child. She denied smoking. Feeling manipulated and lied to, Alan threw Alicia down to the ground and kicked her—a punishment for smoking and lying to him.

Alan's behavior represents one twist in the braid of a batterer's pattern around sex, family planning, pregnancy, and childhood. His motivations tap into strong cultural beliefs about how "good mothers" should behave, reinforced by the power of the health establishment. This example also illustrates how culture and institutions actually extend batterers' leverage beyond their ability to intimidate or inflict physical harm. Given the medical establishment's warnings about the dangers of smoking during pregnancy, Alicia might even feel guilt and shame for her behavior, wrongly blaming herself in some degree for the assault perpetrated by Alan.

Alan's violence affects Alicia's perceptions of herself as a mother and, through its effects on her feelings about the fetus, her relationship with her unborn child. Research indicates that mothers can project the batterer's violent motivations upon her unborn child's kicking in the womb—"He's beating me up." These feelings during pregnancy carry over into childhood. Some survivors indicate that they struggle with children whose personalities and presentation remind them of the batterers.[3]

This next example further illustrates both how cultural attitudes toward the control of women's sexuality intersect with domestic violence and how batterers use children as weapons against survivors.

> Simon was a successful businessman who had three children with Tanya. His emotional abuse started early in the relationship when he said he wouldn't marry her because she wasn't a virgin when they met. But he was willing to have three children with her. As the relationship continued, he became physically violent with her. He assaulted her while she was pregnant with one of their children. He sometimes made her sleep

on the floor when he was angry with her. After one of the arrests, the local child welfare agency became involved. When he violated a court stay-away order, they removed the three children from both Simon and Tanya. It was only after a court hearing that the children were returned to their mother. But the children now treated her with disrespect, and passed along nasty messages from their father. For her part, Tanya struggled with remaining close with her youngest child, who reminded her the most of his father.

In this scenario, Tanya ended up paying three times over for Simon's abuse. She directly experienced his physical, emotional, sexual, and financial abuse. Her children were removed from her for a period of time by the local child welfare agency because Simon violated a court order not because of anything she did. Finally, her relationships with her children were strained because Simon had undermined her authority with the children and actively worked to turn the children against her. Sadly, Tanya's experience is not unusual. Women often report that their contacts with child welfare reinforce the impact of abuse. One result is that many battered women fear child welfare agencies as much or more than they fear their partner. Alongside the fear of their children being removed, they often feel punished by child welfare for the actions of their partners and are angry that they are made responsible for or expected to exert absolute control over his actions.

Not all batterers want children. The common theme is simply that they are willing to use coercion to get what they want. Sometimes a batterer pressures a partner to end a pregnancy, threatening to leave or seriously hurt or kill her if she doesn't. He may abuse her physically and emotionally during the pregnancy, sometimes intentionally trying to cause a miscarriage. Some batterers begin or escalate their physical violence during pregnancy. Interestingly, another group of batterers seem to stop their physical violence during pregnancy, a dynamic I explore in a subsequent discussion of the positive aspects of parenting by batterers. With or without physical abuse, many batterers continue emotional abuse of their partner during pregnancy. As we saw with Alan and Alicia, this process can be unwittingly supported by medical professionals who encourage a batterer to "help" his partner follow certain health guidelines while she is pregnant. When she resists his efforts, she can be perceived as "noncompliant" with medical recommendations. In this process, she may be isolated by medical providers at the very moment when she needs their intervention most.

ONCE THE CHILDREN ARE BORN: VULNERABLE NEWBORNS AND TODDLERS

Starting during pregnancy, a batterer can create a broad array of obstacles to his partner's parenting. He may prevent her from going to the doctor because he is afraid her bruises will lead to questions about the abuse or that she will frankly discuss her fears at home. His control of the phone and the car may make it difficult or impossible for her to keep prenatal visits. With each of these choices—and it is important to remember that he is making *parenting* choices when he denies a partner the right to make the best decisions for herself or her baby—the batterer puts his needs ahead of the needs of his child and selects some combination of coercion and control to meet these needs.

Safety, stability, routine, and nurturance are as important once a child is born as they are during pregnancy. Batterers often interfere with these critical needs, putting their children at risk. A self-centered batterer may demand attention from his partner when the child needs her. One father in my practice demanded that his partner stay in bed with him in the morning when their young children were already up and needed supervision and tending. Batterers commonly isolate their partners to ease their own fears of abandonment, keep the abuse secret, and create a growing dependency that makes it more difficult for her to leave. Tactics designed to isolate and control his partner may also interfere with her parenting. In my work, I have encountered men who have isolated their partners by not letting her:

- Take a child to well-baby visits
- Receive medical or other professionals into the home to help a child with special needs
- Get child care from family and friends.

In addition, they have taken financial control by taking their partner's money or credit cards, making her beg for money or explain every penny spent. Conversely, they have squandered the family's money on alcohol, drugs, or gambling, leading to eviction and moving away from supportive networks of friends or family.

Physical violence in the home by the batterer can threaten the physical safety and developmental needs of young children. Children can develop problems ranging from attachment issues and speech delays to problems with toilet training or walking. Young children are uniquely vulnerable to physical violence because they are unable to remove themselves from a dangerous situation. In one case, the abuser left his infant alone at home for hours as he drove around looking for his partner to continue his physical violence. The trauma of violence in the home can also cause regression from normal developmental milestones. In another case, a child who had been normally breast-feeding stopped abruptly the day after his mother was physically assaulted by her partner.

Abusive men often have expectations for their children's behavior that are inconsistent with their age and become abusive when the child

fails to meet their standard. These expectations may relate to everything from walking and toilet training through reading and playing
sports. Conversely, mothers may be blamed and abused for children's
issues, real or perceived, or when children disturb the abuser's tran-
quility (by crying or being sick, for instance) or violate his "rules"
(such as not touching his things). In one instance, a batterer punished
his three year old because he believed he should never have to repeat
his instructions. In turn, these punishments can elicit developmental
delays in children. The combination of abuse and blame can create an
escalating cycle that looks something like this:

Batterer-created stress
↓
Developmental delays in child
↓
Abuse in the form of blame, verbal degradation, and violence at mother's
parenting
↓
Further developmental delays in child

As children learn to walk and talk, their exposure and risks evolve.
Toddlers can now place themselves in the path of the violence of the
abuse. As language skills develop, young children may repeat degrading and humiliating words and phrases. A small child who innocently
parrots his father referring to his mother as a "stupid bitch" will eventually learn the significance of this phrase. Even young children may
insist that "Daddy, stop!" Batterers may use young children as spies,
betraying their trust by asking them to report on their activities with
mother during the day.

Preschool children can suffer from a range of consequences from
their father's violence. The emotional development of preschool children makes them very vulnerable to blaming themselves for the abuse
in the home. Psychologically, this is an egocentric stage. The child
believes, "Good things happen because I'm good; bad things happen
because I'm bad." Young children categorize things in simplistic and
categorical ways. A father's arrest may lead a child to see all police as
bad. Young children may experience fears of the violence reoccurring,
nightmares causing sleeping problems, and aggressive behavior.
Focused on keeping the family together, preschool children may be
very distressed by a move into shelter or being separated from father
by the court.

Fathers loom large in the emotional lives of preschool children.
Rarely do batterers fully understand the impact of their violence on
their young children. In conversations with batterers, their children's
exposure to violence is often denied or rationalized with comments like

"The children were asleep" or "They're too young to understand." When we consider that children's exposure may be auditory or emotional as well as visual, however, and that even infants appear to be affected by exposure, it is clear that virtually all children are affected in some way by abuse in their families. Batterers minimize the impact they have on children to shield themselves from external consequences, the judgment of others, and their own self-judgment. Professionals also may lack sensitivity to the connection between abusive fathers and children. After we had worked together for a while, a woman who ran a domestic violence program confessed that while they regularly provided emotional support for young children in their shelter, her staff never asked these children how they felt about their fathers. It is often easier for professionals working with battered women and their children to avoid rather than confront the combination of relief, anger, sadness, and loss that burdens many children who have to flee from an abusive parent. While it may be simpler to exclude the father or define him simply as the "bad guy," we do children a disservice by not helping them work through their complex feelings about a violent father.

School Days, School Daze: Violent Fathers and School-Age Children

As children grow up, the impact of the batterer's behavior extends to their lives outside the home—school, friends, sports. Children can be physically uprooted and moved to avoid violence or because the batterer's behavior has led the family to be evicted from their home, disrupting their friendships, academic progress, and social development. Even though the decision to move, enter a shelter, or even go into hiding may have been made with the mother's own and her children's safety in mind, it can lead to behavioral, emotional, or academic problems in children. In these circumstances, internalized low expectations of fathers and high expectations of mothers can compound a mother's guilt, particularly if she believes the children's problems are the direct result of her actions.

Agencies that work with survivors can help them acknowledge and cope with the effects of separation from the familiar, including angry outbursts that may be directed at the mother. This is facilitated, and a mother's guilt at leaving relieved, if she is reminded that the problems her children are suffering are not the result of her decision to flee toward safety, but instead are the continuing impact of the batterer's behavior. The following example illustrates the need for professionals to clearly conceptualize the batterer's responsibility for creating certain problems—even when the batterer is no longer physically present in the home.

> A social worker was telling me one day about a mother who had done "everything right." When her boyfriend got violent with her, she called

the police and went to a domestic violence shelter. While she was in the shelter, she decided that she couldn't go back to live with him. She found a new apartment for herself and her children. I asked the social worker if the children had to change schools because of the move. She said "Yes, the children transferred schools and they are both having some trouble. The teenager is getting into fights. He had been fine, no behavioral issues, at the old school. His sister is falling behind in her grades. At the old school, she had a tutor. This school isn't providing the tutoring services." I asked if she had considered that it was the batterer's actions that had created these social and academic problems for the children. She said, "No, I was focused on what the mother needed to do to get the children stabilized. I never thought about how all this is the result of the Dad's behavior. But now I will. And I'll make it my business to tell the mom that what's going on now isn't her fault. I think she needs to hear that."

A range of professionals may inadvertently collude with the batterer by blaming the surviving mother for her children's academic and behavior problems. School counselors, child welfare agencies, pediatricians, and other professionals may focus on the mother's so-called parenting deficits instead of the abuse she suffered, then refer her to support services to improve her parenting skills, sending the message that she is at fault. Failure to understand the dynamics of abuse prevents these professionals from providing effective support by helping abused mothers appreciate how the batterer has undermined her parenting, sabotaged her relationship to her children, and created the stress to which the children's problems are a response. In this case example, the social worker could play an invaluable role with this mother, helping her and the children make sense of what is going on her home.

In other cases, a mother may have done everything in her power to shield their children from many of the batterer's behaviors. But a paradoxical result of these efforts may be that her children blame her for leaving the batterer and creating problems in the family. The probability of this happening is greatest where the batterer has continually insulted, humiliated, or otherwise blamed his partner for problems in the household in front of the children; is adept at emotional manipulation; pits one family member against another; and presents himself as the "real" victim to others. Again, unless professionals working with the family are absolutely clear that the father alone bears responsibility for the family's disruption, they will reinforce the message that the problems with the children are the mother's fault.

As children come into contact with people outside the family, there are new opportunities for disclosures about what is going on the home and interventions from helping professionals. While these new opportunities can lead to positive changes—such as support from a school counselor, or productive reports to child welfare agencies—the batterer may extend his manipulation and coercive control to target outsiders, successfully exploiting their involvement to his own advantage. Some batterers are quite skillful at using the system as a tool to continue to hurt their partners. In one case, a batterer who was violating a court order to be in his home reported his own violation of this mandate to the local child welfare agency. He had repeatedly threatened that he could have her children taken away from her. Now, based on his report, the child welfare agency investigated his claim, found it to be true, and used his violation of the court order as grounds for removing the children from their mother—which was his entire purpose for calling.

The following are some sound bites from violent fathers who were attempting emotionally manipulate their children, even after they were out of the home.

- "Don't go to that counseling, son, it will make you crazy."
- "While daddy's away [in jail], be a good son—give mommy a hard time."
- Calling from jail with his one call: "It was your mother who got me arrested. It's her fault I'm here."
- "You shouldn't take those pills—they will make you sick."

In each of these families, a father who was supposed to be supporting the health and well-being of his children was actively sabotaging their physical and mental health. In some of the cases, they were seeking to turn the children against their mother. These are fundamental betrayals because the abuser is using his special relationship as the children's father, and the trust they have for him, against them. These acts are not ancillary to their violent acts. To the contrary, violence, emotional manipulation, and betrayal are part of a single process that solidifies a batterer's power over his wife and children.

Batterers' interference with children's medical and mental health care deserves special attention because it is poorly understood, is often kept off the radar by the double standard of parenting, and represents one of the more corrosive behaviors batterers engage in because it directly aggravates a child's health problems. The quotes above illustrate how a batterer can make a child afraid of outside help. His motivation may be a fear that the involvement of a health professional will lead to a disclosure of his behavior or otherwise disrupt the system of mental and emotional control he has established over his wife and children. For some men, any sort of counseling or outside professional help symbolizes a threat to their narcissistic image of a "perfect family." In these cases, his sense of self—and his denial of his abusive behavior—may be tied to the illusion that everything is OK at home. In these instances, it is only his needs that matter, no one else's.

In a number of instances over the years, I have seen violent fathers exercise control over children when they were most vulnerable. In one case, the father intercepted an ambulance that was taking his child to the hospital to get him help for an emotional breakdown. In another case, a father denied recommended counseling for his son, who later took his own life. In another family, the batterer had interfered with the medical care and physical therapy his stepdaughter needed to deal with a congenital disease. Ironically, he boasted that he was taking care of his family.

The statements above also exemplify the almost universal trait of batterers, blaming their partners for their own behavior as well as the misbehavior of their children and the resulting problems. Social workers and other professionals, seeking to engage batterers about their children's medical and other needs, frequently ask me how to talk to batterers about the impact of their abuse on their children. Rarely are they appropriately trained to interview or work with violent fathers and they are worried, often justifiably, about the potential for their intervention to increase the risk to survivors, the children, or even themselves. Speaking to fathers directly about their abuse or confronting their manipulative behavior also frightens them.

To avoid manipulation by batterers, I encourage child welfare professionals to talk to men about the specifics of their violence. I also suggest they expand their interview to questions about the broader pattern of coercive control, like what they told their children about the violence or about the problems caused for the family by their arrest or child welfare involvement. If the children are school-age, the batterer can be asked whether he told them, "I'm not home because your mother called the police. As soon as she says I can come home, I will." Does he tell the children that all the problems in the home "are mommy's fault"? By shifting the responsibility for his absence from his behavior to her calling the police or her behavior, he avoids having to deal with any shame, blame, or anger in his relationship with his children and sends his children back to their mother as guided missiles. Because of this explanation, it is more likely they will act out, direct their anger and blame at her, and advocate for their father's return.

Thus, the child welfare workers now understand that effective intervention must address how he is talking to his children about the violence as well as the behavior itself. Conversely, a battering father who is sincere about changing would not only be working to stop his violent patterns, but also explaining to his children that he alone is responsible for the family's current troubles. He would also encourage the children to be honest with him about how they felt when he was arrested and put out of the home and not encouraging them to be angry at their mother for calling the police. By focusing on positive ways he can relate to the children, the worker is forming an educational bond with the abusive father, but not aligning with his abuse.

In *Batterers as Parents*, Lundy Bancroft and Jay Silverman outline the varied ways that batterers act to harm children.[4] They change rules, play favorites, and create all kinds of instability. They disrupt holidays, vacations, and children's relationships with their friends. They demonstrate that the way to get what you want is through the use of force and manipulation. They also can physically abuse their children. Research shows that more than half of the children living with domestic violence are also experiencing physical maltreatment themselves.[5] In this example, Jerry's violent behavior toward his children continues even after his partner drops out of the picture.

Jerry and Patty lost their children to the state for a period of time because of their use of cocaine and Jerry's violence to Patty. Jerry eventually got clean and sober, and their girls were returned to him. Unfortunately, Patty couldn't stay clean. Perhaps she continued to use drugs to help her not feel the shame, fear, and other emotions and memories from his violence. Whatever the reason, she floated in and out of their lives. As the girls grew up and went to school, Jerry was their primary parent. Jerry remained very conflicted about Patty's attempts to contact the girls. He showed very little awareness of and compassion for how his behavior may have contributed to her troubles. Whenever he spoke of her, his voice dripped with contempt and hatred as he talked angrily about how she had abandoned him and the girls. In treatment, he struggled to connect his lack of compassion toward Patty's addiction with his overall pattern of control and history of violence. Over time, Jerry became aggressive with the girls. He would grab the youngest and yell in her face when she failed to listen. He grabbed the older one by the arm and dragged her up the stairs. When they "wouldn't listen," he would escalate into rage, yelling and screaming and blaming their behavior for his actions. Despite some efforts to take responsibility for his actions, Jerry eventually had both of his children removed by the state.

I never knew Patty because I started working with Jerry only after he and Patty split up. So it is impossible for me to say with certainty what damage his abuse did to her or how he may have disrupted her attempts at recovery. What was clear to me was that, like many violent fathers, Jerry eventually directed many of the same emotions at the children, including anger, that he did toward Patty, perhaps because they were a constant reminder of the failure of his relationship and his perception that she had abandoned him. His resentment at being alone in parenting his children was always palpable.

Jerry's case illustrates a critical point: that despite protestations by many abusive men to the contrary, the attitudes, beliefs, and behaviors batterers direct toward their partner are often intimately inseparable from the attitudes, beliefs, and behaviors they bring to their children. In several of my cases, the batterer's control and violence toward his partner were part of his effort to gain sexual access to his stepdaughter. In another case, the father abused his wife as she lay dying from a terminal disease. Then he fought her family for custody of their children, won, and then continued to abuse the children until the eldest child spoke out at school.

The impact of an abusive parent on a child depends on a range of factors. Research and clinical experience suggest that if the batterer is a child's biological father, he looms larger and that their emotional experience can be more complicated and confusing than if the batterer is unrelated to them. They may feel doomed to become like him or blame themselves for their negative feelings toward him. Even as they grow into adulthood, children of batterers may struggle with their feelings toward their father. In this example, Al, a man in his thirties, maintained a complicated relationship with his father.

> Al was extremely violent. In and out of jail, he alternated between being proud of his toughness and afraid of the demon of his violence. He grew up in a home where his father constantly belittled his mother and was violent with her. He abused and demeaned Al. Al remembers the time he was dragged to counseling by his father because he was getting into trouble at school. He remembers how his father blamed everything on him and never once admitted to being violent and abusive. As a grown man, his love for his father was still palpable. I could feel how he still wished his father was a different man, that he could be close to him. And he was tortured by the violence he had perpetrated against his father to stop him from abusing his mother. You could still hear the little kid in him who felt it was wrong to hit your father even if you were doing it protectively.

Al's story was complex, like his relationship with his father. While he went further than his father ever appeared to in terms of admitting he had a problem with violence and by seeking help for his behavior, he continued to remain dangerous to others (and to himself). Even after working with him for a number of years, I never felt fully confident that his risk for violence had been reduced significantly. His semiannual visits with his parents were ongoing sources for distress, anxiety, and anger. He alternated between anger at his father for not seeming to live up to his expectations, and contempt for the person who he felt failed as a father and as a man. Al eventually dropped out of counseling while continuing with a series of failed romantic relationships, every one damaged by some level of his abusiveness.

Sweet 16? The Role of Violent Fathers through the Teen Years

Teenage years are a time of serious changes and growth. Teens usually have more contacts outside the family, learn more about independence, and are further developed in their thinking, communication, and capacity to identify emotions than their younger peers and siblings. These differences create opportunities and risks for teens growing up in violent homes. School routines and activities may provide safety and a place to excel.

School staff often have no idea what a child is suffering at home. This was true, for instance, in two of my cases that ended with a homicide. In one, a high school boy killed his father to protect himself and his mother. In another, the father of the teenager killed the boy's mother and then himself.

Greater contact with the wider world can also increase the opportunities for teenage children to get involved in drugs, gangs, and other illicit activities. As they grow in size, strength, and independence, teens are more likely to physically and/or verbally try to stop the batterer, sometimes with catastrophic results. In this example, John responded to his father's violence with his own act of violence.

> John was 15 when he shot and killed his father. He and his mother, Jeannie, had endured years of abuse from this man. At one time, the two fled halfway across the country only to be tracked down by John's father. Calling the police had never led to any real safety. So those calls had stopped long ago. Jeannie decided that since calling the police and fleeing didn't make things better, she and her son would just have to make the best of it. They moved back to their hometown, where at least they had a support network and were in a familiar environment. The assaults continued until one day John's father struck his mother outside their house. John saw his mother's head hit the ground and thought she was dead. He ran inside and grabbed a gun that his father had given him "to protect him from bullies" in the neighborhood. John pointed the gun at his father, who said, "If you are going to point that at me, you better use it." John pulled the trigger and shot his father. John's mother recovered from the assault. She stood by John during the trial, explaining the years of abuse and her efforts to protect them both. John wrote a letter to the court outlining the abuse, most of which was unknown to his friends and teachers at school. Considered college material, John's school administrators spoke for him at his trial. John ended up serving almost five years for manslaughter—his sentence considered light under the state's laws. While in prison, John completed his GED. He was eventually released early into a halfway house.

John's story is filled with irony and tragedy. It is sadly ironic that his father gave him the gun to use against neighborhood bullies when the most significant risk in his world was his father. It is also ironic that his father's frequent use of violence was reflected in his son's willingness to use violence to prevent further violence against himself and his mother. In perhaps the ultimate tragedy, John's father's father had killed his grandmother. The thread of violence connects John's grandfather, his father, and him.

By the time children reach their teens, many if not all of their developmental stages may have been influenced by a violent father's behavior. In some cases, children have experienced multiple traumas in addition to domestic violence. In the short life of a child, he or she might have experienced war, sexual abuse, violent dislocations from one country to another, the death of close friends, and the ravages of substance abuse on the health and well-being of caretakers. John not only experienced his father's violence at different ages. His father's violence also led to significant moves and other dislocations. Each trauma potentially disrupts a different development task such as learning, attachment, establishing autonomy, or developing healthy gender roles and integrating multiple roles into a distinctive self.

Age, birth order, gender, and degrees of violence and abuse may impact how a child experiences a parent who is a batterer. Older children may bear the brunt of the violence while trying to protect their mother and their younger siblings. Some children turn inwards in the face of the abuse, retreating into school or depression. Others may be consumed with guilt. One boy attempted to kill himself because he blamed himself for failing to protect his mother. Another adolescent away at a juvenile detention center spent his time worrying about the safety of his family when his father got out of jail.

Like Al, a number of children adopt their father's patterns. Still, most children who grow up in homes with violence do not repeat those actions as adults, either as victims or as perpetrators. In many instances, this is a testament to their own resilience and the support and love of their mother, other family members, teachers, and other significant adults. These networks of support can provide children a place to talk about and make sense of their experience, influence how they interpret the abuse and relate to the battering parent, and give them a new experience—that the world has more to offer than the reality created by the batterer.

Finally, as strange as it may sound and as difficult as it may be to admit, a child's development may also be supported by the positive things given to them by the batterer—whether it is financial security, encouragement to achieve in school, or the development of a talent or skill.

BATTERERS AS PARENTS: DILEMMAS AND DECISIONS

During a meeting of domestic violence professionals, a leading criminal court judge leaned over to me and said, "You know, I issue court orders telling these guys to stay away from their families for six months and then one day the criminal case is over. Maybe he goes to jail for a few months, maybe he doesn't—but then he goes home. What have we done to deal with what it's going to be like for him and his family when he goes home?"

This judge was honing in one of the true dilemmas we face when dealing with batterers as parents. Criminalizing partner violence was a watershed in our commitment to protect women and children and in our moral progress as a society. Despite this, we are just beginning to address the day-to-day realities of how most batterers remain legally and emotionally connected to their families, especially their children, or to confront the challenge posed to working with batterers as parents, regardless of whether they are biological or social fathers. We are also challenged by our deep ambivalence about engaging violent men in general and toward facilitating batterers' access to their children in particular.

I believe the difficulties of working with batterers as parents is a subset of two things—the difficulties we have thinking about batterers in general as people who are embedded in families and communities, and the limitations of our institutions in constructively engaging men, in general, about their role as parents.

News coverage of a murder illustrates how hard it is to think of batterers not merely as "violent men" but also as "violent men embedded in networks of relationships."

> The newspaper article of Tawanda's death and her cousin's serious injury at the hands of Tawanda's boyfriend, Tyrone, explored the history of their relationship, including the boyfriend's violence and her attempts to stay safe. The article described how her friends and family implored her to go into shelter and to end the relationship. The implications were that she might still be alive if only she had listened to her friends and family and so, therefore, that it was her failure to take the "correct" action that led to her murder. As importantly, the reporter treated Tyrone without exploring any of his interactions with his family and friends. How did they respond to his early arrests? To his violent behavior? Were there friends or relatives who were filling him with negative talk about Tawanda or women in general?

In essence, the news story treated Tyrone as an isolated actor versus someone who was probably like most of us—embedded in a web of relationships. Since most batterers will remain in or be quickly returned to the communities in which they were abusive and continue to play multiple roles, including roles as fathers, it behooves us to treat their lives in this context, as the lives of persons who are loved and needed as well as feared.

Our ability to engage batterers as parents is also hampered because many professionals lack the competencies needed to engage men. Educational institutions that instruct social workers, psychologists, and therapists provide little or no training on male adult development. These educational gaps repeat themselves at the policy and practice levels. Human service agencies designed to serve "families" are primarily geared to serving women and children. In part, this reflects who comes for help as well as a possible bias about who *should* be "fixed" if families are to function properly. Planned Parenthood or agencies that address reproductive health and family planning almost exclusively serve women, even when men are intimately involved in the many of the activities concerned.

Ten years ago, when I first started working with child welfare workers, I asked a roomful of seasoned workers, "How many of you have worked with a father?" and the response was that only a quarter had ever met with a father. Today, if I ask a room of 200 human service professionals, "How many of you took a course on male socialization?" and "How many of you did your internship with a primarily male population?" only a handful will answer affirmatively or indicate they've had training to work with men.

Children (and Their Mothers) Want Safety and Contact

In this example, the daily routine and emotional life of a young child are intimately connected to his violent father.

> Cameron was a young child, four years old, whose father was arrested and sent to jail because he had been violent with the child's mother. Cameron's father had been his primary care taker while his mother worked, supporting the family. When he disappeared from Cameron's day to day experience, Cameron cried, often inconsolably.

Cameron's circumstance highlights the bond that can exist between a batterer and his children. Betsy McAlister Groves, Patricia Van Horn, and Alicia Lieberman, national experts on working with children affected by violence, acknowledge the importance of battering fathers in the emotional lives of their children.[6] In case examples, they highlight the coexistence of fear and sadness related to their father's violence with a desire for connection, and a concern about their father's well-being. In one case, a young girl expresses her fears that the police would kill her father. In another example, a girl expresses her sense of abandonment by her father who is in jail.

In each of the cases they present, the children's fathers had committed serious violence against the children's mother, causing fear, significant stress, disruption, and upheaval in the lives of their family as well as physical injury. The dramatic violence perpetrated by some batterers can make it difficult to recognize the day-to-day stress created by their choices. In Cameron's case, or cases with similar circumstances, a father's incarceration may force his mother to scramble to provide child care. A likely source of such care would have normally been his father's family. But if they blame his mother for the arrest and so become estranged, the victim can be further isolated and stressed. At the very moment when the children are trying to cope with the trauma of the violence and their father's incarceration, their daily routine is altered. They may also be deeply affected emotionally by losing their connection with their extended family, aggravating the sense that they had lost their father.

To meaningfully support the children of batterers and their mothers, we need to acknowledge their desire for *both* safety *and* connection. One of the most basic mistakes bystanders, friends, family, and professionals can make when trying to help battered mothers and their children is emphasize one, their safety for instance, without acknowledging the other. Reaching out to battered mothers and their children is most successful when we can accept the importance of the batterer to them and appreciate their visceral desire that he change and become a better person. As with individuals who reject a man's violence, but want to sustain a relationship, so too do families look to "change" as a process that will provide them with everything they want—safety and togetherness as family. The children would have two loving parents and the mother would not have to choose safety for herself and her children at the cost of financial and emotional hardship. Even when the batterer is incapable or unwilling to change and even as we acknowledge how unlikely significant change may be in a particular case, we can still honor the desire for it to happen.

Looking in from the outside, it is easy to believe there are only two simple choices, either to permanently separate the abusive father from his wife and children or to guarantee him continued access to his family regardless of what he has done. If left unexamined, either of these beliefs can lead to the vilification of battered mothers.

If you believe that the only answer is to "get rid of the bum," you are likely to harshly judge any battered mother where contact continues, even with the children. This "get rid of the bum" attitude frequently boomerangs back on battered mothers. In the child welfare system, this attitude is often embedded in the expectation that she take unrealistic and even personally dangerous steps to prevent a batterer who is a father from having access to his children. Such steps might include a guarantee that the children will have absolutely no contact with their father, even in the face of family court orders that he be allowed visitation. In what Evan Stark terms the "battered mother's dilemma," she is caught between the potential of her children being removed by one court or being charged with contempt in another court.

Moreover, these expectations are often placed on battered mothers regardless of whether a separation is in the best interests of the children's emotional attachment to the batterer. Where access continues, even if the woman has made every effort in her limited power to prevent it, it may be alleged that she is "failing to protect" the children and the full weight of the child welfare system may come crashing down on her and her children.

Conversely, a similarly tragic outcome for victimized mothers results when the belief is adopted that fathers have an unqualified right to access their children regardless of their history of violence and abuse toward their mother. Here, the battered mother is judged harshly when she acts protectively based on her legitimate fears for the safety and well-being of the children. Battered mothers who attempt to bring their concerns for their children forward in family court may be accused of trying to alienate the children from their father (see chapters 7 and 5 by Joan Meier and Evan Stark, respectively, in this volume). Actively benefiting from this attitude and the positive regard given to fathers who appear to be expressing interest in parenting their children (even when it's primarily a façade to win in court), batterers are frequently treated better in custody and visitation than nonbattering fathers. Researcher Cris O'Sullivan found that men who had protection orders filed against them were significantly *more* likely to be granted visitation with their children than men without such orders against them.[7] When combined with the compromised parenting that battering has caused or with the portrayal of the victimized mother as an inadequate parent, it easy to see how a batterer may gain custody or the victim lose it in courts that fail to appreciate the gravity of abuse and its effects on parenting. Moreover, batterers utilize an adversarial legal system to their advantage. Coercive control, limited previously to the privacy of the home, can be extended through the family court system in motions that harass and intimidate the other parent.

Equal before the Law? Maybe Not

It happened halfway through a evening talk I was giving to a group of law school students. I was discussing how to hold batterers accountable for the physical and emotional damage their violence does to their children. A raised hand. The student identified himself as a police officer. He shared that he had been an officer for 11 years and that he felt compelled during some calls to homes to speak to the mother privately and say, "How could you put your children through this?" I waited a moment and asked if I could ask him a question. "How many times in your 11 years on the force have you ever sat down one of those fathers who were being violent to say to him, 'How can you treat the mother of your children like this?'" Dead silence. He had never chastised an abusive father in the same way as he felt license to address a domestic violence survivor who in all likelihood was the person who had called the police for help.

This brief exchange summed up the challenges we all face when try-ing to tackle the conundrum of the relationship between batterers and their children. And this conundrum affects a child welfare social worker trying to help a child living with a violent father as much as the battered woman fighting in court for the custody of her children.

THE DOUBLE STANDARD REVISITED

As we have seen, in most families mothers are expected to meet the emotional, physical, and social needs of their children, arranging child care, taking them to medical appointments, and maintaining contact with the children's school. Beyond this is our general belief, perhaps because they have given birth, that mothers will be more attentive to their children's emotional needs. By contrast, our expectations are that father's roles in their children's lives will be extremely limited at best, or nonexistent. Although we are mixed in our expectations about who has primary responsibility for discipline and homework, most people believe that a father's primary responsibility is to provide for their fam-ilies financially. Of course, while these cultural stereotypes may typify the reality in most households, they do not reflect the division of labor in millions of families where single mothers or fathers carry the total load of parenting or where parents have consciously chosen to parent differently.

Our double standards around parenting are of great significance when it comes to thinking about batterers as parents. Without appreci-ating what men *can* do and how children look to them to provide physically and emotionally, it is almost impossible to fully articulate the damage that batterers cause children when they neglect them or to conceptualize how a batterer interferes with a battered mother's par-enting. And it is extremely difficult to describe the extent to which he gains leverage in his control from expectations of parenting based on gender stereotypes.

To return to an earlier point, the double standard is also played out at the institutional level, where cultural beliefs influence decision mak-ing in cases where batterers' behavior creates concerns for child safety and well-being. Batterers' behavior frequently leads to the involvement of child welfare agencies in the lives of families. The mission of these agencies is to promote the safety and well-being of children, protecting them from abuse and neglect that might be perpetrated by parents or other caretakers. While statutes governing abuse and neglect make no distinctions between mothers and fathers in terms of their responsibil-ity for the safety and well-being of children, in practice, because the expectations of mothers are different and higher than for fathers, bat-terers are at a significant advantage when child welfare becomes involved. For example, social workers who are exploring a child's medical and immunization history will almost always turn to the mother for information. When a child is not clean or is poorly dressed, the automatic assumption is that the mother has somehow been negligent in her duties. In homes where the batterer's control over the phone, car, and finances may have limited the mother's ability to take the children to the doctor or her ability to purchase new clothes for growing children, the batterer's role in the neglecting the children may be invisible. Similarly, when a batterer who has been ordered out of a home can manipulate a child into blame and anger at their mother, social workers may blame the mother, who is the custodial parent, for the child's emotional and behavioral issues.

Social workers may naïvely offer a battered mother in-home services to support her "parenting deficits," inadvertently reinforcing her partner's message that she is a bad mother, making her more vulnerable to his threats to report "violations" to child welfare and making his responsibility for the emotional damage suffered even less visible. Because these misdirected services do little or nothing to address his coercive control, the root cause of the problems in the home, they inevitably fail. The social worker may then document the mother's incapacity to improve her parenting.

Alternately, reflecting their stereotyped beliefs about gender roles, social workers may develop case plans for families that rely almost entirely on steps taken by the battered mother. Backed up by the court, the child welfare agency may get a battered mother to agree in writing to ensure the children go to medical appointments and attend counseling, and even promise that the children will not be exposed to any more violence in the home. She may sign these agreements "voluntarily," but under the implicit or direct threat that if she fails to "accept services" her children will be removed. Often the father is not a party to these agreements, sometimes because he is not the child's biological father, is ignored in court proceedings, or is simply held to a much lower standard of compliance. This situation makes it easier for him to sabotage a mother's efforts from outside the view of the social services agency and the court. A batterer may control access to a car, fail to give the mother messages from a medical provider or therapist, or turn his child against counseling. And since the batterer is in control of whether he is violent or not, he can choose to expose his children to violence even if there is a court order of protection. In the end, what the institutions see is the children who miss appointments, fail to attend counseling, or witness more violence, and a mother who has "failed" in her agreement to meet her obligations as a parent. This dynamic is illustrated in the following example.

> Joan and Sam were both addicts living with their two children. Sam had a history of being violent with Joan. Child welfare became involved in

their family because of their drug addiction. The social worker involved also identified the domestic violence in the family. The social worker asked both parents to sign service agreements outlining what they would have to do get their case closed. Joan's service agreement had twice as many items on as it Sam's. While both their plans included expectations that each of them would remain clean and sober, Joan's plan made her alone responsible for feeding the children, getting them to medical appointments, and avoiding any further violence.

So what happens if Sam relapses and takes the car when Joan needs it to take the children to a medical appointment? Or decides, in the course of his coercive control, that Joan *really* wants the car to have a sexual liaison? Who will be held responsible for the missed appointments? I have found that even many professionals who recognize the challenges faced by battered women expect them to work miracles, meaning completing their rounds of child care, nurturance, and protection whatever the obstacles created by the batterer.

The paradox is that more effective intervention with batterers starts by raising our standards of men as parents, equalizing our expectations so that it becomes possible to ask what we would expect from an emotionally engaged, responsible parent regardless of his or her sex. Only with this standard in hand are we likely to objectively evaluate the source of the neglect and emotional damage suffered by the children in abusive homes and hold batterers accountable for change.

POSITIVE SIGNS AND CLEAR EXPECTATIONS: SETTING THE BAR FOR CHANGE HIGH

For most men, fatherhood is a watershed event, possibly the most important in their adult development. In a batterer's identity as a father, there is a potential source of motivation to change, to become a better person. Psychologist Rob Palkovitz, a noted fatherhood author, reports that many men point to becoming a father, not marriage, as the catalyst for becoming "less self-centered and more giving."[8] Other research indicates that men involved in criminal and antisocial behavior may make a significant turnaround when they have their first child.

Authors Janna Lesser, Jerry Tello, and their colleagues share stories from young men on how becoming fathers changed their behavior including leaving gang life, giving up drugs, and improving their respect for their partner. One young father relates how he made the decision to stop doing drugs after he saw his one-year-old son pick up a crack pipe and try to imitate him. Other men discussed how becoming a father made them more empathetic and led them to turn away from a life of violence. A 22 year old said, "I just don't want to have all that anger come out in a negative way one day toward my daughter or toward anybody else.... One of the things that I've seen is domestic violence. It could be from putting your kids down to putting your wife down. That would be something I wish no kid would have to go through." Becoming the father to a daughter can challenge a man to consider male disrespect and abuse of women.[9]

In sum, therefore, while fatherhood provides batterers with a new arena and new "tools" to control a partner, it also offers perhaps the single most important opportunity to promote changes in their behavior. Given the sensitivity that children have to batterers, real changes in how men behave can have immediate and positive outcomes for how children think and feel. It is in the interest of children, their mothers, batterers, and the community at large for us to explore how batterers' relationships with their children may be a catalyst for change. And this process begins by advancing the dialogue about what we should expect from men generally as fathers, facilitating the changes that help position men to meet these expectations, and clearly fixing responsibility for the harms caused by men who fail to make these changes. Setting clear expectations for batterers as fathers will allow us to create opportunities for meaningful positive change and clearly articulate the failure of men who do not change.

Awareness Indicates Potential for Change

Some batterers seem to understand the negative impact of their violence on their children, their own co-parenting relationship, and their own identity as a father. Research I conducted with over 1,000 batterers in batterer intervention programs across Canada and the United States produced results indicating that most batterers involved with these programs could identify that physical and emotional abuse of their partner caused their children or their partner's children to feel sad, scared, or confused. Between two-thirds and three-quarters of the biological fathers identified that their violence against their partner negatively impacted their children's behavior at home and school, their mental health, and their relationship with their mother and with them. Fifty-three percent indicated that they were worried about the long-term effect of the abuse on their children and even more were worried that their boys were going to grow up to be abusers and their girls to be victims. The same percentage said they thought less of themselves as fathers because they were abusive to their children's mother. (It is important to note that within this study there were a significant number of men who showed little or no concern for the impact of their behavior on the children in their lives. For example, almost one-quarter said they wouldn't be upset at all if their children thought violence was normal.)

Other evidence exists for believing that batterers may be interested in change because of their children. Researchers Einat Peled and Jeffrey Edelson, in their article about barriers to children's domestic violence counseling, quoted a batterer who felt excluded from participating in a parenting program: "I understand the women's needs, being intimidated, but I felt I was left out. I really wanted information as a parent." Another man expressed his desire to work on himself before he could help his son heal from his violence.[10] Peter Jaffe, in his book on the children of battered women, quotes one batterer who wrote about his attempts to change his behavior: "Dear Dad ... I'm not as abusive to my kids as you were to me but I put them through hell.... Dad, this is my last chance for a family life.... Wish me well."[11]

In Australia, researchers explored the attitudes of batterers toward change as part of their efforts to construct a domestic violence social marketing prevention campaign.[12] Their results underscored the important role children can play in the change process for abusive men. This is what they had to say about the results of their focus groups.

> Various themes were tested in the groups (e.g., the threat of criminal charges; the damaging effect on the female partner; accusing violent men of cowardice/social disapproval; the effect of intimate partner violence on children; etc.). The most effective motivating theme for those accepting of their need to change was the consequence of the perpetrator's behavior on children. This applied whether or not they themselves had children. Cognitive response data revealed that a likely explanation for this was that for a number of perpetrators, this theme generated memories of the respondent's childhood exposure to physical or verbal family violence. A further positive for the "effects on children" theme was that it was accepted as true by precontemplator perpetrators. Hence there was the possibility that it could contribute to movement of this group toward contemplation.

The effectiveness of this approach was demonstrated when a social marketing campaign using this theme prompted 2,800 batterers and potential batterers to call a special hotline over the course of two years. Out of those calls, almost 60 percent accepted a referral for treatment. (The conclusions of this research should be approached cautiously. Even if the sentiments expressed by batterers in a counseling group or survey are honest, it doesn't guarantee that they will translate into the changed behavior that is the only real test measure of whether children's situations will improve.)

Batterers who are parents need to examine their own lives and behaviors in light of what they have done and how it has impacted their children, their children's mother, and themselves. The first step a batterer can take as a parent is to admit that his behavior is solely his responsibility and not the fault of children or their mother. This admission made directly, honestly, and in an appropriate way without any strings or expectations attached can be significant step toward healing a family. Admission of responsibility also opens the door to make credible changes in behavior. A batterer can also make himself available to listen to his children's experience of his abuse—without pressuring the children into talking, trying to change how they feel, or imposing his own viewpoint. Batterers who are serious about change can also support children in getting the professional help they need and openly describe their abusive behavior to the professionals working with their children. A batterer can support his children's relationship with their mother and express to the children (and Mom) his respect, gratitude, and appreciation for her as a person and a parent.

Challenging batterers to change is not the sole responsibility of the courts and law enforcement. Many of us have friends and family members we know to be abusive. We should ask how we can use our relationship with this person and awareness of their love for their children as a jumping off point to discuss how their abuse is harming their children. Medical and mental professionals, clergy, and others can build into their assessments and interventions questions about anger, jealousy, and control. When indicators of abuse are present, these professionals can educate clients or congregants to the impact that abuse has on children. Prevention efforts can target new fathers with educational information about abuse. Premarital counseling can include similar information. And clergy can develop sermons addressing the connection between being a good father and treating a partner with respect.

A gratifying result of my own research is that it has helped stimulate public awareness campaigns directed primarily at men who are fathers. The posters in this campaign ask men to consider the connection between their treatment of their partner and their child's well-being. One says, "How does your child feel when you abuse her mother?" Over the face of a young girl looking out from the poster are the words "sad" "scared," and "confused," the top three emotions the batterers I surveyed attributed to children. Designed to raise awareness and as vehicles for outreach, the posters are hung in courthouses, social services agencies, and even men's rooms, frequently with the phone number for a local domestic violence agency, and have been incorporated into public awareness campaigns that utilize bus ads and billboards.

Although service providers may feel uncomfortable working with abusive men, I am convinced that we cannot end violence and abuse in our homes unless we increase our capacity to address men who are violent. They are our fathers, friends, brothers, and sons. They are the source of the risk to our families, and this risk can only be significantly reduced if we devise ways to change their behavior. Importantly, more and more domestic violence advocates are embracing this approach, in part because working directly with perpetrators has increased their ability to be better understand and advocate on behalf of domestic violence survivors and their children.

Nothing I have said in this chapter is meant to diminish the responsibility that abusive men bear for the harms they cause to the women and children in their lives through their violence and control. To the contrary, I believe that holding these men solely accountable for the harms they cause is fully consistent with the central messages here; that if we want our families to thrive, we must raise our expectations of men as fathers, address batterers directly about their violence and abuse, and afford them the education and opportunity to change.

NOTES

1. I want to thank my wife, Rosalyn Dischiavo, for her extensive editing and comments as I developed this chapter.

2. The extracts are based on real cases or composites of real cases. The names and other potential identifying features have been changed.

3. A. Levendosky, "The Effects of Prenatal and Postnatal Domestic Violence on the Psychosocial Functioning of Children from Infancy through Preschool," presentation at the 3rd International Conference on Children Exposed to Domestic Violence, London, Ontario, May 10, 2007.

4. L. Bancroft and J. Silverman, *Batterer as Parent: Addressing the Impact of Domestic Violence on Family Dynamics* (Thousand Oaks, CA: Sage Publications, 2002).

5. An excellent review of the literature on the impact of batterers on children was produced by the National Council of Family and Juvenile Court Judges, "Children's Exposure to Domestic Violence: A Guide to Research and Resources," http://www.ncjfcj.org/content/blogcategory/356/425.

6. B. M. Grove, P. Van Horn, and A. Lieberman, "Deciding on Fathers' Involvement in Their Children's Treatment after Domestic Violence," in *Parenting by Men Who Batter: New Directions for Assessment and Intervention*, ed. J. Edleson and O. Williams (New York: Oxford University Press, 2007), 65–84.

7. C. O'Sullivan, "Estimating the Population at Risk for Violence during Child Visitation," *Domestic Violence Report* 5 (2000): 77–79.

8. R. Palkovitz and G. Palm, "Fatherhood and Faith in Formation: The Developmental Effects of Fathering on Religiosity, Morals, and Values" [electronic version], *Journal of Men's Studies* 7, no. 1 (1998): 33–51.

9. J. Lesser, J. Tello, D. Koniak-Griffin, B. Kappos, and M. Rhys, "Young Latino Fathers' Perceptions of Paternal Role and Risk for HIV/AIDS," *Hispanic Journal of Behavioral Sciences* 23, no. 3 (2001): 327–43.

10. E. Peled and J. Edleson, "Barriers to Children's Domestic Violence Counseling: A Qualitative Study," *Families in Society: The Journal of Contemporary Human Services* 80, no. 6 (1999): 578–86.

11. P. G. Jaffe, D. A. Wolfe, and S. K. Wilson, *Children of Battered Women* (Newbury Park, CA: Sage, 1990).

12. R. J. Donovan and D. Paterson, "Targeting Male Perpetrators of Intimate Partner Violence: Western Australia's *Freedom from Fear* Campaign," Paper presented at the 5th Annual Innovations in Social Marketing Conference, Montreal, Canada, 1999.

Chapter 5

The Battered Mothers' Dilemma

Evan Stark

This chapter concerns the significance of domestic violence in disputed child custody cases and the response by family courts. It critically reviews research on exposure of children to domestic violence in light of new knowledge about coercive control, and argues that the current approach by professionals responsible for evaluating custody leaves millions of women and children at extreme risk. The focal point of the chapter is the "battered mother's dilemma," the forced choice these women face between fighting to protect their children and possibly losing them as a result, and sharing custody with an abusive partner.

BACKGROUND

Over the last few decades, the proportion of U.S. marriages ending in divorce, typically in the first 10 years of wedlock, has hovered around 45 percent, though it is considerably lower (only about 25 percent) for men and women with college degrees. The vast majority of these divorces (between 85 and 90 percent) are uncontested. Mothers are solely responsible for about 84 percent of children who live with a single parent, and most of these children (about 55 percent according to the U.S. Census in 2007) live with women who are divorced or separated. Importantly, since the 1970s, the proportional increase in children living with their mother (the rate has tripled) mirrors the proportional increase in divorce during this period. In other words, whether by agreement, choice, judicial decision, or default, the vast majority of women who divorce end up with sole or primary custody of their children.

The most widely accepted estimate is that one woman in five in the United States is the victim of physical and/or sexual assault by a male partner. Since the risk that a woman will be victimized by a male partner is many times greater if she is single, separated, or divorced than if she is married, an even larger proportion of women who do *not* come to family court to resolve custodial disputes are victimized than of those who do, either because they never married or because their partner has no interest in custody. Among married couples with children who divorce, however, there is some evidence that those engaged in custody disputes are more likely to have been victims of their partners than those who do not. Somewhere between a third and a half of contested custody cases appear to involve abuse, considerably higher than in the general population, even after we control for the younger age of divorcing mothers. As we shall see, fighting for custody is a tactic many abusive men use to extend control over their wives and children into the postseparation period. Still, most abusive husbands do not contest custody when they divorce.

The effects of exposure to domestic violence on children's well-being obviously extend to millions of families that never come to family court. But this chapter primarily concerns the subset of cases where three facts combine: partner abuse, divorce, and disputes over child custody. Just under 1 million divorce petitions are filed each year in the U.S. If 10 to 15 percent of these involve contested custody (approximately 125,000), the number in which domestic violence is an issue can be conservatively estimated at around 50,000 annually, affecting around 75,000 children. Over time, these numbers add up.

The prevailing conceit in family court is that children are best served when their access to both parents is preserved to the maximum extent feasible. Indeed, 17 states plus the District of Columbia have statutory presumptions favoring joint custody. Nowhere are the prospects for future contact by both parents more in doubt than where one or both of the parties allege violence or other forms of abuse. No other problem encountered by family judges or evaluators is comparable to battering in its prevalence, duration, scope, dynamics, effect on personhood, and significance for the health of everyone involved. Domestic violence can be a major context for a range of medical, behavioral, and mental health problems that can affect parenting as well as for almost half of all child abuse. Moreover, when couples for whom domestic violence has been an issue separate, the risk for both partners of being killed or severely assaulted by the other partner increases dramatically, though the absolute numbers for men at risk are small. Some researchers believe that mere exposure to parental violence can have traumatic and long-term effects on children that resemble child abuse. Moreover, as this chapter will make clear, the spectrum of harms in partner abuse cases extends far beyond the violence that has been widely studied. These less tangible harms affect basic dimensions of personhood such as autonomy and decision making and may threaten children's well-being even more fundamentally than threats to their or their parent's physical safety.

Despite the significance of domestic violence in disputed custody cases, judges, lawyers, evaluators, and advocates who work with families remain sharply divided about the appropriate response. So do litigants. Horrific stories are commonplace of women who have lost custody to abusive partners or been punished, even jailed, for disobeying court orders to provide unsupervised visitation to these men. On the basis of interviews with female custodial litigants in Massachusetts, the "Battered Women's Testimony Project" at the Wellesley Center for Women documented a pattern of discrimination, mistreatment, and arbitrary or biased rulings they named as human rights violations.[1] These results were replicated in Arizona.

But mothers aren't the only ones who claim bias. Fathers also tell dramatic stories about being unjustly accused of physical or child sexual abuse by their wives and exiled by the family court to a lifetime of alienation from their children. Building on these stories, fathers' rights groups and their supporters use their Web sites to insist that husbands, not wives, are the real victims of bias, to discount documented injustice to mothers, and to attack "feminists," "protective mothers," and their supporters (see chapter 8 by Dawson, Fathers' Rights Groups, in this volume). When PBS aired *Breaking the Silence* in 2006, a documentary that featured critics who dubbed the use of parental alienation syndrome (PAS) to counter abuse allegations as "junk science," a letter-writing campaign spearheaded by fathers' rights publicist Glen Sacks won support from the station's "advocate," a watchdog appointed by President George W. Bush, and PBS hastily produced a more "balanced" film. From California to Maine and Alaska, coalitions of protective mothers and court reformers have challenged legislation making joint custody the default disposition in family disputes, advocated for the presumption of sole custody in abuse cases, and demanded greater transparency and accountability for the range of professionals involved in family court, including judges. In response, researchers from Canada, the United States, and Great Britain recently convened a national conference to challenge what they believe is a "feminist" stranglehold on research and policy in the domestic violence field, asking "Does gender matter?" and answering in the negative. Based on the premise that wives are as violent as husbands, father's rights groups in California sued so that public funds would be equally spent to support shelters for "battered men."

Amidst the practical realities that constrain their work, judges and evaluators are expected to set these political conflicts aside; envision a unique family whose willingness or capacity to resolve critical disputes has broken down, perhaps irretrievably; and dispassionately apply the law as well as their training, their experience, and the limited assessment tools at their disposal to map a workable postseparation arrangement least likely to harm children. Given the complexity of this process, the huge variation in the qualifications of those involved, and the often contradictory legislative contexts in which family court decisions are made, it is inevitable that some proportion of outcomes will appear unfair and leave abuse victims and their children at risk. Biased treatment of even a small proportion of litigants is a concern. But is the number of persons put at risk by court bias and the resulting harm significant enough to merit a public response? Even if bias is commonplace in family court, does it constitute a discriminatory pattern? In other words, even if bias is widespread, is the differential treatment a result of a systemic problem or the by-product of widespread ignorance or malfeasance? If the latter is true, enhanced professional education and training should provide sufficient correctives. More fundamental reforms are needed if the "mistakes" made by family courts reflect systemic bias.

The Long March

Confrontation with the family court is only the latest step in a long march through which advocates for domestic violence victims have tried to rid public institutions of practices they insist are discriminatory against women. Previous efforts have largely succeeded, in part because the arguments defending the status quo are so transparent and the political forces advancing these arguments are relatively weak. When the first battered women's shelters opened in the early 1970s, domestic violence had no standing in the social or family sciences. Psychiatry and psychology assumed it was rare and attributed it to maladaptive family dynamics or to personality problems (such as masochism or "dependent personality disorder"). Today, largely as a result of federal and state legislation promoted by advocates and their supporters, laws and policies throughout the United States and in hundreds in of other countries reflect the prevailing understanding that domestic violence is a widespread and criminal act primarily committed by men to gain "power and control" over female partners or former partners. Equally widespread is the belief that states are obligated to extend protections afforded to women through arrest, court orders, and counseling to their children.

One basis for the societal revolution in how we approach domestic violence were lawsuits arguing that failing to protect persons from partner abuse violated their 14th Amendment right to equal protection. In finding for the plaintiffs in these suits, courts made it clear that neither the site of an assault nor the fact that the parties are married or intimate compromised their right to legal protections, the same view that had extended the protections of rape laws to partners in the 1970s. While the sex discrimination protections afforded in Title VII of the 1964 Civil Rights Act have yet to be formally extended to personal life, the Violence Against Women Act passed in 1994 in the United States defined abuse as a crime motivated by "an animus based on the victim's gender" and allowed domestic violence victims to seek civil rights relief based on the view of abuse as a group-based harm rooted in inequality, giving victims a common point of reference to counter the claim that it is a private concern or the result of their complicity. Although the U.S. Supreme Court would find this provision unconstitutional in *United States v. Morrison* (2000), it received bipartisan endorsement in the Congress.

Separate Planets?

If the belief that domestic violence is a gendered crime from which women and children particularly require institutional protection is widely accepted in policy circles, the criminal justice system, medicine, and the social services, it remains highly controversial in the civil arena and particularly in family court, where the tenet remains strong that the private sphere of family life should be immune from the principles of formal justice that govern criminal law and that "discrimination" (assumed to be a problem best left to federal courts) and the relationship problems seen in state family courts are mutually exclusive phenomena. Resistance to a gendered analysis of abuse in family court and the tenacity with which decision makers in this arena hold arguments long rejected in criminal court also reflect the financial stakes at risk in family proceedings and the relative privilege and political power of the families who typically engage in custodial disputes, particularly but not exclusively the men, compared to the men and women charged in criminal court.

British scholar Marianne Hester (see chapter 6 in this volume) has dramatized the different and often contradictory assumptions that criminal and family courts bring to bear in domestic violence cases by referring to them as "separate planets."[2] In criminal court, a woman who presents evidence of abuse is considered a strong and cooperative witness. But if she presses these same claims in family court, she risks being identified as vindictive or uncooperative with "friendly parent" assumptions. The criminal court addresses equity concerns by using its authority to redress the imbalance of power exploited through abuse; in family court, abusive fathers are assumed to have an equity interest in custody. The "perpetrator" of domestic violence may now be reframed by an evaluating psychologist as the "good enough father." No-contact orders are commonplace in domestic violence proceedings.

But they are extremely rare in custody cases, even in the face of identical evidence. To the contrary, even victims who hold a no contact order from another court may be held in contempt in family court if they fail to provide access to an abusive dad. At best, family courts can help couples set aside long-standing grievances for the sake of the children. At worst, the normative emphasis on cooperation leads court professionals to misread partner abuse as a form of "high conflict," rationalize unworkable proposals for contact and then turn on victims when these plans fail.

In 1997, in part to overcome inconsistencies between family and criminal court practice, Congress passed the Morella resolution, so-named after its sponsor, Maryland Republican, Congresswoman Connie Morella, recommending that state courts give presumptive custody to victims of domestic violence. Some variation of this recommendation has been adapted by most states. While the language of these statutes is gender neutral, it is widely understood that their primary beneficiaries will be battered women. Fathers' rights groups claim these statutes have exacerbated the prevailing antimale bias in the family court.

Somewhat less extreme than the position adapted by fathers' rights groups, proponents of a so-called gender-neutral approach acknowledge that men commit the more serious forms of domestic violence. Even so, they argue, the domestic violence seen in family court is less serious than the types seen by police or criminal courts, typically consists of isolated episodes provoked by the stress of separation rather than of chronic abuse, and is rooted in the dysfunctional interpersonal dynamics specific to a given relationship, in personality deficits or in the sorts of childhood experiences key to other psychiatric or behavioral problems. Research psychologists in Canada and England have extended this claim to abuse generally.[3] This argument echoes the victim-blaming psychiatric explanations of abuse that prevailed when the domestic violence revolution began in basic respects. But this does not mean it is wrong. Naming domestic violence as one among the many personality or behavioral problems seen in family court gives the argument an intuitive appeal to judges and custody evaluators. If a pattern of maladaptive or dysfunctional behavior by men is the core obstacle to family cooperation in these disputes rather than an instrumental pattern designed to subordinate and control a partner, then shared custody can be facilitated by some combination of adjustment counseling, family systems work, or psychotherapy, short-term interventions that are commonly recommended to ease the difficult transition faced by divorcing couples. In contrast to the mainstream view of domestic violence as volitional, instrumental behavior rooted in sexual inequality and sexist cultural norms, the gender-neutral approach holds that the sheer existence of domestic violence is insufficient to justify restricting parental access, particularly when the only evidence is of minor or isolated assaults.

The remaining sections of this chapter set the questions being debated in the context of a new body of knowledge about the scope and dynamics of abuse, distinguishing domestic violence from the pattern of "coercive control" I and others have identified with "battering" and explaining how the current focus on violent episodes masks the most devastating facets of abuse. In making the argument that domestic violence is a sentinel event in custody cases, advocates and researchers have focused on how children are harmed by exposure to parental assaults. Much less is known about the dynamics and consequences of coercive control, a situation in which children commonly become both direct objects of an abuser's control and instruments in his attempts to control their mother. As we will see, coercive control may involve relatively minor levels of physical violence, leading judges and evaluators to conclude that abuse is not serious. In fact, because the tactics used to isolate, intimidate, and control partners in coercive control directly target a mother's autonomy, they often compromise parental decision making even more profoundly than physical assault. If the risks associated with coercive control are typically more far reaching than when domestic violence alone is involved, they are also more difficult to identify, particularly when attempts are made to interpret the significance of abuse through the prism of discrete acts of violence. Because victims of coercive control are subjected to multiple tactics, often over many years, its cumulative effects are likely to include high levels of fear, anger, dependence, and/or confusion. When these effects are taken out of the context of a pattern of abuse extending over time or their credibility is weighed only against documented or alleged incidents of physical assault, most of which are likely to be relatively minor, they are attributed to exaggeration, duplicity, or even malevolence, foundational deficits in parenting that justify limiting or denying access to a protective mother.

Clarifying the real extent and dynamics of abuse mothers experience and the risks it poses to all family members gives us a basis against which to measure evaluation and decision making in disputed custody cases. If the fathers' rights groups and their supporters are correct about the antimale bias in family courts, we would expect to find a pattern of restrictions on men's access to their children in these cases, particularly when partner abuse is merely alleged (falsely in the view of fathers' rights groups) as well as where hard evidence of prior abusive behavior is presented. If the protective mothers are correct and the bias works against their interest, we would expect to find that courts, evaluators, and other related professionals are minimizing or denying the significance of abuse or even responding punitively to women who raise abuse as an issue in custody disputes, possibly by giving custody to abusive dads. A third possibility is that family courts are behaving equitably. In this instance, we would expect to find a greater sensitivity to abuse in family court decisions, but not bias. This would be true, for example, if we found that the courts routinely applied protective measures when abuse is proved, an outcome fathers' rights groups would be hard-pressed to oppose, but not where it is merely alleged. Should public policy address systemic bias against mothers or fathers in these cases or, rather, should we merely press contending parties to present more compelling evidence for their claims? The outcomes of custodial disputes involving abuse bear on the long-term health and safety of millions of children as well as on the happiness, health, and safety of their parents. If a condition of systemic discrimination in abuse cases exists and is allowed to persist, the overall legitimacy of the family court as an institutional arbiter of marital dissolution may be jeopardized.

THE NATURE OF ABUSE SEEN IN THE CUSTODIAL CONTEXT

We have suggested that between a third and a half of disputed custody cases involve allegations of domestic violence. In about half of these cases, somewhere between 15 and 25 percent of all disputed cases, there is substantiating evidence of physical abuse such as a prior arrest for domestic violence, a criminal court finding, or a court order.[4] Given its prevalence and potential significance, it would seem clear that routine assessment for abuse in disputed custody cases is a prerequisite for any reasonable determination of equity and a child's best interest.

From Domestic Violence to Coercive Control

Between the early 1960s, when we learned that a higher proportion of police calls involved "domestics" than all other violent acts combined, and the adaptation of mandatory arrest statutes in the 1980s, society's response to abuse was revolutionized. These changes were elicited by the legal challenges already mentioned, a grassroots movement that opened shelters in hundreds of communities to which women who identified themselves as "battered" flocked in droves, and a burgeoning research literature on the extent and seriousness of abuse and the relative effectiveness of sanctions.

The Hallmarks of Physical Abuse

Since the mid-1970s, more than 12,000 research monographs have been published documenting the prevalence of partner violence in the general population as well among various subgroups, including medical and mental health patients, mothers of abused children, and petitioners for divorce. This research documented the three most salient dimensions of abuse: its significance as a source of injury and a range of other physical and psychological problems, its frequency, and its duration. In the early 1980s, in a program of research known as the Yale Trauma Studies, Dr. Anne Flitcraft and I reported the results of a randomized review of the medical records of more than 3,500 women who came to the medical emergency room. We found that domestic violence accounted for about four times as many injuries presented to the hospital as auto accidents (40 percent versus 11 percent), considered the most common source of adult injury at the time, and affected almost twice as many patients (18 percent versus 11 percent).[5] Physical abuse was also shown to be frequent, with rates varying from 3.7 to 8 assaults annually in community samples and a significant minority reporting being abused daily. Our hospital data and longitudinal studies of battered women show that abuse continues for between five and seven years on average, a fact that has elicited a broad-ranging debate about "why women stay" with abusive men.

Compared to nonbattered women, after the onset of abuse, battered women's risk of attempting suicide, becoming homeless, and developing secondary medical, behavioral, and mental health problems such as alcoholism or drug abuse increases dramatically. Since no comparable risk profile characterizes other populations of assault victims, including persons assaulted by strangers, men abused by female partners, or men or women abused by same-sex partners, an outstanding challenge was to identify what distinguishing features of woman battering by male partners elicit this profile. Another important finding was that the vast majority of abuse seen in the helping system is long-standing rather than "new," a finding consistent with the evidence of its frequency. This fact had two implications: that effective early intervention can substantially impact the burden abuse places on women, children, and the community, and that current interventions are largely ineffective in protecting women and their children from further abuse.

Our research and the work of others has also exposed as myth three beliefs about abuse that bear directly on its reception in family court: that it should be equated with discrete episodes of physical violence, that its seriousness can be gauged by the presence of injury, and that its typical context is an intimate or intact partnership. Many of the changes in institutional policy and practice we lauded were based on these false assumptions. Not only are domestic violence laws geared to discrete assaults but also, even when injury isn't officially required to identify a domestic violence crime, as a practical matter, police, courts, and physicians are unlikely to provide protections in the absence of injury or other tangible harms. Moreover, protection orders and many other interventions are predicated on the notion that separation effectively curtails domestic violence, even if it doesn't end completely.

In fact, the vast majority of abusive episodes are relatively minor, probably more than 95 percent, and involve pushing, grabbing, holding, slapping, hair pulling, and the like. Interestingly, this is even true at those sites, like the military or the emergency room, where we would expect to find the most injurious violence. Of 11,000 substantiated abuse cases reported to the military in 2001, for example, 57 percent involved no injury at all, another 36 percent prompted one visit to outpatient care, and only 7 percent could be classified as "severe."[6] In our study of the emergency medical population at Yale, fewer than 1 woman in 50 required hospitalization. As we've seen, the hallmarks of domestic violence are its frequency and duration, but not its severity or link to injury.

The risk of postseparation violence in custody cases is addressed below. Suffice it to say here that study after study has documented that the majority of victims are single, separated, or divorced from the men who abuse them; that the most serious risk of severe injury and death occurs after couples separate or are in the throes of separation; and that abusers employ a range of criminal tactics, such as stalking, harassment, and surveillance, that make separation ineffective as protection. Indeed, well-designed research shows that a majority of the men being arrested for domestic violence crimes are not physically living with the women they have assaulted.[7] For battered women, the fact that violence "crosses social space" means that physical separation is less an antidote to abuse than a negotiating tactic within an ongoing process of violence reduction.

Interventions based on false presumptions have proved very problematic for victims. Since the vast majority of incidents of partner violence are minor and few of the protections or sanctions won by advocates are set in motion by minor incidents, we need look no further than the incident-specific focus in domestic violence law to understand why, in most states, domestic violence crimes are treated as second-class misdemeanors for which almost no one goes to jail. In family court, the propensity for providers to trivialize the typical pattern of chronic but low-level violence is expressed in the belief that abuse is minor if there have been no injuries reported. When this approach renders the pattern invisible, its cumulative effect, the high levels of fear commonly expressed by protective mothers for instance, seems exaggerated to evaluators and judges, convincing even the well-intentioned professional that the woman is lying, crazy, or actively trying to alienate the children. Indeed, in many cases in which I have been involved, even if a woman has called the police or gone to court for a protection order, the low level of abuse reported can be used to further undermine her credibility and reinforce the claim advanced by the husband that she is simply making trouble for him to gain advantage in the proceeding. The catch-22 is that, absent serious injury, almost no meaningful help is available.

The false belief that separation ends domestic violence leads judges to become extremely frustrated if abuse continues, which it almost always does, a woman returns to an abusive partner or comes back to court for another protection order. Instead of recognizing the futility of separation unless the partner's access can be constrained, the "failure" of the protection order is ascribed not to the inadequate institutional understanding but to the victim's "ambivalence" or "dependence," ascriptions that make it harder for her to muster the continued support she needs.

Coercive Control

Even more far reaching than the problems that result from the incident-specific approach are the dilemmas created for abuse victims in family cases by the equation of battering with physical violence. In 20 to 40 percent of cases, domestic violence is the principal source of abuse, usually accompanied by forms of emotional abuse such as chronic name calling. However, somewhere between 60 and 80 percent of cases involve coercive control, an ongoing pattern of behavior characterized by a range of tactics to hurt, intimidate, humiliate, exploit, isolate, and control a partner (see chapter 9 by Lischick in this volume). Routine but minor acts of violence accompanied by coerced sex or sexual assault are commonplace in coercive control (sometimes termed "intimate terrorism"). But in a minority of these cases, there is no violence at all or violence has not occurred for some time. In a national survey conducted in Finland, for instance, researchers reported that older women who had not been abused for at least 10 years reported even higher levels of fear and abuse-related mental symptoms than younger women who were currently being physically abused.[8] The nonviolent forms of coercion and control are at least as harmful as violence and may also be more consequential for the range of concerns about parenting and child well-being that underlie custody decisions. Although the strategy of coercive control is the most common form of abuse women experience, it remains almost completely outside the scope of evaluation and decision making in family court.

The intimidation tactics that characterize coercive control extend from open threats, stalking, and harassment via phone or computer to more subtle warnings whose meaning is only grasped by the victim. This last tactic was illustrated by one of my male clients, who would show up at his wife's softball games and offer her a sweatshirt when she struck out several batters in a row, a gesture her teammates interpreted as loving. Only his wife understood the real meaning of his sweatshirt offer, that it was an ominous warning that the attention her pitching attracted made him jealous. She would have to "cover up" her arms that night due to a beating. The purpose of intimidation is to instill fear, enforce obedience, and raise the cost of disobedience. Apart from literal threats to hurt or kill a wife or someone she cares for, husbands in my custody caseload have embarrassed their wives on social occasions to get them to do as instructed; forced them to stand and listen to "lectures" at all hours ("We're done when I say we're done"); openly followed them; accidentally left "porno" sites or a love letter open on the computer; given them the "silent treatment" for days after a wife has refused a sexual demand or otherwise displeased them; engaged in frequent sexual inspections; described in detail how they would have them killed without detection; told the children in their wife's presence that if she wasn't home when they returned from school, they could find her in the ground next to the dog; had them followed at the mall, called them repeatedly at work, or showed up there unexpectedly; sent anonymous "reports" about their moral indiscretions to clients, business associates, or coworkers; revealed personal secrets to family members or friends; engaged in periodic house "cleanings" by burning toys, pieces of furniture, or a wife's clothing; secretly monitored their cell phones; driven recklessly with the children in the car; installed surveillance cameras throughout the house; used tracking devices; gone through diaries; called back anyone whose voice they didn't recognize; and allowed children to have "accidents" while they were babysitting. "Gaslighting" is commonly used to make a wife feel she is crazy by sabotaging a common activity: turning the stove back on after she has turned it off and left the room, for instance, or moving her car from its parking space without her knowledge or removing keys, then replacing them in her pocketbook after she has searched. Seemingly anonymous acts whose authorship is transparent are particularly shaming in the context of physical threats and coercion because a partner cannot "know what she knows" without putting herself at risk, a condition termed "perspecticide" in the hostage literature.

Isolation involves a set of tactics designed to enforce dependence on victims; enforce possession; monopolize their time, skills, and resources; and "keep the secret" by cutting them off from core sources of support and reality testing, such as family, friends, coworkers, or helping professionals. Examples from my forensic practice include forbidding a wife to call family or friends; timing or limiting her conversations; demanding she answer his calls within three rings, no matter where she is or what she's doing; destroying mementoes or photographs of family members; forbidding her to go to the gym; calling back numbers the abusive partner doesn't recognize; calling her repeatedly at work or leaving anonymous reports about her sexual behavior on the phones of her business clients; monitoring her e-mail account, phone bill, or MySpace; forcing her to sit in one place ("and don't move") when they're at a bar; sitting in a car outside work and school; publicly embarrassing her at lectures; refusing to provide money for plane trips home; forcing her to check out of the hospital 24 hours after cancer surgery; having a partner in a medical practice write prescriptions for psychiatric medicine (without meeting the woman) so she didn't "need" to see someone else; accompanying her to class; pulling the phone out of the wall; demanding sex just when she has to leave for work; and forbidding her to leave the house, go to church, or remain in a home-schooling network that was a woman's only source of contact besides her children. In one case where the husband continually belittled his wife's failure to attend college, he constructed elaborate lies about the education and careers of his father and his colleagues' wives. When she relied on this information in social gatherings with his family or friends, she was humiliated. Isolation evolves through a cat-and-mouse game in which victims attempt to establish and their partners to locate and destroy "safety zones" where a wife can ponder her options and preserve autonomy. Lest this account seems exaggerated, consider these numbers. Studies in the United States and England reveal that 40 to 89 percent of women who are physically assaulted by their partners are also kept from socializing, seeing their families, or leaving the house.[9] In attempts to placate husbands who fly into a jealous rage when they encounter or chat with forbidden contacts, many women voluntarily cut themselves off from friends and family members. In extreme cases of isolation, battered women can suffer from the Stockholm syndrome, where they cling to the man who is abusing them because he has become their only source of reality, positive reinforcement, and protection.

At the heart of most battering relationships are control tactics that install a husband's dominance directly. This is accomplished by three means primarily: exploiting a partner's capacities and resources for personal gain and gratification, depriving her of the means needed for autonomy and/or separation, and regulating her behavior with formal or implicit "rules" to conform with stereotyped gender roles. These tactics begin with a partner's control over the necessities of daily living, including money and other assets, food, sex, sleep, medication, housing, transportation, and communication with the outside world. But control tactics can extend to taken-for-granted arenas of autonomy such as toileting, eating, or even which chair a wife can use. Husbands in my practice have removed the doors from bathrooms, timed how long their wife and children could use the toilet, and denied them toilet paper when they were "bad." If the exploitation or regulation of access to necessities is the material foundation for coercive control, its infrastructure involves the micromanagement of minute facets of everyday life, particularly in areas like cooking, cleaning, and child care associated with women's default roles as homemaker or mother. In studies of service populations and domestic violence offenders, more than half of the abusive men monitored women's time as well as took their money.[10] In a number of my cases, wives were given written "rules" for daily behavior that covered everything from which clothes they were allowed to buy and which positions they were to favor in sex to how high the bedspread was to be from the carpet. One husband measured the space available in the refrigerator and demanded his wife make a dish that would fit exactly. The more arbitrary or petty the rule, the more women experience compliance as demeaning. Most often, rules are broad enough so that violations are almost impossible to avoid such as "You will be a 'good girl' at all times" or "You will never make me jealous." Or they are contradictory. One wife was punished "for thinking for yourself" as well as for waiting for her husband's permission to purchase a new appliance; another was told she had to answer the phone by "the third ring or else," but then told to pick up the man's stepson at a location that he knew was out of cell phone range. Several well-designed, large-scale studies have shown that control factors predict fatality and the psychological, physical, and psychosocial outcomes heretofore attributed to domestic violence far better than do levels or frequency of physical assault.[11] As importantly, as Lischick reports in chapter 9 in this volume, they may elicit these outcomes even in the absence of physical assault or long after physical assault has ended. With stalking, telephonic harassment, and control over money as the most obvious examples, many of the tactics used in coercive control also cross social space as well as extend over time, making them particularly effective as a way to continue abuse after couples are physically separated.

It has long been known that the violence used in abuse has little or nothing to do with the sort of "conflicts" that are the focus of anger management or various forms of family therapy many evaluators recommend to help couples cooperate post divorce. In fact, 60 percent of victims who use shelters report having been beaten in their sleep. Instead of being an ill-advised response to conflict, these behaviors, like the forms of isolation, intimidation, and control discussed here, are almost always part of a comprehensive strategy built around a husband's privileged access to his wife and the personal knowledge of her whereabouts, habits, and fears.

Although far more widespread and devastating in its consequences than domestic violence, coercive control is far more difficult to decipher, is almost never documented by court or police records, and can easily be concealed from evaluators or made to appear odd, eccentric, even "crazy" rather than malevolent, like the offer of the sweatshirt, despite eliciting high levels of psychological distress in a wife. Unless the diverse tactics deployed, as well as the wife's reactions, are put in the context of the pattern of coercive control and framed as part of a single, continuous strategy, her expressed fears can appear exaggerated, her claims histrionic or paranoid, and her personality "borderline," observations that may be supported by a husband's history of his wife's "acting out" or reports from friends that the wife "acted crazy."

Case Example

In a recent case, violence was minimal. The wife testified her husband had pointed a gun at her on two occasions, slapped her, thrown her off the bed, locked her out of the house in the snow, and choked her once. The largest number of incidents involved shoving, which he claimed had been mutual, a point she admitted. On the basis of having attended a domestic violence seminar, the judge insisted that she knew "real" domestic violence when she saw it and had no need to hear my forensic assessment. After all, she told the wife's attorney, the gun hadn't been loaded when he pointed it and pulled the trigger. What never got into evidence was that isolation and intimidation tactics had been continual in this home. Several times a week, the husband made his wife stand next to the bed while he lectured her about her faults, often for hours. After 9/11, he claimed to have received special information from sources in the Pentagon that their suburban Connecticut town was a target of Al Qaeda and that they would infect the mail with anthrax. On this pretext, he stopped letting her leave the house without him, even to get the mail, which he insisted the cleaning woman retrieve with rubber gloves. Under the interim agreement, the couple was to communicate via e-mails—his consisted of numerous, lengthy and abusive lectures on the areas of her life that needed correction—and to have no personal contact without mutual consent. Although the evaluator made no effort to verify the wife's claims of abuse, she advised her to set clear boundaries with her husband and joined the law guardian in recommending the wife get primary custody, largely because the husband had serious mental health problems. Shortly before the final disposition, the girl had a karate tournament while in her mother's care. The husband told his wife he was coming to observe the tournament with his new girlfriend, which the woman acknowledged. But when he arrived, he insisted on sitting with them; became verbally abusive when she said no, probably because he was intoxicated; followed them when they attempted to leave; blocked their exit; and then shoved the woman down when she tried to get around him, all in front of witnesses. The wife called the police and the husband was arrested. Instead of supporting the woman, however, the professionals agreed the wife's "overreaction" constituted a "selfish, self-centered attitude" that showed "she could not distinguish the child's interest in being with her father from her own." They reversed their earlier recommendation, the husband got primary custody, and the wife got only very limited visitation.

In this case, the husband was in another relationship—the reason he had initiated the divorce; he also had managed to invest a substantial equity loan taken against their home in a new condo that he shared with his partner and was about to get generous visitation with his daughter. He nonetheless became increasingly agitated as the settlement date approached and he faced the prospects of losing not only a substantial portion of the family assets he had controlled but also his hold over his wife. His increasingly accusatory and threatening e-mails (most of which the children's lawyer and therapist saw) caused her to fear he would do something to hurt her or their daughter, as he had in the past. Her reaction at the karate tournament was only intelligible as a by-product of the cumulative fear she felt when he became verbally or physically abusive. Moreover, the limits she had set were consistent with the therapist's advice that she should set strict boundaries with her husband and stick to them. To the guardian and evaluator, however, and ultimately to the judge, assuming the wife's perspective at the karate incident implied the husband was more dangerous than they had suspected, a conclusion that was incompatible with their assessments and recommendations for liberal visitation. The alternative that they adapted was that the wife was "crazy" or malicious, and hence unable or unworthy to be the primary parent. This conclusion protected them from being "wrong."

Victims of coercive control suffer many of the same physical or psychological effects as victims of domestic violence. But the major harms it causes are to autonomy, personhood, and decision making, harms that are less tangible than physical injuries but no less consequential for parenting. In this case, when the effects of the coercive control to which the wife was subjected were decontextualized, the guardian, evaluator, and judge attributed the behavioral consequences of literal regulation, intimidation, deprivation, and control to the wife's psychological dysfunction, compounding the effects of her husband's abuse. Since there had been no serious acts of violence, my testimony in the case was deemed irrelevant.

Domestic violence is committed by women as well as men and is often mutual. But coercive control is almost wholly committed by husbands. There is a growing sentiment among fathers' rights activists and their supporters that abusive men represent a deviant subtype who suffer from some combination of borderline, paranoid, or impulse control disorders that are often manifest in childhood. Well-designed studies of batterers in treatment, however, show that only one in four have serious psychological problems, although the proportion rises to 40 percent among those who commit chronic physical abuse.[12] Psychological models of abuse consistently have been found to predict subsequent risk of violence less accurately than simply knowing whether there has been a previous assault. Whether men who commit coercive control are more or less likely to have psychological problems than men who only assault their wives is not known. Of the several dozen domestic violence assessment tools available, only a handful consider aspects of abuse other than violence. But the long-term strategic planning and instrumental calculations involved in coercive control are generally incompatible with the impulse or borderline disorders and related personality types most commonly identified with violence.

DOMESTIC VIOLENCE, COERCIVE CONTROL, AND CHILDREN

Research on the overlap of woman abuse and harms to children differs greatly in quality, uses varying definitions of harm to children, and often disregards the incredible resilience shown by women who mother through domestic violence and their children or the mediating role of coping skills, parental support, and developmental age. Whatever the limits of this work, however, there is no question that abuse of a female primary caretaker is far and away the most common context in which evaluators are likely to confront behavior that jeopardizes a child's best interest.

Where domestic violence is identified, child abuse is a common consequence. Over 30 well-designed studies using a conservative definition of child abuse show a robust link between physical and sexual child abuse and domestic violence, with a median co-occurrence of 41 percent and a range of 30–60 percent. One large, multicity study found that children were directly involved in adult domestic violence incidents from 9 to 27 percent of the time (depending on the city) and that younger children were disproportionately represented in households where domestic assaults occurred as they are in family court cases.[13] In our Yale research, we found that abused women are more likely than nonabused women to abuse their children. Importantly, however, the man who is abusing the mother is more than three times more likely to be abusing the child than is the victimized mother.[14]

Witnessing and Exposure to Violence

Much of the research on children's response to domestic violence focuses on the psychological, behavioral, and cognitive harms caused by "witnessing," one of the more tangible facets of what is referred to as "exposure," rather than to literal physical or sexual abuse. It can be assumed that any child in a home where abuse occurs has witnessed violence, particularly when we consider the repeated nature of violence in these relationships. Although an abused woman or a perpetrator may deny children have witnessed the abuse, children often provide detailed recollections of the very events they were not supposed to have witnessed.

On average, children exposed to adult domestic violence exhibit more difficulties than those not so exposed. Witnessing violence has been linked to a range of psychological, emotional, and behavioral problems, including many of the same problems classically identified with physical and sexual abuse, with exposure to other behavioral problems such as parental alcoholism, or traumatic events such divorce or the death of a parent. Children exposed to domestic violence exhibit more aggressive and antisocial behaviors (externalized behaviors) as well as fearful and inhibited behaviors (internalized behaviors) when compared to nonexposed children. Exposed children also show lower social competence than other children, lower cognitive functioning, and higher-than-average anxiety, depression, trauma symptoms, and temperament problems than children who are not exposed to violence at home.

The relationship of the child to the violent adult appears to influence how a child is affected. A recent study of 80 shelter-resident mothers and 80 of their children revealed that an abusive male's relationship to a child directly affects the child's well-being without being mediated by the mother's level of mental health. Violence perpetrated by a biological father or stepfather was found to have a greater impact on a child than the violence of nonfather figures (e.g., partners or ex-partners who played a minimal role in the child's life). Children whose fathers or stepfathers were the abusers showed lower scores on self-competency measures when compared to the other children. The researchers concluded that "there may be something especially painful in the experience of witnessing one's own father abuse one's mother."[15]

Despite the importance of domestic violence for children's well-being, it cannot be assumed that all children exposed to any type of abuse in the home suffer long-term or severe consequences or that any manifestation of psychological or behavioral problems in exposed children results from abuse. Whether serious problems will develop depends on the resilience of a particular child, the available support system, the child's developmental age, and the nature and extent of abuse to which children are exposed, with the probability of harm increasing sharply if abuse is chronic. Although infants and small children are too young to appreciate what other people are feeling, they respond to cues like crying, shouting, or bleeding in the same ways as older children.

At the same time, even if they do not suffer behavioral or cognitive difficulties because of exposure, children living with abuse are engaged in ways that the relative passive term "witnessing" fails to capture. They interpret, predict, assess their roles in causing "fights," worry about the consequences, engage in problem solving, and/or take measures to protect themselves, their siblings, and their primary parent physically and emotionally. Psychological defenses may be at work even when children appear unresponsive. As an adult reports her experience with abuse as a child, "I wouldn't say anything. I would just sit there. Watch it ... I was just, felt like I was just sitting there, listening to a TV show or something.... It's like you just sit there to watch it, like a tapestry, you sit there."

COERCIVE CONTROL AND CHILDREN'S WELL-BEING

While the unique effects of coercive control on children have not been studied, given the prevalence of coercive control in partner abuse cases it is clear that many of the harms attributed to physical violence alone are actually elicited by exposure to a combination of abusive tactics, among which assault (because it is often low level) may not be the most important.

The limits that shape the general misunderstanding of domestic violence in family court extend to how the potential harms to children are assessed. Either explicitly or by implication, research on children's witnessing adapts an incident-specific definition of violence that highlights the potentially traumatic effects of exposure, particularly for very young children, showing that even infants exposed to severe violence may experience symptoms similar to adult posttraumatic stress disorder. While children can be traumatized by witnessing a severe assault, particularly if they experience an overwhelming fear that they may lose their mother, their more typical experience is prolonged exposure to repeated, but minor assaults and to the combination of violence, intimidation, isolation, and control in coercive control. The psychological, behavioral, and cognitive harms caused by this type of exposure are not adequately encompassed by traditional trauma models and cannot be accurately measured using these models. With coercive control, what the child "witnesses" is one parent being humiliated and systematically deprived of liberty and autonomy in everyday affairs, an "exposure" that elicits far less tangible signals of distress than are associated with violence and may be more difficult to discern than those induced by seeing a primary parent physically injured. Still, the long-term effects of such exposure may be quite dramatic and affect a child's gender identity, sense of autonomy, as well as their behavior as a "citizen." Few of these effects are picked up by the standard psychological tests used in custody evaluation, and virtually none are ever linked to exposure to parental abuse.

THE BATTERED MOTHER'S DILEMMA

In addition to the direct physical risks children face in any cases involving domestic violence, in coercive control they are also endangered by two common patterns: "the battered mother's dilemma," and when child abuse occurs as "tangential spouse abuse."

The battered mother's dilemma refers to the choices an abusive partner forces a mother to make between her own interests, including her physical safety, and the safety or interests of their children. A particular incident may bring this dilemma into sharp focus, as when a woman realizes that she may be hurt or killed if she attempts to protect her child from her partner's abuse. In custody disputes, common examples involve abusive husbands who threaten extended custody battles unless the wife abandons all claims for financial support or threaten her with physical harm if she pursues custody. Typically, however, the battered mother's dilemma describes an ongoing facet of abusive relationships where the victimized caretaker is repeatedly forced to chose between taking some action she believes is wrong (such as using inappropriate forms of corporal punishment with her child), being hurt herself, or standing by while her partner hurts the child.

Ignorance of the external constraints to which a caretaker is responding often leads courts or service professionals to aggravate the battered mother's dilemma. This happens, for instance, when, instead of providing appropriate protections for an abused mother, a court threatens to shift primary custody to an abusive partner if she fails to facilitate his access to their child. Another common example involves charging a mother who reports domestic violence with "neglect" and removing her child to foster care, a practice found unconstitutional in New York in *Nicholson v. Williams*.

A related dynamic involves child abuse as tangential spouse abuse, when the abusive partner uses the child as a tool to solidify control over a mother's behavior. While this pattern often begins when the couple is living together, it typically escalates when they separate and the perpetrator has less access to his victim. When they are together, the perpetrator may suggest a child's misbehavior is the reason the primary parent must be beaten or encourage children to abuse their mother, frighten children by threatening to harm them or their pets, or use them to spy on the victimized parent. Children may also be held hostage or abducted as a way to hurt or control their mother. This dynamic often underlies a woman's hesitation to separate or secure a protection order. Examples of this dynamic in my practice include threats to report the mother to Child Protective Services, moving for custody despite no real interest in or history of care taking, punishing a mother by denying her access to the children, hurting the children whenever the mother does something that makes him jealous, being passive-aggressive by consenting to care for the children so the mother can work and then neglecting them, and telling a child he will hurt himself or the mother if he doesn't "win" custody. In two large studies, 44 percent of battered women in the United States reported their partner had threatened to take or report the children "at least once" and 40 percent of the women in England reported their partner had done so "often" or "all the time."[16]

Children may also be harmed indirectly because of the secondary consequences of coercive control (e.g., depression, substance abuse, or attempted suicide) or because nonviolent abusive tactics may extend to the child through neglect, manipulation, or undermining a victim's ability to parent. Child outcomes in these instances include depression, suicide, aggression, delinquency, anxiety, developmental delay, substance use, and inappropriate behavior at school. Control over a partner's money and other vital resources, including transportation, is a major facet of coercive control that can jeopardize a child's safety and support. In a randomized sample of low-income women, Susan Lloyd from the Joint Center for Poverty Research in Chicago found that those who had been physically abused, threatened, or harassed by a male partner in the 12 months prior to the study had lower employment rates, had lower income, and were more likely than nonabused women in the sample to exhibit depression, anxiety, anger, and other problems that affect their labor market experience over time.[17] All of these outcomes bear on custodial and support decisions in family court.

Less tangible changes induced in a nonoffending mother by coercive control may also affect children. A victimized woman may believe she is an inadequate parent because her partner has consistently portrayed her as unfit or lose the respect of her children because they adapt their father's view, because she repeats his excuses for his abuse or because he has undermined her authority. She may also change her parenting style. She may become too permissive in response to the authoritarian parenting of an abuser or inappropriately punitive to compensate for her loss of authority or because her partner promises to do "worse" if she isn't tough enough, an example of the battered mother's dilemma. Because of her isolation, a mother in the throes of coercive control may make age-inappropriate or unreasonable demands on children or look to them to meet needs for affection she would normally satisfy in her adult relationships. Children may be angry at a mother for failing to protect them or to evict the abuser or because she is unavailable to comfort them with they are distressed. In some of these cases, children become "parentified," assuming caretaking roles for their mother or other siblings that are inappropriate for their age. Some abused children "identify with the aggressor" and become alienated from their mother either to protect themselves by an alliance with the stronger parent or as a magical way to protect their mothers. Some children become co-abusers of their mother.

MEN'S INTERFERENCE IN WOMEN'S PARENTING DURING CUSTODIAL DISPUTES

All forms of abuse extend into the postseparation period, a major reason why "separated" women actually face a higher risk of abuse than do married or cohabiting women.

Child visitation and shared custody are the most common contexts for reassault during the postseparation period. Of 235 Canadian divorced women interviewed, one in four reported being threatened or assaulted during child visitations. Approximately one-third of violations of court orders occur during child visitation exchanges.[18] Studies of so-called high-conflict marriages and divorce indicate that children continually exposed to abusive encounters between parents in shared custody arrangements or in noncustodial visits have more behavioral problems in childhood and early adulthood than children in sole custodial arrangements.

Typical of control tactics during postseparation is interference with a woman's parenting. In a work that is quickly becoming seminal to our understanding of abuse, Bancroft and Silverman describe a range of tactics men who batter use to systematically undermine their partner's parenting and how this interference often extends into the postseparation period.[19] Fathers who have had minimal involvement in child raising may win over court professionals committed to co-parenting at almost any cost when they suddenly develop an intense interest in custody. The legal system often colludes in a batterers' use of repeated legal motions in an attempt to bankrupt a former partner, protect his assets, and intimidate her into "compromising" her interests in the protection of the children.

Coercive control poses a particular challenge in cases where the child's expressed preference is to live with the abusive father or the child denies witnessing abuse despite compelling testimony that he has. Explanations for a child's apparent closeness to an abusive parent range from identification with the aggressor and frank Stockholm syndrome to the child's belief that he or she can magically protect the victimized parent by placating an abusive father, perhaps in response to his threats to hurt himself if he loses custody or his plaints about abandonment. We were able to expose this pattern in one case when the nine-year-old girl was recorded as telling the mother, "I hope you die, I hope you die," the same thing she had heard her father say at the dinner table on numerous occasions.[20] As an extension of this self-presentation, children often imagine their abusive fathers as the weaker of two parents and as requiring their support. Children may also deny abuse or express a preference for an abusive father simply because they share their mother's fear, which they often observe directly, a reaction which often leads mothers to be charged with "alienation." In one of my cases, two teen boys denied seeing their father use violence though the mother provided convincing descriptions of how they had responded when they saw her hurt, and neighbors told me they had shared their fears of "daddy's big hands," which he used on them as well as his wife. Too great a focus on the child's wishes in these cases can prevent judges, evaluators and children's attorneys from explicating the dynamics of parental abuse and how it shapes a child's expressed feelings or perceptions. The quality of a child's relationship to the abusing parent is important, but less because it points to whether limits should be placed on parental access and protections implemented than because it should influence how separation from an abusive parent should be facilitated. Protective custody arrangements may certainly involve providing an opportunity for a child to say goodbye to an abusive dad or for the abusive parent to relieve the child's burden of guilt by accepting responsibility for creating chaos in the home, particularly if a supervised visitation center is available in the area where this meeting can take place safely.

THE RESPONSE TO ABUSE IN FAMILY COURT

How have family courts and evaluators responded to the realities of abuse and its effects on children?

All but two states have implemented some version of the Morella resolution, most either prohibiting giving perpetrators sole custody or unsupervised visitation or adapting a "rebuttable presumption" that the victims in these cases should receive primary custody, the position promoted by The National Council of Juvenile and Family Court Judges (NCJFCJ) through its Greenbook initiative. But there is a growing concern that this legislation has not affected actual judicial decision making in abuse cases, particularly relative to changes in the institutional response in other arenas. For example, sole physical custody was given more often to fathers than to mothers in states where statutes favoring joint custody or friendly parent (FP) statutes competed with statutes denying custody to perpetrators of abuse. In fact, in New York, fathers were more likely to receive visitation when the mother had a protection order than when she did not. At best, family courts remain deeply ambivalent about the changing normative response to abuse.

In addition to statutes favoring joint custody or "friendly" parents, the family court's response to abuse is constrained by its reliance on "the best interests of the child" as a guide to custodial decisions. Since children's actual wishes are rarely polled directly, in practice this has meant relying on "therapeutic jurisprudence," an approach in which psychological interpretations of what children need, however weak their empirical foundation, trump the sort of justice concerns put in play by abuse allegations. By placing a significant proportion of custody cases outside the realm of psychological evaluation, presumptive custody rules threaten the professional infrastructure of therapeutic jurisprudence. By contrast, absent evidence of direct harm to a child, the "best interest" standard allows family judges to exclude domestic violence evidence as tangential to a child's psychological well-being. Because the psychological and behavioral harms to children caused by the most common forms of abuse are rarely detected using conventional models of assessment, forcing victims of domestic violence or coercive control to adapt a psychological argument to convince courts to provide needed protections disadvantages victimized mothers.

With marked exceptions, most family courts continue to interpret partner violence as different only in degree, but not in kind, from other types of animosities and family problems that bring disputants in custody litigation to court. The most relevant fact for our current purpose is that, in a disturbing proportion of cases, abusive partners continue to be given primary or shared custody and to be allowed unrestricted access to protective mothers and children. Moreover, even when abuse is well documented, it rarely surfaces as a major determinant of case outcomes.

When asked, psychologists, mediators, and other professionals charged with evaluation in family court claim that they assess for domestic violence and make specialized referrals or protective recommendations when appropriate. Studies of their actual practice suggest otherwise. Like the study in New York, research in Kentucky and California found domestic violence was not only overlooked by evaluators as a general rule but also played no role in recommendations even when it was mentioned in the report. Domestic violence couples were as likely as those without such allegations to be steered into mediation and mediators held joint sessions in nearly half of the cases where domestic violence was substantiated in an independent interview, even though this was against the regulations. In San Diego, California, mediators failed to recognize domestic violence in 57 percent of abuse cases. As importantly, revealing domestic violence was found to actually be detrimental to outcomes for victimized mothers. Mediators who said they were aware of abuse were less likely to recommend supervised exchanges than those who were not so aware.[21] Because of this reality, family lawyers in many areas are now advising clients not to discuss domestic violence with evaluators.

Research in Seattle illuminates the current status of decision making in abuse cases. Kernic and her colleagues studied all couples with minor children petitioning for dissolution of marriage in the target year, merged the marital dissolution files with police and criminal court files, and compared the outcomes for mothers with a documented history of abuse (as well as those with allegations of abuse in the dissolution file) with those without this history. Of the cases with a documented preexisting history of abuse, more than three quarters had either no mention of domestic violence in the marital dissolution file (48 percent) or only unsubstantiated allegations (29 percent). In other words, the court was made aware of abuse in fewer than one case in four where it could be documented. After adjusting for a range of potential confounders (such as allegations that the mother had used violence), mothers with a history of abuse were no more likely than the nonabused mothers to be granted child custody. Fathers whose abuse was substantiated in both criminal and family court files were significantly more likely to be denied child visitation and assigned to relevant services than comparison fathers, an outcome consistent with recommended best practice. But the vast majority (83 percent) of abusive fathers had no such restrictions. Sadly, the outcomes in cases that involved fathers with a documented history of abuse but whose abusive history was not included in the dissolution file and those with a documented history whose abuse was included only as an allegation by their wives were no different than the outcomes for nonabusive fathers. This last finding is particularly disturbing because the low level of violence typical of domestic violence and coercive control rarely prompts an arrest or protection order.[22]

The Seattle study addresses one of the questions raised earlier as to whether fathers are disproportionately denied visitation when their wives allege abuse. Not only is there no support for this claim, but no special restrictions are being placed on visitation even in the vast majority of cases where there is documented evidence of abuse. Thus, family courts, evaluators, and other professionals involved in therapeutic jurisprudence appear to be failing battered women and their children at every point in the custodial process. The fact that some judges who possessed information about abuse were more likely to take protective action suggests that better communication between criminal and family proceedings might improve the response, as would proper investigation of abuse allegations by evaluators. Still, the fact that the vast majority of judges failed to respond to documented abuse points toward a systemic constraint on appropriate decision making that is not likely to be remedied by training alone.

THE NATURE OF ABUSE IN CUSTODY CASES

Some defenders of therapeutic jurisprudence acknowledge that domestic violence harms children, but insist that the type of violence seen in custody disputes is substantively different and less serious than abuse seen in other service settings such as shelters or criminal courts. Instead, they insist, much of this violence is new rather than long standing and reflects "separation-engendered violence" or "postdivorce trauma" elicited by the tension surrounding divorce. Instead of being rooted in a well-established pattern of power and control in the marriage, they claim that violence in custodial settings is rooted in dysfunctional marital dynamics rather than in individual behavior and poses little long-term risk to children, largely because it is episodic, unlikely to continue once the finality of separation is accepted, and is not linked to other forms of violence or control. Rather than "cast a dark shadow" over the perpetrator's life by labeling him abusive, they argue that courts should treat the episodic violence they see as transitory, search for its cause in "family factors," and recommend therapeutic interventions that can manage trigger events or otherwise facilitate the ongoing cooperation and access of both parents.

The concept of "separation-engendered violence" was developed in a single study in which two well-respected custody researchers tested a typology of violence in a convenience sample of divorcing couples.[23] As an assessment of abuse, the study was flawed in major respects. For instance, it limited the definition of abuse to cases where unilateral violence "rises to dangerous, life threatening levels." This definition excluded most cases of coercive control or domestic violence as well as what they termed "male-controlled interactive violence," where a controlling male who is willing to use force to win compliance escalates his assaults when his partner resists his efforts at control. Excluding cases from the abuse category if women have reacted protectively to their husband's violence and control raises a range of ethical concerns. For our purposes, however, the important fact is that the research was designed to test a preset typology and had no way to determine what proportion of actual divorce cases fell into any category or even whether any substantial number did so. Interestingly, the researchers attributed separation-engendered violence to the "intolerable sense of abandonment and loss" that prompts some partners to engage in "one, two, or several incidents" of violence, including "sometimes very serious ones." In my experience, this same feeling is commonly elicited in perpetrators who lose control over a wife due to separation or divorce and is associated with a murderous rage that can culminate in murder-suicide, the vast majority of which (over 95 percent) involve female (and often child) victims. The controlling husband obsesses over his loss, deprives himself of food or other basic necessities, "slips" in his personal hygiene, and experiences many of the same health and behavioral symptoms due to the loss of control over his partner that we observe in women who are being abused. Even if the violence in these cases only surfaces during a divorce proceeding, it can almost always be identified with a history of violence and control. When the couple separates, the husband blames his wife for disloyalty, uses the court system to the fullest extent his assets allow, and takes every opportunity, including visits with his children, to denigrate his wife for abandoning him, an example of child abuse as tangential spouse abuse.

There is no evidence that the types of abuse found in disputed cases are any different or less severe than in other cases. Researchers have identified three factors that increase a woman's risk of severe or fatal violence nine fold: separation, the presence of a weapon, and the existence of control. Since separation is a constant in divorce cases and control is also likely to be present in a majority of abuse cases, there is good reason to suspect that, if anything, the types of abuse in the custodial setting are more dangerous than abuse seen in other service settings, not less so.

For the family court, the critical questions are how the power dynamics at work in an abusive relationship jeopardize the physical and psychosocial integrity of a partner and their children and how to protect them during separation and after divorce. As has already been suggested, therapeutic jurisprudence is little help in answering these questions.

In any given case, violent outbursts can be isolated, related to stress, and respond well to short-term counseling and arrangements for "parallel parenting." But we cannot know this without a full assessment by a qualified domestic violence professional who rules out the more likely and more dangerous possibility that a pattern of abuse or coercive control is involved. So widespread is abuse in custody cases; so critical is the presence of abuse to the future prospects of a primary parent's relationship to her child; so elusive and eclectic are the signs and symptoms of intimidation, isolation, and control; so easily are the behavioral dynamics of coercive control hidden from view; and so commonly are a victim's reactions to control mistaken for psychological dysfunction that, much like a cardiologist confronted by complaints of chest pain, any professional called to advise the court in these cases should conduct a full workup for abuse in all cases in which an evaluation of parental dynamics is requested.

CONCLUSION

Three decades of advocacy, professional education, and legal reform have greatly enhanced the response of hospitals, police, child welfare, the criminal court, and other services to battered women and their children. But the family court remains largely outside this process. Here, the same pattern of denial, minimization, and victim blaming that heretofore characterized other institutions continues to dominate practice, particularly in disputed custody cases. As the research described in this chapter illustrates, even when a history of abuse is well documented in a man's criminal records, domestic violence is rarely identified or validated by custody evaluators and is even less often included in custodial recommendations to the court. One consequence is that, despite state legislation to the contrary, in a disturbing proportion of cases, abusive husbands are given sole custody, joint custody, or unsupervised access to children to whom they continue to pose a significant risk. Moreover, as chapter 3 by Hilary Saunders in this volume suggests, this response does not distinguish family courts in the United States from similar proceedings abroad.

Well-designed research in New York and California suggest something more: that victims and their children may actually fare worse in the family court when abuse is identified than if mothers remain silent about domestic violence, a dramatic example of the battered mothers' dilemma. Stories abound of abused mothers who have been forced to provide access to perpetrators, been given pseudo-psychiatric labels because of their aggressive attempts to protect their children, and had severe constraints placed on their own access, been ordered to supervised visitation, denied access altogether, or even been jailed for their reluctance to "cooperate."

In sum, although domestic violence is far and away the most prevalent threat to children in disputed cases, the family courts not only deny its significance but also appear to discriminate against battered women and their children as a class, even when state policies explicitly direct judges to give presumptive custody to battered women. The question is, Why?

One explanation is structural. The family court occupies a unique place in the legal system because of its substantive concerns with personal life and character, its informal evidentiary procedures, and a decision-making process that lacks the sort of accountability to formal law, public scrutiny, and empirical validation that characterizes other legal, medical, or criminal justice institutions. To some extent, this reflects its function, to reconcile the conflicting needs and wishes of particular individuals rather than to administer equity and justice, for example. But its combination of a personalistic focus and relative insularity also allows social prejudice with respect to gender, sexual identity, race, or social class to take on enormous importance in decision making. Although therapeutic jurisprudence may cushion the application of bias to some extent, in the case of domestic violence it gives stereotypes the imprimatur of science.

Another explanation for the inappropriate response by the family court is paradigmatic. The prevailing conceit favoring co-parenting implies that fathers have an inalienable "right to contact" if they choose to exercise it. Therapeutic jurisprudence recasts the same man who appears as a perpetrator in criminal court as a "good enough father" in family court, rationalizes this interpretation as in the child's best interest, and reframes women who persist in seeking protective interventions as "uncooperative" or worse, punishing them for vindictively alienating their children from their fathers and giving these fathers primary custody, a process examined in chapter 7 by Joan Meier. At the same time, when courts equate abuse with violence, take an incident-specific approach and apply a calculus of injury to assess severity, the result is to trivialize partner assault—which typically involves frequent, but minor violence—and to render coercive control, the context of violence that is most devastating to victims and their children, virtually invisible. This approach makes the cumulative fear expressed by victims of battering or coercive control appear exaggerated or, in the case of children, to be a by-product of deliberate alienation, two of the more common rationales for dismissing allegations of domestic violence.

A third explanation reflects the socioeconomic and political context in which custodial decisions are made. Without a principled theory of primary parenting or equity to constrain the exercise of prejudice in disputed family proceedings, decisions follow the dollar; in this instance, the advantaged status of husbands both relative to their wives and to the offenders seen in criminal court. Therapeutic jurisprudence rationalizes this dynamic. By applying psychological theories discredited in other settings, evaluators reframe legitimate allegations of abuse as transparently self-interested efforts to sabotage the benefits of co-parenting and father's access to children.

A final explanation involves the nature of abuse itself. Battering and coercive control are behavioral strategies intended to exact privileges by oppressing and exploiting an adult partner. Although these strategies have psychological dimensions and effects, they are not psychological conditions, nor are they typically rooted in psychological problems. Like other miscreants up to no good, perpetrators of abuse have a self-interest in concealment, minimization, and blaming others for their strategies that far exceeds the detection capacities of evaluators, family judges, and most other professionals who work in and around the family court. Appropriate assessment in abuse cases requires a new type of forensics, including new types of evidence, assessment conducted by persons with extensive experience working with abuse perpetrators and their victims, and expert testimony from persons whose investigative skills more closely resemble those of police detectives than psychologists. Given the prevalence of domestic violence in disputed custody cases, adapting this approach means sharply reducing the role of therapeutic jurisprudence in custody cases. Nor are most family lawyers prepared to appropriately present a case for abuse, let alone to decipher its more subtle dimensions. Scattershot training for judges or evaluators, the current approach, is as likely to reinforce as to curtail the prevailing bias evident in family court decisions in abuse cases. In the end, mounting an effective response to abuse in disputed custody cases requires major changes in family court procedure as we know it.

Given convincing evidence of abuse, the primary concern of the family court should be to limit access by the perpetrator to his former wife and children, provide appropriate protections against future assault, and offer support services to all parties. Adhering to this program would help a significant proportion of abusive husbands (and some wives) reframe their behavioral choices, as many now do in the context of criminal proceedings and some perpetrators do in batterer programs. But there should be no illusions. Appropriately retooling family courts to respond to abuse would dramatically up the ante in custodial disputes, lengthen the time and cost of these proceedings, add a level of conflict to already acrimonious proceedings, and make evaluators and judges targets of criticism by fathers' rights groups and their supporters. Frank assessments of abuse would also challenge the prevailing ideology of family courts by pitting justice concerns, the importance of safety, and moral judgments about right and wrong against deeply held beliefs in equity, fairness, privacy, and cooperation. But it is also likely that strengthening the family court commitment to just outcomes in abuse cases may actually move us toward rather than away from an ideal of joint parenting after divorce. As Justice Wall, the Lord Justice of Appeal in England, put it in a recent paper,

> It is ... high time that the Family Justice System abandoned any reliance on the proposition that a man can have a history of violence to the mother of his children but, nonetheless, be a good father.[24]

Incorporating this insight into family court practice may be a first step toward responsible fathering, an issue addressed by David Mandel in this volume, and allowing victimized women to properly protect and mother their children.

NOTES

1. K. Y. Slote, C. Cuthbert, C. J. Mesh, M. G. Driggers, L. Bancroft, and J. Silverman, "Battered Mothers Speak Out: Participatory Human Rights Documentation as a Model for Research and Activism in the United States," *Violence against Women* 11, no. 11 (2005): 1367–95.

2. M. Hester, "Future trends and developments: Violence against women in Europe and East Asia," *Violence against Women* 12, no. 10 (2004): 1451–8. This argument is elaborated in L. Radford and M. Hester, *Mothering through Domestic Violence* (London: Jessica Kingsley, 2006), as well as in chapter 6 by Marianne Hester in this volume.

3. D. G. Dutton, "Domestic Abuse Assessment in Child Custody Disputes: Beware the Domestic Violence Research Paradigm," *Journal of Child Custody* 2, no. 4 (2005): 23–42; and D. G. Dutton, "On Comparing Apples with Apples

Deemed Nonexistent: A Reply to Johnson," *Journal of Child Custody* 2, no. 4 (2005): 53–64.

4. M. A. Kernic, D. J. Monary-Ernsdorff, J. K. Koespell, and V. L. Holt, "Children in the Crossfire: Child Custody Determinations among Couples with a History of Intimate Partner Violence," *Violence against Women* 11 (2005): 991–1021.

5. E. Stark and A. Flitcraft, *Women at Risk: Domestic Violence and Women's Health* (Thousand Oaks, CA: Sage, 1996).

6. Calibert Associates, *Symposium on DV Prevention Research* (Washington, D.C.: U.S. Department of Defense, 2002).

7. E. Buzawa, G. Hotaling, A. Klein, and J. Byrne, *Response to Domestic Violence in a Pro-Active Court Setting: Final Report* (Washington, D.C.: National Institute of Justice, 1999).

8. M. Piispa, "Complexity of Patterns of Violence against Women in Heterosexual Partnerships," *Violence against Women* 8, no. 7 (2002): 873–900.

9. R. M. Tolman, "The Development of a Measure of Psychological Maltreatment of Women by Their Male Partners," *Violence and Victims* 4, no. 3 (1989): 159–77; A. Rees, R. Agnew-Davies, and M. Barkham, "Outcomes for Women Escaping Domestic Violence at Refuge" (paper presented at Society for Psychotherapy Research Annual Conference, Edinburgh, 2006).

10. Ibid. Also see op cit. Buzawa et al., 1999.

11. N. Glass, J. Manganello, and J. C. Campbell, "Risk for Intimate Partner Femicide in Violent Relationships," *DV Report* 9, no. 2 (2004): 1,2, 30–33. See also Piispa op cit. and C. Lischick, "Coping and Related Characteristics Delineating Battered Women's Experiences in Self-Defined, Difficult/Hurtful Dating Relationships: A Multicultural Study" (PhD diss., Rutgers University, 1999).

12. E. W. Gondolf, *Final Report: An Extended Follow-Up of Batterers and Their Partners*, Grant no.: R49/CCR3l0525-04-06-1, 1997–2001 (Washington, D.C.: Centers for Disease Control and Prevention, 2002).

13. J. W. Fantuzzo and W. K. Mohr, "Prevalence and Effects of Child Exposure to Domestic Violence," *The Future of Children* 9 (1999): 21–32.

14. E. Stark and A. Flitcraft, "Women and Children at Risk: A Feminist Perspective on Child Abuse." *International Journal of Health Services* 18, no. 1 (1988): 97–118. Reprinted in *Women at Risk: Domestic Violence and Women's Health* (Thousand Oaks, CA: Sage, 1996).

15. C. M. Sullivan, J. Juras, D. Bybee, H. Nguyen, and N. Allen, "How Children's Adjustment Is Affected by Their Relationships to Their Mothers' Abusers," *Journal of Interpersonal Violence* 15, no. 6 (2000): 587–602, 598.

16. Op. cit., note 11.

17. S. Lloyd, "The Effects of Violence on Women's Employment," Joint Center for Poverty Research, MacArthur Foundation, 1997, http://www.spc.uchicago.edu/PovertyCenter/violence.html.

18. B. Leighton, *Spousal Abuse in Metropolitan Toronto: Research Report on the Response of the Criminal Justice System*, Report no. l989-02 (Ottawa: Solicitor General of Canada, 1989); and M. McMahon and E. Pence, "Doing more harm than good: Some cautions on visitation centers." In *Ending the Cycle Of Violence: Community Responses to Children of Battered Women*, ed. E. Peled, P. Jaffe, and J. Edleson (Thousand Oaks, CA: Sage, 1995), 186–206.

19. L. Bancroft and J. Silverman, *The Batterer as Parent: The Impact of Domestic Violence on Family Dynamics* (Thousand Oaks, CA: Sage, 2002).

20. *Knock v. Knock*, 621 A.2d 267, 272–73 (Conn. 1993).

21. See op. cit., Johnson et al., 2005. Also see L. S. Horvath, T. K. Logan, and R. Walker, "Child Custody Cases: A Content Analysis of Evaluations in Practice," *Professional Psychology: Research and Practice* 33 (2004): 557–65; and A. M. Hirst, "Domestic Violence in Court-Based Child Custody Mediation Cases in California," Research Update, Judicial Council of California, Administrative Office of the Courts, November 1–12, 2002.

22. Op cit., note 4, Kernic et al.

23. J. Johnston and L. Campbell, "A Clinical Typology of Interparental Violence in Disputed Custody Divorces," *American Journal of Orthopsychiatry* 63, no. 2 (1993): 190–99.

24. N. Wall, "Report to the President of the Family Division on the Publication by the Women's Aid Federation of England Entitled Twenty-Nine Child Homicides: Lessons Still to Be Learnt on Domestic Violence and Child Protection with Particular Reference to the Five Cases in Which There Was Judicial Involvement," 2006. Available online at www.judiciary.gov.uk/docs/report_childhomicides.pdf, accessed January 31, 2009.

FURTHER READING

Bancroft, L., and Silverman, J. (2002). *The Batterer As Parent: The Impact of Domestic Violence on Family Dynamics*. Thousand Oaks, CA: Sage.

Radford, L., and Hester, M. (2006). *Mothering through Domestic Violence*. London: Jessica Kingsley.

Stark, E. (2007). *Coercive Control: How Men Entrap Women in Personal Life*. New York: Oxford University Press.

Chapter 6

The Contradictory Legal Worlds Faced by Domestic Violence Victims

Marianne Hester

It is now more than 30 years ago since work to combat domestic violence began in the United States and United Kingdom, with other countries—especially in Northern Europe—following suit from the 1980s. In the past couple of decades, these developments have been particularly rapid, with a wide range of agencies and interventions across governmental and nongovernmental organizational (NGO) sectors, and involving criminal, civil, and family jurisdictions. However, despite this prolific activity, and despite some limited successes in tempering men's violence against their female partners, domestic violence has continued largely unabated.

This chapter considers one aspect of this conundrum: the problem created by the separate development of three different areas of work with a direct bearing on families experiencing domestic violence. These areas are work with victims and perpetrators of domestic violence, work on child protection, and work on child contact or visitation. The chapter discusses key tensions and contradictions that have resulted between the professional discourses and practices in relation to these three different areas. The contention here is that the work related to domestic violence, child protection, and child visitation should be conceptualized as being located on three separate planets with their own separate histories, culture, laws, and populations (sets of professionals). From the vantage of the victims or survivors, the perpetrators, and the children who are the subjects of domestic violence work, this is indeed how domestic violence, child protection, and child visitation work appear to operate.

Alongside the notion of the planets, another important force is at work: the process of gendering that results from the continual replication and reconstruction of the gender-based social inequalities prevalent in both the United Kingdom and United States, let alone elsewhere. The "planets" provide a way of understanding some of the systemic problems across criminal and welfare systems. However, the ways in which approaches to perpetrators, victims or survivors, and children are played out is underpinned by gender inequality. Stark talks about the gender inequality processes involved in domestic violence as "coercive control."[1] These processes have previously been written about as involving the gendering of meanings and expectations about victims and perpetrators, where woman blaming is an integral feature and where even as victims women may be construed as the main problem.[2]

In each of the three "planets" of domestic violence work, child protection, contact, and visitation, there are distinct "cultural histories" underpinning practices and outcomes, and these also involve different understandings of and approaches to gender inequality. Domestic violence work has been influenced by feminist understanding of domestic violence as gender based, which is carried out mainly by men against women and rooted in gender inequality. Organizations and agencies working with domestic violence, such as shelters and providers of advocacy, have developed with the adult victim or survivor as their central focus and are working in a context where there has been increasing criminalization of and intervention with domestic violence perpetrators. Consequently, domestic violence work tends to see the problem as (mainly) male perpetrators impacting on (mainly) female victims or survivors. The work of child protection services has a very different history to those organizations and agencies focusing more specifically on domestic violence. Child protection agencies have the child as the central focus of their work. The prevalent social work view has been to see the family, and in particular "dysfunctional" families, as central to the problem. Within this approach the focus is on the child and her or his main carer, usually the mother. Consequently there has been a tendency to see the mother "as colluding with the man's behavior and failing to protect her children."[3]

These differences between child protection and domestic violence services create tensions and contradictions, and have made it more difficult for coherent and consistent practice to be developed that takes into account needs for the safety of both children and adults. These structural factors, with domestic violence and child protection work on different "planets," have made it especially difficult to integrate practice, and have resulted in child protection work where there is a tendency to see mothers as failing to protect their children rather than as the victims of domestic violence, and where violent male perpetrators are often ignored.

These difficulties are made even more complex when both child protection and arrangements for child visitation after separation of the parents intersect. Mothers have to be seen by child protection services to be actively, indeed aggressively, protecting their children. Yet in relation to divorce and separation, the message is very different. Within the contexts of divorce proceedings, mothers must be perceived as proactively encouraging child contact and must *not* be attempting to "aggressively protect" their children from the direct or indirect abuse of a violent father. Here, mothers who bring up problems related to domestic violence or child abuse issues have often been construed as "implacably hostile" or "unreasonably hostile" and seen to be acting against the children's best interests of contact with the father. As a result of this problem, contradictory outcomes may be established: on the one hand, there may be an expectation that mothers should protect their children; but, on the other hand, formally constituted arrangements for visitation may be implemented that do not adequately take into account that in some instances mothers and/or children may experience further abuse.

The remainder of this chapter looks in more detail at the operation of the "three planets" and the implications for women's and children's safety.

THE DOMESTIC VIOLENCE PLANET

In North America, the United Kingdom, and most Westernized countries, the "domestic violence planet" tends to be the most sophisticated of the three with respect to the safety of women and children living with violent men. As well as providing a range of victim- or survivor-focused support including shelters, rehousing, advocacy, and so on, it also involves criminalization and protection via civil injunctions and rehabilitative work with perpetrators. The criminalization of domestic violence has been especially important in symbolizing the shift from considering domestic violence as merely a "private" problem to its being seen as an issue of public concern.

Since the mid-1970s, the increasing recognition of domestic violence as a crime has shifted how it is approached as a social problem. There has been a move away from emphasizing a woman's own responsibility to solve the problem or protect herself toward a view of domestic violence as unacceptable behavior that all agencies should try to prevent. Safety has been reframed as everybody's business.

Started in the United States in the late 1970s, the policy of criminalizing domestic violence began to impact the United Kingdom by the late 1980s, particularly police intervention and practice. Where police had initially not taken domestic violence seriously and were reluctant to intervene in what they saw as merely private "domestic disputes," there was a reassessment of this approach following lawsuits in the United States and criticism of police practice, especially from women's groups. In the United Kingdom, as in the United States, and since the 1990s in particular, a plethora of policy initiatives has aimed at developing criminal justice approaches to domestic violence, in particular via pro-arrest policies and increases in prosecution and conviction. The English Domestic Violence, Crimes, and Victims Act 2004 places further emphasis on criminalizing domestic violence by making it a criminal offense to breach a civil protective order and increases the possibility of arrest of perpetrators in domestic violence situations.

At the same time, the use of a criminal or civil justice approach deals with only a minority of domestic violence cases, and only a small proportion of cases proceed to prosecution or conviction. In the United Kingdom, about 23 percent of incidents are ever reported to the police, and of those incidents reported only about a quarter result in arrest and only about one in 20 end in conviction. Consequently, many men do not appear before the courts. Where there is conviction, the result is likely to be only small fines of perhaps $200 to $500. Many abused women are also ambivalent about calling the police, fearing they will not be believed or taken seriously; they may believe that the police can only respond to actual physical assault; they may fear it will provoke further or greater violence by challenging the man; or they may not want their partner or ex-partner to be taken to court.

Research indicates that criminal justice interventions are unlikely to be effective on their own, and are most effective when carried out in a context of wider support and advocacy for those victimized.[4] Dedicated advocacy for victims, where women are provided with an advocate who can provide information and support throughout the criminal justice process, increases reporting to police and use of protection orders. Ensuring close links between the police and domestic violence support services, for instance by having a police officer attached to the support service, also increases reporting to the police and leads to a greater proportion of arrests. A further approach in both the United Kingdom and United States has been the setting up of dedicated domestic violence courts, with the judges receiving specialist training in domestic violence issues. Such courts are found to increase conviction rates.[5]

The focus by the UK and US governments on criminalization suggests that criminal justice interventions can be used to reduce or manage domestic violence. However, this is not without contention. In the United States—where criminalization has been taken much further than in the United Kingdom and has included mandatory arrest and prosecution policies—some feminists have argued that criminal justice interventions should no longer be pursued because they are directly disempowering for women. In the United Kingdom it has been argued that the adversarial criminal justice system cannot in any case deal with crimes where the victim and perpetrator know each other, as with domestic violence. More importantly, the criminal justice system deals primarily with individual incidents and mainly physically violent incidents and thus is unable to adequately deal with or reflect the actuality of domestic violence: that it is ongoing and involves coercively controlling behaviors by the perpetrator as well as assaults. The emphasis on individual physical assault has also meant that when women retaliate against violent male partners, it is the women who may end up being prosecuted rather than the main, male, perpetrators.

There are also specific questions about the outcomes of using a criminal justice approach. Research in the 1980s in the United States initially indicated that use of arrest helped to reduce repeat offending in relation to domestic violence. Later work was less clear-cut, and in both the United Kingdom and United States has increasingly shown that while arrest may act as a deterrent for some domestic violence perpetrators, it does not appear to have such an effect on the more chronic domestic violence offenders. The more limited research on court outcomes appears to indicate that conviction, especially where it involves jail or probation rather than fines, may reduce repeat offending. However, to reiterate, the proportion of domestic violence cases resulting in conviction tend to be very small.

Women victimized by domestic violence may see criminalization as a positive approach if they feel it will enhance their safety, but are critical if their safety is not ensured. For instance, research in the United Kingdom examining attrition in domestic violence cases found that women's perception of the ability of the different actors and processes of the criminal justice system to provide safety was key in their decisions about engaging with the system.[6] Two main categories of need emerged from this research:

1. For the immediate violence to be stopped and the situation to be calmed down
2. The need for longer-term protection and measures to be put in place to ensure the violence did not continue

The women in the first category tended to be satisfied with the police intervention because the police had arrived quickly, had been effective in calming the man down, and/or had separated the two of them. They did not want their case to be pursued further, and thus attrition was in this sense positive. This was the situation, for example, for Ada:

Ada's partner had been drinking, and beat her up. She rang the police and they took him away. She did not want him charged. This pattern had happened a few times, and Ada felt the police had been very supportive—there when she needed them. She has now been able to give her partner an ultimatum to stop drinking or she would leave.[7]

The women in the second category, needing longer-term protection and measures put in place to ensure the violence did not continue, were more likely to be dissatisfied, especially with the court process. As echoed by other research, the fines and bind-overs, or short custodial sentences, did not stop the men from continuing their violence and harassment in the longer term. The men in this category were more likely to be "chronic" offenders—as was the case for Celia:

> Celia had been married for five years. Her husband gradually became more violent. First he used the "odd slap," then started isolating her from friends and family. She tried to leave three times, but her husband became more violent each time. Police were eventually called. Her husband was arrested for breach of the peace, but she would not press charges and he was released. More violence ensued: broken ribs, nose, an arm, chin split, teeth loose. Police were eventually called again. Celia gave a statement, and her husband was charged with grievous bodily harm. He was placed in a bail hostel and she felt safe, but he was then allowed out to see the children. The court case resulted in conviction: he was fined £100, paid £5 a week, and was ordered to attend a perpetrator program. She felt none of this had an impact on the offender, as he continued to pester her daily.[8]

For women in this second category, the apparent inability of the criminal justice system to impact on or control the male partners' behavior was viewed especially negatively. The women felt let down by the court process and the frequently inadequate outcomes. The women were generally bewildered and shocked by the plea-bargaining and reduction in sentences that tended to take place in a court system that they thought was there to provide justice and protection. Feeling safe as a result of the court outcome was very important if women were to contemplate pursuing a case again. Nonetheless, many of the women felt stronger because of having taken the cases through the courts and thus having "stood up to" their (ex-)partners. In some instances, this meant the men were less likely to be violent again.

Thus, although the domestic violence planet is focused on providing women's safety, there are limitations, and there is the potential to negate or undermine women's safety. Even so, on the domestic violence planet a domestic violence perpetrator's (male partner's) behavior may be recognized by the police and other agencies as abusive in relation to the victim or survivor (female partner). His behavior is seen as a potential crime and he may even be prosecuted for a criminal or public order offense. He might also have a restraining or protective order taken out against him. Crucially, he is thus perceived as a *violent male partner* and the woman in need of protection and support. The support services for female victims or survivors provided on this planet may also use an approach that seeks to empower women and attempts to equalize her position in relation to that of the abusive male partner.

CHILDREN'S SAFETY: THE CHILD PROTECTION PLANET

Whereas the focus on the domestic violence planet is on adults, the focus on the child protection planet is on children and what is considered by the state to be in their best interests. The legal framework is provided by the laws on safeguarding children, which in the United Kingdom are the Children Act 1989 and 2004, the Adoption and Children Act 2002, and to a lesser extent the Domestic Violence, Crime, and Victims Act 2004. Child protection is largely within public law because the emphasis is on intervention in families by the state to ensure that a child does not suffer significant harm. The approach is to attempt partnership with parents rather than prosecution, with removal of children from families of origin into public care and/or adoption supposedly as a last resort.

The Children Act of 1989 is underpinned by the principle that the child's welfare is paramount. There is no overt acknowledgement of the context of domestic violence in which many children live or the well-documented fact that children may be impacted detrimentally in such circumstances. An amendment in 1996 (via the Family Law Act 1996), in recognition of the impact of domestic violence on children, shifted this emphasis and allows the courts to exclude from the home someone who is suspected of abusing a child within the home, including a domestic violence perpetrator. However, at the same time there has been an expectation that the carer, usually the woman, will herself eventually exclude the abuser either by using civil protection remedies or through the intervention of criminal justice agencies. This was also lodged in the 1996 amendment, which states that the exclusion of the abuser is linked only to an interim order and "by the time the court considers making a final care order a proposed carer, usually the woman, will be expected to have excluded the abuser either by her own legal remedies or through the intervention of criminal justice agencies."[9]

Reflecting this emphasis, practitioners on the child protection planet—social workers in the UK context—have increasingly seen separation of mother and child from the violent male perpetrator as the favored approach. That women and their children may be better off by leaving such men is perhaps a positive step forward in social care practice from the earlier emphasis on families remaining intact, and the approach has developed alongside a greater public awareness of domestic violence. However, many women experience this current "failure to protect" approach as especially punitive. The problem is linked to an inability by practitioners to see the gender inequalities that underpin domestically violent relationships. The emphasis on "dysfunctional" families and ungendered "parents," rather than male perpetrators and female victims or survivors, leads to a hidden gendering of the meanings and expectations associated with victims' behavior. Thus, all the responsibility for protecting children is placed on mothers—because they are deemed the main caregivers—rather than tackling those responsible for the violence, the male abusers. Moreover, the dynamics involved in domestic violence and the impacts on and needs of the women living in violent relationships have often not been understood by the professionals concerned. This has led to frustration about why women "don't just leave." Professionals, whose prime focus is on protecting children, have tended to respond by threatening removal of the children—partly as a means of "pushing" women to leave violent relationships. Or they may have decided that the woman is no longer able to parent effectively for her children in the context of the violent relationship, and have therefore removed the children into care. These may appear sensible courses of action, but have in reality been counterproductive because they have largely ignored the (primarily male) abuser and have created fear for women that their children will be taken away if they disclose domestic violence. As Farmer argues,

> Relying on women to protect their children is clearly a flawed policy.... When women who live with violent men are clearly unable to protect themselves, the chances of their being in a position to protect their children may be remote.[10]

Farmer is not implying that women being abused by male partners are bad parents, but that they can only provide effective protection for their children if they are provided safety and support. A range of studies indicate the problems associated with the "failure to protect" approach. For instance, in Humphreys and Thiara's study of women using domestic violence outreach services in the United Kingdom, 44 percent had contact with social services children and families' teams. Concerns of social workers about child protection issues led to a significant number of these women being coerced into leaving their abusive partners before they were ready, or without the support needed to carry through such a difficult and dangerous process.[11]

Research in the United Kingdom during the past decade looking at social work practice indicates that social workers tend to be uncomfortable about working with domestic violence, and until recently have had few or no policies or guidelines on domestic violence to which they can refer. Social workers are likely to ignore domestic violence perpetrators, focusing instead on the women and children who are more accessible, with whom they are more familiar and more confident, and who are possibly more open to social work influence. Some professionals also assume that women are able to influence or prevent the men's violence against them. In Farmer and Owen's study on child protection practice, they note that not only was there a striking shift in focus *"away from an abusing father figure onto the mother"* in relation to physical and emotional child abuse, but also this *"shift of focus from men to women often also allowed men's violence to their wives or partners to disappear from sight"*[12] (emphasis in original). This was based on an assumption about parenting by social workers that mothers, but not fathers, were mainly responsible for the children's well-being. Similar findings have been highlighted since then in other studies. Williamson and Hester's study of a perpetrator program in the United Kingdom suggests that social workers are beginning to take a more active approach in relation to domestic violence perpetrators, urging them to attend such programs for the sake of the children.[13] However, this has not changed their focus on seeing female carers as responsible for protection and blaming them for "failure to protect" where the men still continue their violence and abuse.

Clearly, child care professionals avoid violent men or minimize their behavior for a number of reasons that include their assumptions about parenting as well as concerns regarding their own safety. Farmer also discusses the ways in which violent men assist in deflecting the focus of social work attention away from themselves and onto mothers. They might, for instance, be absent when the social work visit takes place, might refuse to discuss with the social worker issues concerning the child, or can be intimidating to (often female) professionals. Farmer provides three main examples:

> One occurred when the social worker considered the father figure to be a serious risk to the child and tried to arrange for him to move out. If no charge had been brought by the police, workers could only try to put pressure on mothers to exclude their partner. If ... unsuccessful, workers might concentrate their attention ... on the mothers and on general child-care issues....

> A second process ... was when a male social worker became strongly identified with the father's view of the family situation ... that the children were disobedient. The father's abuse was reconstructed as discipline, albeit occasionally excessive....

> The third process occurred where, either because the man denied causing the child's injury or because, in the absence of any direct evidence, it was unclear which parent had abused the child, the worker focused on some other area of family difficulty.[14]

There have been some attempts in welfare policy and practice to move away from this approach and the resulting problems identified in relation to mothers. In particular, supporting mothers' safety from violent men was first seen as a positive approach in child protection in the United States and then echoed in English policy directives. For example, in England the Department of Health issued guidance in relation to the Family Law Act 1996 suggesting that "[w]here domestic violence may be an important element in the family, the safety of (usually) the mother is also in the child's welfare [sic]."[15]

However, in practice neither the family courts nor welfare practitioners have ever generally applied this approach to any great extent, and the problems identified above remain. In their discussion of the North American juvenile courts, psychologist Peter Jaffe and his colleagues cite numerous cases of mothers losing their parental rights due to a perceived failure to protect their children from abusive partners, while abusive men are still being perceived as good enough parents and even being given custodial rights.[16] They also identify a specific and increasing problem involving family law cases in the United States where the victimized mother was held to be neglectful solely because the child has witnessed her being abused by her male partner, the child's father. For instance,

> in *In re Lonell J* (N.Y. App. Div., 1998), 973 N.Y.S.2d 116, in which the battered mother was found to have emotionally neglected her children because they witnessed her being abused by the father, in spite of evidence that police were called repeatedly, the father was arrested, and a protective order was issued.

And similarly,

> in the *Matter of Deandre T.* (N.Y. App. Div. 1998), 253 A.D.2d 497, the father's abuse of the mother in front of one of their children was sufficient to sustain a finding of neglect of that child's sibling.[17]

Although some such cases have been reversed on appeal, the general trend remains. A similar trend can be seen in the United Kingdom. In 2002, the Adoption and Children Act extended the definition of "harm," as stated in the Children Act of 1989, to include "impairment suffered from seeing or hearing the ill treatment of another." This came into effect in January 2005, and since then there has been a steady increase in the use of "emotional abuse" as a category for registering children with the child protection services as at risk of significant harm, with resultant pressure on mothers to be shown to be protecting children from their violent partners. Examples from my own research with Williamson in the northeast of England show the difficulties and contradictory messages that are resulting for mothers. One instance involved a very physically and psychologically abusive male ex-partner who was attending a perpetrator program. There were fears about a significant emotional impact of the man's behavior on two children, who had been placed on the child protection register as a result. The parents were separated, and as part of a safety plan developed by social services the mother was provided with an alarm with direct access to the police so that she could easily call for help if the ex-partner or father came to the house. However, social services used the evidence of the woman's attempts to increase her own and her children's safety by triggering the alarm as evidence against her of "failing to protect," and the children were removed into local state care:

> So every time he came 'round and kicked the door in because he couldn't get what he wanted off me on the phone, or you know he couldn't get me sort of say, "Yes no" or whatever ... I'd hit the alarm. Or when he did something I hit the alarm. And they used it against us in court to prove how many times he'd been to the house to take the children. And, so you stop using them, because you think, "No. Fuck you. I'd rather have a slap 'round the face and a black eye than lose my family." ... But at the end of the day, it didn't matter what I did. It didn't matter how far I went, it didn't matter what I agreed to, it didn't matter what groups I went to, appointments I went to. You know, they took 'em anyway. (Interview with mother)

Thus, while recognition of domestic violence as a context for child abuse should be a positive step, in reality the processes of gendering lead to the opposite. As Jaffe and his colleagues conclude, while phrases such as "witnessing domestic violence is child abuse" are useful to draw attention to the interlinking of woman and child abuse, they should be used with caution. If witnessing domestic violence is seen as child abuse, women experiencing domestic violence will continue to be accused of "secondary abuse" or as having "engaged in domestic violence."

As in the United States, in the United Kingdom legislation ostensibly aimed at dealing with situations of child homicide where neither parent indicates that they are guilty is creating a further context for mother blaming and criminalizing mothers for "allowing" a child to be murdered. The English Domestic Violence Crime and Victims Act of 2004 (section 5—introduced March 2005) has a new offense of

> causing or allowing the death of a child or vulnerable adult, whereby a person is guilty of such an offence if a child or vulnerable adult dies as a result of an unlawful act, and the defendant either was or should have been aware of the risk and failed to take steps to protect them.

The legislation has been used against a number of mothers who were acknowledged as not carrying out the homicide but who "stood by," often in circumstances where the mothers were themselves experiencing domestic violence from the same individuals. As Herring points out regarding the new clause:

> The motivation behind it is undoubtedly good. It is designed to protect children's rights. The offence must, however, be viewed in the social context in which it operates.... It leads to the prosecution of women who are themselves victims of domestic violence. It involves criminal proceedings against women when they and their children have been let down by the state's failure to provide adequate protection from domestic violence or adequate services for those seeking to flee from it.[18]

Again we see how the gendering of meanings and expectations about women's behavior as mothers places a focus on a mother's "failure to protect," even if the father is the actual abuser. The following, one of the first cases under the new clause, typifies the approach:

> In May 2005 Rebecca Lewis, aged 21, was sentenced for failing to prevent the murder of her baby, Aaron Gilbert, at the hands of her partner, Andrew Lloyd, with whom she had lived for six weeks. She was sentenced to six years in prison. Lloyd was sentenced to 24 years in prison for murder. The court was told that Lewis was largely absent during Lloyd's attacks and was not present when he killed the baby. However, she knew that Lloyd had flicked Aaron's ears and feet when he cried; had picked him up by his ears and ankles; and had thrown him onto a bed. (Crim. L.R. 927) ... In sentencing her, the judge said: "You put your own interests first, above and beyond that of your vulnerable child. You could have stopped the violence that Lloyd was subjecting Aaron to. You could so easily have got the authorities to stop it." At the trial Lewis had explained that she did not summon help because Lloyd had said he would kill her if she left.[19]

The apparent culpability of mothers and invisibility of abusive fathers are further highlighted by media coverage of the cases:

> "Woman lets boyfriend kill her baby"; "Mother allowed baby son's murder"; and "Mother first to be convicted of failing to stop violent lover killing her baby."[20]

To reiterate: on the child protection planet, the focus is on protecting children, not adults—even if making mothers safe might actually provide a better way of also ensuring children's safety. On the child protection planet, the father's abuse of the mother may lead to the involvement in the family of social services or other child protection agencies, and result (in England) in the children being placed on the child protection register for emotional abuse. In order to protect the children, social workers are likely to insist that the mother removes herself and her children from the male abuser's presence, and leaves the relationship if she has not already done so. If she does not, then it is she who is seen as "failing to protect," and the children might be removed into the care of the local authority. It is highly unlikely, however, that the father will be prosecuted for such abuse because a predominantly welfare, rather than criminalizing, approach prevails. Criminal proceedings will mainly apply in cases of homicide, and there the abused mother might also end up with a serious criminal conviction for "allowing" the murder. On this planet, therefore, despite the violence to the mother being from the male partner, it is the *mother who is seen as responsible* for dealing with the consequences. In effect, the violent man disappears out of the picture.

POST SEPARATION: THE CHILD CONTACT AND VISITATION PLANET

On the child contact and visitation planet, the focus is on outcomes and arrangements for children when parents separate or divorce. While the domestic violence planet perceives domestic violence as a crime, and the child protection planet uses a public law "welfare" approach, these two planets both have as a general ethos intervention to deal with risk of further violence and harm, whether to an adult (the domestic violence planet) or a child (the child protection planet). By contrast, the child contact and visitation planet draws on a private law framework, underpinned by the notion that the state does not normally need to intervene in families, and if parents find it difficult to agree on arrangements for their children post separation, then a negotiated or "conciliated" approach is preferable. While the domestic violence and child protection planets are concerned with past behavior and abuse, on the child contact planet the focus is specifically on the future. Despite the copious evidence that domestic violence is likely to continue post separation, a relationship history of domestic violence is deemed to be in the past and thus largely irrelevant to arrangements for the children. The overarching ethos is one of children having two parents even if the parents are no longer living together. The presumption is that contact between a child and the nonresident parent is the desired, and indeed inevitable, outcome of any court proceedings, whatever the history of the relationship.

The following assumptions about "responsible parenting" have thus been especially influential in the family courts in the United Kingdom and the United States:

1. Most parents are "reasonable parents" who can be encouraged to make decisions that are the best decisions for their children.
2. It is best if parents can agree to decide things for themselves rather than bother the courts.

3. Co-parenting, "shared care," and generous contact are the top three outcomes for children when parents separate.

Furthermore, the gendering of expectations and meanings related to parenting by mothers has led to the following assumptions:

1. Mothers who do not facilitate shared care or generous contact are selfish and unreasonable and possibly child alienators.
2. The best cure for maternal resistance is the enforcement of orders that support the father's contact with the child.

In the United Kingdom, as in the United States, when a woman leaves home because of her partner's violence, she is most likely to take the children with her and will probably wish to continue to care for them and make a home for them. Usually, this is in the children's own interests. The children and the absent parent may wish to see each other regularly, and sometimes this can be arranged without major problems. But in many cases, the mother will be reluctant for her children to see her abusive ex-partner because she is fearful for their or her own safety. These fears may, however, be ignored or minimized by professionals who believe, mistakenly, that if there is no clear evidence of substantial risk to the child then contact with both parents is in the child's best interests. This failure to recognize the risks of domestic violence to the safety of both the mother and the child has sometimes been compounded by the apparent lack of hard evidence of previous or present violence in the home. This itself results from a number of other problems, including lack of coordination of information and evidence across criminal justice and family proceedings; absence, until very recently, within statutory responses of full recognition of the impact of domestic violence on children living with it; court pressure to reach agreement on arrangements for children; inadequate legal representation leading to the full nature of the abuse being hidden or minimized; and the intrinsically private nature of the abusive behavior itself.

Following much pressure from women's organizations and evidence from research, starting in the late 1990s, the English judiciary began to look more closely at the problems of children's contact and visitation in circumstances of domestic violence. For instance, a report on the topic from the Children Act Sub Committee (CASC) of the Advisory Board on Family Law in May 2000 took a large step forward in acknowledging that there are links between domestic violence and possible harm to children and that this needs to be addressed in cases relating to children's contact with a violent parent. A notable set of cases followed this report (*Re: L (A Child)*, *Re: V (A Child)*, *Re: M (A Child)*, and *Re: H (Children)*). While involving very different circumstances of race and ethnicity and family relationships, the four cases all concerned fathers who had previously been denied direct contact with their children against a background of domestic violence. The fathers, who had been allowed indirect contact, were all appealing against the refusal of direct contact, and one father was in addition appealing against the refusal of custody or "parental responsibility." The judgments are important in indicating a potential shift in emphasis and understanding with regard to the impact of domestic violence on children, and linked to this, a cautious critique of the contact presumption operating in the courts. In her case commentary, the most senior judge involved supported the plea for courts to be more aware of the possible effects on children of domestic violence, "both short-term and long-term, as witnesses as well as victims," and also of the impact of violence on the residential parent, as identified in a range of research:

> There has, perhaps, been a tendency in the past for courts not to tackle allegations of violence and to leave them in the background on the premise that they were matters affecting the adults and not relevant to issues regarding the children.[21]

However, this approach has been applied infrequently and inconsistently by the family courts.

A second Children Act Sub-Committee (in 2001) consultation paper and a report, *Making Contact Work*, in 2002 focused on facilitation of contact and enforcement of court orders.[22] Legislation on this topic followed in 2005 (the Children [Contact] and Adoption Act 2005). The idea of enforcement of court orders for contact relies on a strong reemphasis of the contact presumption—that contact is inevitably in the best interests of children. The concern is in particular with the cases where agreed contact arrangements are not adhered to, and there is an underlying assumption that women deliberately set out to prevent fathers from caring for children. The approach adopted is an active facilitation via mediation and conciliation in such cases as well as the strengthening of legal enforcement. Discussion leading up to the new legislation indicated how domestic violence was being remarginalized in the contact discourse. Thus Margaret Hodge, the minister for children at the time, in public statements about the new proposals for a law on enforcement of contact indicated that she considered issues related to domestic violence as merely extreme and thus a minor concern.

During this period, cases in the English courts illustrated how the risk of losing contact continued to be seen as a weightier concern than the risk of harm to a child. For example, in *Re W Brothers* (2002) EWCA Civ 1052, a father who was a convicted murderer released from prison from a life sentence in 1995 was given contact with his three-year-old son after his mother had died despite expert testimony that the father was a risk to the child. In another case, *Re R* (2003) EWCA Civ 455, expert testimony supported the conclusion that a five-year-old child had been sexually abused by her father and a recommendation was given for very carefully supervised contact. The senior judge argued, however, that the child should not be deprived of the benefits of being able to visit her father's farm and to play with the animals. He granted contact with the father on the basis the child would be safe if the grandmother was there.

Another concern is the emphasis on implacable hostility. This was an issue mentioned in relation to the 2000 Appeal Court cases in England, where the court accepted that the impact of domestic violence may make the residential parent (mother) wary of contact. However, there is no guarantee that women with "reasonable" fear of their ex-partners and concerns for the safety of their children will not in fact be considered "unreasonable." For instance, in *Re L* (contact, genuine fear), a case heard by the family division in November 2001, the father had a long history of extreme violence, including stabbing his former wife, her solicitor, and her boyfriend; domestic violence against the mother in question; as well as stalking and harassment of her after they separated. The mother resisted contact between the father and the child (aged seven) "on the basis of her own fear of the father and on the basis he would be a bad influence on the child." The court, however, on the basis of psychological evidence, decided that the mother merely had a "phobia" in relation to the father that would necessitate psychological intervention to overcome her fear. The impact of this phobia was such that only indirect contact could be ordered. The expression of interest in the child by the father was, on the other hand, perceived as genuine, and despite listing a catalog of "character flaws"—including his tendency to violent behavior and showing "a startling lack of insight"—the judge considered that, if possible, the father should be considered for direct contact.

A number of reports as well as court inspections in the United Kingdom have continued to highlight domestic violence as a contentious issue within family policy, and also that professionals on the child contact and visitation planet, despite increasing awareness of the issue, continue to promote contact with a violent father rather than safety for the child and mother.

While professionals working in the family courts increasingly acknowledge that cases involving contact often have domestic violence as a feature, there continues to be a lack of understanding what this may involve, and consequently a minimizing of the issue in relation to outcomes and arrangements for contact. In *Re S* (a child) (contact), heard in the English Court of Appeal in January 2004—a case that the principal of the English Family Division, Dame Butler-Sloss, describes as paradigmatic—there had been two nonmolestation orders against the father, he was described as "a fairly aggressive person," and the child (aged seven) was reluctant to see him after witnessing his angry and argumentative behavior. Nonetheless, the Appeal Court accepted that his behavior was "at a very minor level," and thought that his consistent attempts to obtain contact indicated that he was a "good enough parent" and that direct contact should be pursued. Instead, it was the mother who was perceived as the problem, being seen as having influenced the child against contact and not showing willingness for contact to take place.

Failure to deal adequately with the risk to children from domestic violence perpetrators was also highlighted in inspections by the UK government of family court practice. A series of inspections in recent years in different parts of the country have been critical of a lack of attention to the impact of domestic violence on children, including the failure to obtain relevant information about criminal convictions. As exemplified by one of the most recent reports:

> Whilst allegations of domestic violence were a common feature in cases, its impact on children was assessed adequately in only a minority of cases. One case involving domestic violence had such serious deficits in practice that inspectors referred it to the regional director for immediate review.[23]

Thus, despite attempts to shift policy and practice on the child contact and visitation "planet," the contact presumption continues to be central. As a recent study of the family court process found, the contact presumption was in some instances becoming a "self-fulfilling prophesy" that would override any allegations of risk arising from domestic violence. As exemplified by one of the judges they interviewed,

> I have to say I do try and steer the parties away from the past, I tend to say "look, statistics show that there is a very high likelihood that there is going to be contact. At the end of the day the Court is going to order contact, so the more fruitful exercise is to concentrate on how that contact is going to progress."[24]

Research in the United Kingdom has also indicated that where criminal justice and private family law cases are pursued in relation to or by the same perpetrator, such intersection of "planets" may prioritize contact to the detriment of the criminal outcomes. Court observation and case file analysis undertaken as part of the study of attrition of domestic violence cases through the criminal justice system revealed that reference to contact between children and alleged offenders was likely to lead to more lenient outcomes, whether bail conditions or sentences. One of the prosecutors interviewed explained that a custodial sentence following a conviction for actual bodily harm and harassment was unlikely because the offender had almost daily contact with his three children. Yet, it was not questioned whether contact should be allowed to continue in such circumstances. Defense attorneys also explained that contact between the children and offender was an obvious area for the defense to exploit.

To reiterate, in both the United Kingdom and United States, while family courts have started to take domestic violence into account when contact decisions are made, fear of hostile mothers alienating children from fathers has been the greater concern. In family law, separated fathers are put into the position of the aggrieved, seen as deprived of their children. This has reinforced violent men's tendency for legal persistence and litigation abuse. The law's response to domestic violence and contact for children is a victim- and woman-blaming response. The primary concern in the family courts is in getting women to overcome their fears for the apparent sake of their children rather than challenging the violence of men. Courts may order supervised contact or attach conditions to an order to keep parents apart, but the purpose and value of contact for the child are rarely considered. Keeping in contact with fathers is almost always viewed as being in a child's best interests. On the child contact and visitation planet, a violent male perpetrator is most likely to be perceived as a *good enough father*. There is a distinct conceptual gap between being a violent man on one hand and being a father on the other.

For mothers, the situation created by the child contact and visitation planet is especially contradictory. She may have attempted to curb her partner's violent behavior by calling the police and supporting his prosecution on the domestic violence planet. She may have left her violent partner following instruction from social services on the child protection planet that she leave to protect her children. However, the child contact and visitation planet, in effect, has the opposite approach: that families should continue to be families even if there is divorce and separation. On the contact and visitation planet, therefore, she is ordered to allow contact between her violent ex-partner and the children, leaving her not only bewildered and confused but also yet again scared for the safety of her children, let alone herself.[25]

CONCLUSION

In this chapter, it has been shown that the serious systemic contradictions between the work on domestic violence, child protection, and child contact and visitation justify viewing these as operating on separate "planets" each with their own cultures, laws, policies, and practices. The systemic contradictions are further compounded by gendered inequalities and associated processes of gendering. Mothers end up being subject to both formal and informal pressures from the separate planets, resulting in impossible choices about how they might or should be acting in order to ensure safety for themselves and their children. Moreover, children's welfare and interests are by no means achieved. Tackling the "three-planet problem," and dealing more effectively with domestic violence as it impacts on adults and children, requires both a unified approach across the separate areas and acknowledgment of the processes of gendering that are situating women as culpable victims.

NOTES

1. E. Stark, *Coercive Control* (New York: Oxford University Press, 2007).

2. M. Hester, "Patriarchal Reconstruction and the Early Modern Witch Hunts," in *The Witchcraft Reader*, ed. M. Oldridge (London: Routledge, 2002).

3. N. Parton, "Taking Child Abuse Seriously," In *Taking Child Abuse Seriously*, ed. Violence against Children Study Group (London: Unwin Hyman, 1990), 15.

4. E. S. Buzawa and C. G. Buzawa, *Domestic Violence: The Criminal Justice Response* (London: Sage, 2003); and M. Hester and N. Westmarland, *Tackling Domestic Violence: Effective Interventions and Approaches*, Home Office Research Study 290 (London: Home Office, 2005), http://www.homeoffice.gov.uk/rds/pdfs05/hors290.pdf.

5. D. Cook, M. Burton, A. Robinson, and C. Vallely, "Evaluation of Specialist Domestic Violence Courts/Fast Track Systems" (London: CPS/DCA/Criminal Justice System Race Unit, 2004).

6. M. Hester, "Making It through the Criminal Justice System: Attrition and Domestic Violence," *Social Policy and Society* 5, no. 1 (2006): 79–90.

7. Summary from interview with Ada, in Hester, "Making It Through," 87.

8. Summary from interview with Celia, in Hester, "Making It Through," 87.

9. M. Hester, C. Pearson, and N. Harwin, with H. Abrahams, *Making an Impact—Children and Domestic Violence: A Reader*, 2nd ed. (London: Jessica Kingsley, 2007), 101.

10. E. Farmer, "Using Research to Develop Child Protection and Child Care Practice," in *Domestic Violence and Child Protection*, ed. C. Humphreys and N. Stanley (London: Jessica Kingsley, 2006), 125.

11. C. Humphreys and R. Thiari, *Routes to Safety: Protection Issues Facing Abused Women and Children and the Role of Outreach Services* (Bristol: Women's Aid Federation of England, 2002).

12. E. Farmer and M. Owen, *Child Protection Practice: Private Risks and Public Remedies* (London: HMSO, 1995), 223.

13. E. Williamson and M. Hester, *Evaluation of South Tyneside Domestic Abuse Perpetrator's Programme (STDAPP)* (Bristol, UK: University of Bristol, 2009).

14. Farmer, "Using Research to Develop," 127.

15. Department of Health, *Family Law Act 1996. Part IV Family Homes and Domestic Violence*, Local Authority Circular LAC(97) 15 (London: Department of Health, 1997), 12.

16. P. Jaffe, N. Lemon, and S. Poisson, *Child Custody and Domestic Violence: A Call for Safety and Accountability* (Thousand Oaks, CA: Sage, 2003).

17. Jaffe, Lemon, and Poisson, *Child Custody and Domestic Violence*, 103.

18. J. Herring, "Familial Homicide, Failure to Protect and Domestic Violence: Who's the Victim?" *Criminal Law Review* 923 (2007): 7.

19. Ibid., 3.

20. Ibid., 5.

21. Appeal Court Transcript, 2000, 10. *Re L (A CHILD) Re V (A CHILD) Re M (A CHILD) Re H (CHILDREN)*, heard in the Court of Appeal, 19 June 2000, before the President of the Family Division Dame Elizabeth Butler-Sloss, Lord Justice Thorpe, and Lord Justice Waller.

22. Children Act Sub-Committee, *Making Contact Work* (London: Lord Chancellor's Department, 2002).

23. Ofsted, "Ofsted's Inspection of Cafcass Southeast Region: An Inspection of Service Provision by the Children and Family Court Advisory and Support Service (Cafcass) to Children and Families in the South East" (London: Ofsted, 2008), http://www.ofsted.gov.uk/reports, 11.

24. District Judge, in L. Trinder, J. Connolly, K. Kellet, C. Notley, and L. Swift, *Making Contact Happen or Making Contact Work? The Process and Outcomes of In-Court Conciliation*, DCA Research Series 3/06 (London: Department of Constitutional Affairs, 2006), 96.

25. L. Radford and M. Hester, *Mothering through Domestic Violence* (London: Jessica Kingsley, 2006).

Chapter 7

The Misuse of Parental Alienation Syndrome in Custody Suits[1]

Joan S. Meier

Parental alienation syndrome (PAS), a term used almost exclusively with reference to custodial disputes, typically refers to two intersecting behavior patterns: (1) systemic attempts by one parent (usually the mother) to turn a child or children against the other parent (usually the father) and (2) a child's hostility toward that parent, usually the father, often expressed in a resistance to visitation. The most common use of PAS is to counter claims of partner or child abuse and to reframe a child's reaction to a parent who is alleged to have committed this abuse. PAS may be raised as a concern during a custodial dispute or after custody has been assigned. PAS may also be alleged when one element is present, but not the others, e.g., when a mother claims to have been abused but the child shows no hostility toward the other parent, or when a child is hostile toward a noncustodial parent even though there is no evidence the custodial parent has discouraged contact or denigrated a former spouse. PAS and parental alienation (PA) are also invoked in legal and legislative contexts when the custodial rights of fathers and mothers are being determined, again when the question of how courts should weigh allegations of domestic violence or child abuse is on the table. Indeed, alienation claims have become ubiquitous in disputed custody cases and have elicited a wide range of commentary from judges, evaluators, psychologists, attorneys, and their professional organizations, as well as from protective mothers and fathers' rights organizations. This chapter will provide an overview of PAS and PA, raise some strategic issues raised by its popularity, and suggest a better approach to dealing with questions of alienation.

THE EVOLUTION OF "PARENTAL ALIENATION"

The concept of parental alienation as a child's pathology in the context of divorce was first recognized by divorce researchers who characterized the phenomenon of a child's rejection of a noncustodial parent and strong resistance or refusal to visit that parent as a pathological alignment between an angry parent and an older child or adolescent. This alignment was seen as a result of the dynamics of the separation, including the child's reaction to the divorce. While this construct had merit, it did not become a routine part of custody evaluations or judicial determinations, nor did it receive significant public attention.

Beginning in the early 1980s, attention to a purported parental alienation syndrome exploded as the result of the dedicated efforts of Richard Gardner, M.D., a psychiatrist loosely affiliated with Columbia University, who ran a clinical practice counseling divorcing parents. Based solely on his interpretation of his own clinical experience, Gardner posited that child sexual abuse allegations were rampant in custody litigation, and that 90 percent of children in custody litigation are suffering from the PAS "disorder." He described PA as a "syndrome" whereby vengeful mothers employ child abuse allegations as a "powerful weapon" to punish the ex and ensure custody for themselves. He further theorized that such mothers enlist the children in their "campaign of denigration" and "vilification" of the father, that they often "brainwash" the children into believing untrue claims of abuse by the father, and that the children frequently fabricate their own added stories. He claimed—again, based solely on his own clinical practice—that the majority of child sexual abuse claims in custody litigation are false, although he suggested that some mothers' vendettas are the product of mental illness rather than intentional malice. Gardner posited that when children reject their father and abuse allegations are made, this behavior is most likely the product of PAS rather than actual experiences of abuse. PAS theory thus inherently implies that an abuse claimant's veracity should be doubted, and dissuades evaluators and courts from seriously considering whether abuse has actually occurred. At a minimum, it implies that abuse is a rare occurrence despite the frequency with which it is alleged. While acknowledging that if the abuse was real there could be no PAS, Gardner's "diagnostic criteria" focus on the personalities of the parties rather than expert assessment of abuse or the other reasons offered for a child's hostility to a parent. Thus, only one conclusion is implied.

PROPOSED PAS REMEDIES

Gardner presumes that a child's hostility toward a father is a pathological by-product of a mother's attempts to undermine the father's relationship with the child. His "remedy" for PAS thus includes total termination of the child's contact with the mother and "depro-gramming" the child through a concerted brainwashing effort to change the child's beliefs that he or she has been abused. Some observ-ers consider the removal of such a child from the parent who is trying to protect him or her to be Draconian, particularly since children sub-jected to these procedures have become suicidal—and in some cases died—in reaction to court orders to live with the father they believed abused them.

In the tragic case of Nathan Grieco, on the strength of a Gardner "diagnosis" of PAS, a judge ordered a form of "threat therapy" that Gardner recommended and that is the stock and trade of psychologists who specialize in alienation assessments. Sixteen-year-old Nathan and his two brothers were informed that if they did not attend visits with the father they hated and feared and claimed had abused them (and behave in a positive frame of mind, respectfully and obediently), then their mother would be sent to jail. Prior to his death, Nathan wrote an essay in which he stated, "Many things (mostly bad), have happened in my life.... Eight years ago my parents got a divorce and my father threw us out of the house ... he is still harassing us through court case after court case.... There are more stories ... but I don't have the time or the sanity to go on. Thus ends this chapter in my life of endless tor-ment." Two weeks later his mother walked into the 16-year-old's room to make sure he was getting ready for school. She found him kneeling on the floor by his bed, a leather belt around his neck, blood spilling from his mouth. He was dead. It was later discovered that the night before, he had searched his mother's desk for a copy of the court order refusing to lift the threat therapy.

Courts have also ordered children into jail and juvenile homes as a form of threat therapy. In one such case, on the advice of such a psy-chologist, a judge ordered a nine-year-old boy seized by three police officers and placed in a juvenile detention facility when he refused to get into his father's car for a scheduled visitation. The boy alleged that the son of the father's girlfriend had sexually molested him dur-ing a previous visit. He had also witnessed the father's violence against his mother. After three days in the detention facility, where he was bullied by other boys, he agreed to cooperate with the court order. The judge concluded that his "treatment" for parental aliena-tion had worked.[2]

PAS is ideal fodder for attorneys representing accused abusers because all evidence a mother presents to refute it can simply be reframed as further evidence of the syndrome. The child's repeated claims of abuse are characterized as further evidence of extreme "pro-gramming" and brainwashing by the mother. If the mother points to a therapist's opinion that the child has been abused, the therapist is char-acterized as contributing to the disorder. If the mother gathers other corroboration of the allegations, this too is seen as further evidence of her pathological need to "alienate" the child from the father. If the mother then continues to attempt to protect her child after an evaluator has stated that her allegations are unsubstantiated, she is deemed an even more extreme alienator.

SCIENTIFIC AND LEGAL REJECTIONS OF PAS

Gardner and PAS have many adherents. Still, perhaps because the theory itself lacks any basis in empirical research, few researchers have endorsed PAS. To the contrary, the prevailing view in the research community is that there is no scientific evidence for the existence of a distinct "syndrome" concerning parental alienation. Leading researchers, including some who view alienation itself as a real problem, have stated that "the scientific status of PAS is, to be blunt, nil."[3] The Presidential Task Force of the American Psychological Association on Violence in the Family stated as early as 1996 that "[a]lthough there are no data to support the phenomenon called parental alienation syndrome, in which mothers are blamed for interfering with their children's attachment to their fathers, the term is still used by some evaluators and Courts to discount children's fears in hostile and psychologically abusive situations."[4]

In support of this scientific consensus, a leading judicial body, the National Council of Juvenile and Family Court Judges, has published guidelines for custody courts stating that "Richard Gardner's theory positing the existence of 'parental alienation syndrome' or 'PAS' has been discredited by the scientific community. Testimony that a party to a custody case suffers from the syndrome should therefore be ruled inadmissible."[5]

At most, PAS is a label that offers a particular *explanation* for a breach in relationship between a child and parent. However, insofar as the same condition could be (and often is) explained in other ways, it is not in itself a medical or psychological diagnosis, but rather a particular legal hypothesis.

In contrast, the factual claims on which Gardner based the PAS theory *have* been subjected to empirical testing, and been refuted. Gardner claimed that child sexual abuse allegations are widespread in custody cases and that the vast majority of such allegations are false. Both assertions have been shown to be false. For instance, the largest study of child sexual abuse allegations in custody litigation ever conducted—across 12 jurisdictions—found that child sexual abuse was alleged in fewer than 2 percent of cases and that approximately 50 percent of the claims were deemed valid. An additional 17 percent were inconclusive, leaving one-third that were believed to be unfounded. But this does not mean the claims were false. To the contrary, in most instances, determinations that an allegation of sexual abuse is unfounded reflect the lack of sufficiently definitive evidence, usually of a physical nature, to prove the allegation to the satisfaction of an evaluator or investigator.[6] Other studies have found such allegations to be valid approximately 70 percent of the time. Given the volatility of sexual abuse allegations, the sorry state of the art in sexual abuse evaluations, and the difficulty of providing conclusive physical evidence and of assessing young children's expressions and behaviors, 50–70 pecent is remarkably high, certainly high enough to suggest that such allegations not be dismissed without a thorough evaluation. Gardner's assertion that child sexual abuse is typically false when raised in the context of custody litigation, but *true* when raised in the general population, has also been disproved. A study of approximately 7,000 Canadian child maltreatment cases found only 12 percent of allegations in custody litigation were intentionally false (compared to 4 percent in the general population). Interestingly, the majority of those false claims were made by noncustodial fathers, not by custodial mothers or children.[7]

Gardner attributed the alleged propensity of women to lie about sexual abuse in custody cases to the supposed titillation they derive by imagining their child having sex with the father and because "hell hath no fury like a woman scorned." Needless to say, there is not a shred of empirical support for these offensive assertions.

Widespread criticism has made the invocation of PAS slightly less common in court and in the research literature. But it has continued to gain popular and political recognition. Indeed, the American Psychological Association and state and local bar associations continued to sponsor workshops on PAS through the first half of the decade. Since approximately 2005, roughly 10 states' governors have issued proclamations calling attention to the purported problem of PAS. Moreover, the media continue to popularize PAS, most famously when Alec Baldwin invoked PAS to rationalize his recorded abusive phone message to his teenage daughter.

PAS IN PRACTICE

Gardner's claims have powerfully influenced custody courts and forensic evaluators. It has become virtually an article of faith in these venues that child sexual abuse in particular, and abuse in general, are widely and falsely alleged by mothers in custody litigation. In addition, PAS has not been limited to its original context. PAS is commonly invoked in any custody litigation where abuse is alleged, even without evidence that a child is actually "alienated" from his or her father, and is also often raised whenever a mother objects to full shared custody with the father. At least one researcher has found PAS allegations to be correlated with a high rate of custody awards to documented spouse abusers.

PAS is routinely raised by a father in response to abuse allegations lodged by the mother or children. But it is raised with equal frequency by custody evaluators appointed by the court to provide an objective assessment of the children's best interests. Such evaluators, presumably "neutral" psychological professionals, often suggest alienation is at work when they are confronted with abuse allegations that they find not credible. Usually, this finding reflects the fact that the evaluator lacks the knowledge and training to do a proper abuse evaluation or is predisposed to believe that fathers don't do these things and women often lie. For example, in one case, the court's evaluator posited alienation as an alternate explanation for the mother's and child's sexual abuse allegations after observing a single brief visit in the court-supervised visitation center, in which the father and child were "relaxed," "comfortable," and "affectionate." This evaluator, who was seen by the court as a highly respected expert, did not seem to believe that such affectionate interactions would be likely if the sexual abuse allegations were true. In fact, child sexual abuse experts state that one cannot assess the veracity of such allegations by observing the parties' interactions; most abused children continue to love their abusive parents, and crave loving attention from them. Their affection may be most evident when they know they are in a safe setting.

In other instances, even evaluators with a passing knowledge of abuse may be skeptical of allegations of partner abuse for any number of reasons even where no harm to the children is claimed, including the lack of witness corroboration, the compelling and sympathetic persona of the accused, an unappealing personality of the accuser, and/or the timing of the allegations. Alienation then becomes the explanation of choice for why a mother would be making false abuse allegations in a custody case: she is doing it in order to minimize the father's access to the children. This viewpoint presumes, as did Gardner, that many women are vengeful and use child custody to hurt their ex-partners. Such neutral evaluators often do not accept the views of domestic violence experts that many men are hidden abusers; that abuse is often kept secret for years until the family separates; or that women rarely lie about it. Moreover, many evaluators believe the widely discounted myth that abuse cannot have been serious if the relationship is long standing, the abuse wasn't reported to authorities, or there were no serious injuries. Alternatively, some evaluators and judges fail to see discrete acts of "minor" violence as serious enough to constitute abuse or to signal real risk to the children. Lacking information or understanding of power and control dynamics, and reluctant to believe that seemingly "decent" or "nice" men genuinely pose a danger to their children, such professionals often turn to alienation as an explanation for the mother's claims of danger.

COURT RULINGS ON ADMISSIBILITY

Very few appellate courts have actually published opinions regarding the scientific validity and admissibility of PAS. Two primary cases (both in New York) that actually analyze and adjudicate the legal admissibility of PAS in a criminal proceeding both found that PAS lacked sufficient scientific validity to meet admissibility standards. A third Connecticut court has come to the same conclusion in a tort case.

In contrast, PAS' prevalence in family courts is a testament to their sloppy evidentiary standards. Gardner's Web site (and his followers' publications) touts over 50 cases that he asserts held it admissible, and custody evaluators and lawyers routinely rely on these assertions and string cites to support their PAS arguments. However, a thorough review of the cases cited on Gardner's Web site revealed that *not one* precedent-bearing decision has ruled PAS admissible. Four trial-level decisions found it admissible, but the appeal of each decision resulted in *no ruling* on the PAS issue. No published decision exists for several of the purportedly favorable trial court opinions. A handful of appellate courts have recognized PAS, but without addressing validity or admissibility.

THE SHIFT FROM PAS TO PARENT ALIENATION

The combination of criticism of PAS and the transparency of the empirical claims made by its proponents has resulted in a shift—at least among some leading scholars of custody evaluation—from support for the *syndrome* to support for a "reformulation of PAS," called instead parental alienation or "the alienated child." Among the more credible researchers spearheading this trend are Johnston and Kelly, who clearly state that PAS does not exist, that Gardner's version of it is "overly simplistic" and tautological, and that the data do not support labeling alienation a syndrome. Instead, they speak of "parental alienation" or "child alienation" as a valid concept that describes a real phenomenon experienced by some children in the context of custody disputes.[8]

The redefined alienated child is one who the evaluator deems to have "unreasonable" negative feelings and beliefs toward a parent that are not based in actual experience with that parent. Children who are strongly (and unreasonably) rejecting of one parent "with no apparent guilt or conflict" are considered especially clear cases.

In contrast to the syndrome, the idea that some children are alienated from a parent is both a less scientific and more factual assertion. It is thus easier to raise "alienation" in court without triggering a battle over the admissibility of scientific evidence. However, debate continues to rage over the extent to which parental alienation is something that can be measured, is caused by a parent, and/or has harmful effects, or whether it is simply "old wine [i.e., PAS] in new bottles."

What is the difference between PAS and the reformulation as PA? The primary shift in the *theoretical* focus is from the purportedly alienating *parent* and toward a more realistic assessment of the multiple sources of the child's hostility or fear of his or her parent, including behavior by both parents and the child's own vulnerabilities. Another notable difference between PAS and PA is the relaxing of the use of draconian "remedies," including custody switching to the "hated" parent. Proponents of PA favor instead individualized assessments of both the children and the parents' parenting and maintaining a focus on the children's needs rather than the parents' "rights." Reconciliation with the hated parent is given less importance than cultivating a more realistic and healthy attitude toward both parents.

HOW DIFFERENT IS PARENTAL ALIENATION?

The new approach recognizes the many reasons children can become alienated from a parent and blunts some of the most disturbing elements of Gardner's theory, particularly its insistence that abuse allegations are largely fabricated, almost always by a malevolent mother. In practice, however, the failure to draw clear lines between "alienation" and PAS has resulted in PA evaluations that often mirror PAS evaluations in both the interpretation of the facts and, to a lesser extent, the recommended remedies. One consequence, ironically, is to make the fallacious core of PAS—that is, the belief that mothers litigating custody frequently fabricate false abuse claims—more palatable to the family court and more difficult to challenge.

In a recent case in which I was involved, the court's forensic expert substituted the label "parental alienation" for her earlier suggestion of PAS, without changing anything significant about her analysis. In her first analysis, her written report had raised "alienating tactics" as an alternative explanation for the allegations of child sexual abuse "levied" by the mother. At that time, on cross-examination, she defended PAS as valid science and not "controversial." Several years later, in 2005, she testified that PAS is indeed controversial, and that the concept has been "reconceptualized and refined" as "alienation." When pressed to describe the difference between the new alienation and PAS, she said only that Gardner's approach was "much more black and white and much more rigid." At the same time, she asserted that there are "many studies" on "the existence of PAS." She also disagreed with statements in the *Handbook on Child Maltreatment* by the American Professional Society on Abuse of Children that PAS has no scientific validity. As cross-examination continued, the court expressed impatience with the focus on the distinction between PAS and PA, asserting that the mother's expert herself had "admitted that the process of alienation could occur. It doesn't have to be labeled."

PA was reconceptualized in part expressly in order to shed PAS' insistence that children's alienation is caused solely by bad custodial parents. Nonetheless, advocates of PA continue to contribute to the demonizing of mothers through a troubling degree of psychoanalyzing of mothers' conscious and unconscious desires. For instance, PA theorists assert that a mother's "warm, involved" parenting can powerfully fuel alienation in a child. This counterintuitive position posits that the deeper and warmer the bond between mother and child, the easier it is for the mother to poison the child's attitude toward the other parent. Thus, just like PAS, PA can become a self-fulfilling prophecy: even evidence that common sense suggests would refute it can be neatly turned against the mother and reframed as further evidence of PA. The evaluator in the above case responded to my pointing out that the mother appeared to have a very warm, nurturing relationship with her daughter with the comment that that is perfectly consistent with alienation.

Similarly, according to Johnston, a parent could unintentionally and subconsciously denigrate the other parent to the child due to his or her own deep psychological issues that cause them to resent or fear his or her ex-spouse. Even putting aside the obvious danger that such psychoanalyzing facilitates ignoring the potentially real basis for that fear (i.e., abuse), it even more efficiently does away with any means of refuting the alienation charge: evidence that a mother has consciously and intentionally attempted to support the child's relationship with his or her father can be dismissed with the uncontrovertible claim that it is her subconscious, not conscious, behaviors that are impairing the relationship.

Finally, if PA has shifted the emphasis from demonizing the "aligned" parent to the "alienated" child, it can still be used to pathologize women who allege abuse, minimize the role of abuse in "alienating" children from an abusive parent, and obscure the relevance of even adult abuse to the child's well-being. Like PAS proponents, advocates for PA sometimes discuss the damage caused by "alienation" without adequately distinguishing between alienation and the abuse that may have caused *both* the psychological damage and the child's alienation. Further obscuring the importance of abuse is a failure to distinguish the presentation of PA among alienated, nonabused children from the presentation of the same "symptoms" as the natural response to an abusive parent. Apart from confounding very different sources of a child's rejection of a parent, this obscuring of potentially real danger undermines courts' ability to identify risks or adopt appropriate protections for mothers or children.

ABSENCE OF EMPIRICAL EVIDENCE OF ALIENATION AND ITS IMPACT

While clinicians who use PA insist that they do see "alienation" in their caseloads, there is no objective proof that relationship breaches between children and parents are caused by a disorder (alienation), as opposed to healthy or otherwise adaptive responses to the child's experiences with the parent. Moreover, experience suggests that the most common parental alienators are not the mothers—upon whom discussions of PAS and PA focus—but their male partner abusers. (Some alienation research has confirmed that abusive men are more likely to commit alienation than abused women.) Indeed, most battered women's lawyers or advocates have multitudes of examples of batterers denigrating the mother to the children. One case involved an abuser who dragged the children out of their bedrooms to watch him beat up their mother while he instructed them that she was a slut and a whore. In that case, the court responded to the request to instruct the abuser not to denigrate the mother in front of the children with an order to both parties to that effect. In a more recent case, a five-year-old child, who had been torn from his protective mother and given to his sexually and emotionally abusive father, when being handed over for a visit with his long-missed mother appeared awkward and uncomfortable until he was driving away out of the father's sight—and then kissed and hugged her and expressed his relief to see her. Indeed, it is rare to work on a case involving abuse in which the abuser does *not* in both overt and subtle ways undermine the children's relationship with and respect for their mother, including derogatory names, disrespectful treatment, calling her incompetent and irresponsible, and, at worst, directly warning the children not to be close to her. And as family courts under the influence of PAS and PA forensic evaluations increasingly strip custody from mothers and allow allegedly abusive fathers full control over their children, we are beginning to see teenage children telling courts they do not want to see their mothers because it is too "disruptive." In the case of Wendy Titelman, this was accomplished by a father whose sexual abuse of the girls had been identified and recognized by multiple expert professionals. PAS was the trump that neutralized these opinions and resulted in custody to the father and the ultimate complete exclusion of the mother from their lives at their own requests, after years of living under the control of the father and his then-wife.

Nor is there empirical support for PA advocates' deeply held belief that alienation—even when genuinely at work—is devastating for children. So, Johnston, one of the leaders of the PA "reconceptualization," acknowledges that "there is very little empirical data to back up these clinical observations" that "alienated" (i.e., unreasonably hostile children without basis in experience with that parent or normal developmental conditions) children will be significantly undermined in their emotional and psychological development.[9] In fact, she states that "there are no systematic long-term data on the adjustment and well-being of alienated compared to non-alienated children so that long-term prognostications are merely speculative."[10]

Empirical research has also demonstrated that there is no clear link between purported alienating behavior by a parent and actual alienation of a child. In one of the leading studies of child alienation in divorcing families, the researchers found that only 20 percent of children were actually alienated, *despite the alienating behaviors of both parents in most of the families*. Importantly, these 20 percent had multiple causes for their alienation, *including abusive or other destructive behaviors by the disliked parent*. There are two critical inferences that can be drawn from this data: first, alienating behavior by parents is far less destructive (i.e., effective) than is commonly assumed, that is, mothers are far less powerful than alienation evaluators would have us believe. Second, when children do become alienated, they often have good reasons, regardless of the preferred parent's alienating behaviors; these data also reinforce domestic violence experts' concern that the courts' focus on alienation behavior by parents is a major distraction from the accurate assessment of abuse and concomitant risks to children.

Finally, casting doubt on some alienation advocates' assumption that abuse claims are often indicative of a "campaign of alienation," research has found no correlation between domestic violence and alienation: battered women are no more likely to engage in alienating behaviors than other women. This finding is consistent with the experience of domestic violence advocates and survivors.

UNRELIABLE SCIENTIFIC CLAIMS BY PAS AND PA PROPONENTS

This field is especially challenging because those who advocate that PAS and PA are serious and real conditions have an extensive literature upon which to draw. Many articles make assertions about PAS and PA without any citation to scientific literature. Yet their publication or dissemination on the Internet and their association with apparently credentialed authors and/or supporters give them an aura of credibility. Some articles *do* cite research selectively but contain numerous unsupported assertions as well, about PAS, PA, and how they operate.[11]

The field of "expertise" on these issues has been created largely by two dominant forces: first and most significant are forensic psychologists' repeated assertions that PAS and PA exist, usually backed up by referencing Dr. Gardner's views or other sources similarly devoid of sound research. As we've seen, credible assessments of the literature, such as that of the American Psychological Association's Presidential Task Force on Violence in the Family, have emphatically rejected the belief that PAS is a real syndrome.

Second, the belief that mothers who seek to restrict fathers' contact with children are sacrificing the children's interests to their own wishes has been fueled by fathers' rights advocates, who are extremely well-organized and persuasive advocates who perceive fathers as being discriminated against in custody litigation and who have sown doubts about the credibility of women's abuse allegations. (See chapter 8 by Dawson in this volume.) The claims of both these advocates and many forensic evaluators in PA and PAS are linked to the belief that children are likely to be worse off, and even at risk for significant psychic harm, if they are in sole custody of a mother rather than in joint custody arrangements. This is not the place to engage the debate about whether this assertion has independent empirical validity. It suffices to say that here, as with PAS and PA generally, the studies most often cited fail to actually support these assertions.[12]

STRATEGIC ISSUES

What if you are a parent who confronts allegations of PAS and PA in the context of a disputed custody case involving abuse allegations? The ideal strategy for combating PAS and PA claims leveled against an abuse survivor is to recruit a psychological expert to testify that PAS is not valid "science" and to explicate the limited science surrounding PA. Such an expert should also explain how PAS and PA are easily misused in custody litigation to distract from and undermine an objective assessment of past abuse and future risk. Without a psychological expert, lawyers can attempt to make such arguments, but they are unlikely to get very far without an expert to validate the critique of the science, the assessment of what research does and does not demonstrate, and the critique of how the forensic professions have gone awry. If a PAS or PA evaluation has already been submitted, or argued, a knowledgeable and well-credentialed social science expert is the optimal response. While this can be expensive, experts in this field are sometimes willing to charge on a sliding-scale basis.

Of course, few custody litigants can locate, let alone afford, an appropriate expert on these subjects. Moreover, not all courts are persuaded by such testimony, and PAS and PA claims in custody litigation can be particularly difficult to refute. Because PAS theory is so circular—reframing all claims, evidence, and corroboration of abuse allegations as further evidence of the "syndrome"—direct rebuttal may sometimes seem impossible. In this situation, a lawyer or his or her abused client may need to reluctantly consider not pressing their claims about domestic violence or child abuse. Because claims of PA or PAS are often raised as bargaining chips in the husband's arsenal, withdrawing allegations of abuse may sometimes be the only way to reduce the courts' focus on purported alienation by the mother. A troubling number of mothers have lost custody of, and even all contact with, their children as a result of seeking to protect them from their fathers' abuse.[13] With the risks this high, tolerating unsupervised visitation or even joint custody with an unsafe father can be seen as the lesser of two evils. Nonetheless, allowing a child or his or her mother to remain at risk is a high price to pay for the politics of junk science in family court.

Where alienation is unavoidably part of the case, protective parents and their lawyers and experts should argue that PA be treated—at most—as merely a factual behavior, using the same standards of evidence used for other factual claims. That is, before PA or PAS can even be considered, there must be evidence that a child is strongly hostile to the parent and engaged in some kind of vendetta against him. Mere fear or ambivalence should not be sufficient to raise the specter of PAS or PA; on the contrary, those concepts are built from the premise that alienation is evident in children's strong, unambivalent "campaign" against their noncustodial parent, not mere ambivalence, fear, or even partial anger. Once it has been factually established that a child is at least resistant and notably hostile, the next step should be a careful assessment of the child's full range of attitudes and the reasons for them, including any claims of abuse.

In the contemporary context, this threshold alone would be sufficient to end PA and PAS inquiries in many cases. This is because these terms and concepts are widely used not only when children are reluctant to visit or hostile to their father, as the theory itself purportedly posits, but also whenever mothers seek to restrict fathers' visitation while alleging adult or child abuse. For instance, in one case in which I was involved, PAS became a central focus merely because the mother in this upper-middle-class family was alleging a 30-year history of abuse and was opposing joint custody. The children opposed joint custody but were willing to visit their father, and none of them expressed significant or irrational hostility to him. Nonetheless, the PAS framework of suspecting the mother, characterizing her allegations as a "campaign of denigration" and "vilification" (both code phrases from Gardner's PAS publications), was applied, resulting in the court treating joint custody as the appropriate penalty or remedy for this misconduct. The PAS analysis focused not only on the abuse allegations and opposition to joint custody but also on a small number of fearful or unfavorable comments made by the mother regarding her ex-husband.

As noted above, empirical research has found that, while most divorcing parents in disputed cases engaged in derogatory behaviors or comments about the other parent, only 20 percent of the children became "alienated" (and many of these had good reasons stemming from the disfavored parent's behavior). Given this reality, courts' and evaluators' focus on purportedly alienating parental behaviors is misplaced. The harsh truth is that some hostility between divorcing spouses may be unavoidable. Indeed, given human nature and frailties, some (hopefully limited) exposure of children to their parents' hostility may also be unavoidable. But unless the children are actually showing signs of being negatively affected, courts should not be seriously weighing alienation claims.

Perhaps the most obvious, yet difficult to implement, goal in these cases should be to ensure that the court thoroughly assesses any claims of abuse or risk to the children or mother. It cannot be strongly enough stated that such an assessment must be *by someone with the knowledge and expertise* to do so. The typical forensic custody evaluator lacks real training, knowledge, and understanding of abuse—although many (such as the one described earlier) believe their experience in cases with such allegations constitutes sufficient expertise. The problem with experience-based "expertise" is that how experience is interpreted is in the eye of the beholder. For instance, Gardner himself came to his conclusions about PAS based on his "experience" with his caseload. Evaluators who have seen domestic violence allegations in past cases and viewed them as fabrications aimed at gaining an advantage in custody are unlikely to possess the real expertise necessary for sorting between valid and invalid allegations.

It should also be noted that even in cases where the custodial parent's "alienating" behaviors have fueled a child's alienation or ambivalence about a noncustodial parent, there may still be valid claims of real past and threatened future abuse. In other words, evidence of alienating behavior is not, in itself, proof that claims of domestic violence or child physical or sexual abuse are false. Although credible research has indicated that battered women engage in alienating behaviors no more frequently than nonabused women, it would be naïve to assume that all abused women are able to take the high road and avoid denigrating their abuser to the children. Still, courts and evaluators must be wary of discounting abuse even when critiquing alienating behaviors by the victim. In the rare case where both alienation and abuse exist, courts must keep their eye on the ball and prioritize the child's well-being over fairness to the parents. If the child is fearful or hostile toward an abusive parent, and the mother is also somewhat hostile or alienating in her behaviors, there is good reason to fear future abuse of the child, the mother, or both. It is hard to conceive of a case such as this where the alienating behaviors should be given more weight than the risks of abuse in assessing the child's best interests.

Finally, another strategic dilemma arises for mothers who have observed the abusive *father* to be actively alienating the children from their mother. As those who work with abuse victims well know, abusers are the first to engage in active denigration of their children's mothers—undermining a mother's authority and capacity as a mother is a common aspect of abuse. Such alienation is most likely to be effective and extreme where custody is awarded to the abusive father; but it can certainly also occur to a lesser extent in any joint custody or visitation arrangement where an abusive father has unsupervised access to the children. In such cases, the mother and her lawyer must decide whether to invoke alienation (or PAS) *against* the father. On the nay side, to do so would be to validate a concept that is widely misused against mothers, has been vigorously opposed by domestic violence experts and advocates, and is not scientifically valid. On the plus side is the importance of pointing out to the court the psychological damage the abusive parent is causing the children, and the "alienation" label may be the most efficient and powerful way to make the point. In response to this dilemma, one advocate has coined the term "maternal alienation" to distinguish the phenomenon from the much maligned "parental alienation." Others have suggested "estrangement." Neither term has yet to catch on in most court settings. Given the hostility of many courts to alienating behaviors, as well as the genuine harm that such "coaching" and/or alienating can engender by undermining children's safe relationship with their protective parent, the decision as to whether or not to use the charge of alienation is not easily made. However, if alienation *is* raised in support of a mother's case, the thresholds and requirements discussed above should be employed: that is, specific behaviors and the impact on the child should be described factually—and the term should not be referred to as a purported clinical category à la Gardner.

NOTES

1. Courtesy of VAW Net, Minnesota Center Against Violence and Abuse, University of Minnesota. The full document is available at http://www.vawnet.org.

2. E. Stark, e-mail communication with Joan Meier, May 2007.

3. R. E. Emery, R. K. Otto, and W. T. O'Donohue, "A Critical Assessment of Child Custody Evaluations: Limited Science and a Flawed System," *Psychological Science in the Public Interest* 6, no. 1 (2005): 1–29.

4. American Psychological Association, Presidential Task Force on Violence in the Family, *Report on Violence in the Family* (Washington, D.C.: American Psychological Association, 1996).

5. C. Dalton, S. Carbon, and N. Olesen, "High Conflict Divorce, Violence, and Abuse: Implications for Custody and Visitation Decisions," *Juvenile & Family Court Journal* 54, no. 4 (2003): 11–33.

6. N. Thoennes and P. Tjaden, "The Extent, Nature, and Validity of Sexual Abuse Allegations in Custody/Visitation Disputes," *Child Abuse and Neglect* 14 (1990): 151–63.

7. N. Trocam and N. Bala, "False Allegations of Abuse and Neglect When Parents Separate," *Child Abuse & Neglect* 29, no. 12 (December 2005): 1333–45.

8. J. R. Johnston and J. B. Kelly, "Rejoinder to Gardner's 'Commentary on Kelly and Johnston's The Alienated Child: A Reformulation of Parental Alienation Syndrome,'" *Family Court Review* 42, no. 4 (2004): 622–28.

9. J. R. Johnston and J. B. Kelly, "Commentary on Walker, Brantley, and Rigsbee's (2004) 'A Critical Analysis of Parental Alienation Syndrome and Its Admissibility in the Family Court,'" *Journal of Child Custody* 1, no. 4 (2004): 77–89.

10. J. R. Johnston, "Children of Divorce Who Reject a Parent and Refuse Visitation: Recent Research and Social Policy Implications for the Alienated Child," *Family Law Quarterly* 38 (2005): 757–75, 770.

11. See, for example, P. Stahl, http://www.parental-alienation-awareness.com/awarness-articles.asp?articleid=60.

12. See, generally, http://www.thelizlibrary.org/~liz/liz/those-jointcustody-studies.html.

13. See, for example, "Petition in Accordance with Inter-American Commission on Human Rights," http://www.stopfamilyviolence.org/media/web%20-Petition-B.pdf; and A. Neustein and M. Lesher, *From Madness to Mutiny: Why Mothers Are Running from the Family Courts—and What Can Be Done about It* (Boston: Northeastern University Press, 2005).

BIBLIOGRAPHY

Critiques of PAS, PA, and Gardner

Adams, M. A. (2006). "Framing Contests in Child Custody Disputes: Parental Alienation Syndrome, Child Abuse, Gender, and Fathers' Rights." *Family Law Quarterly* 40, no. 2: 315–38.

Childress, S. (2006). "Fighting over the Kids: Battered Spouses Take Aim at a Controversial Custody Strategy." *Newsweek*, September 25.

De Moraes, L. (2007). "Alec Baldwin, Still Angry at the Wrong Person." *Washington Post*, April 28, C01.

Ducote, R. (2002). "Guardians Ad Litem in Private Custody Litigation: The Case for Abolition." *Loyola Journal of Public Interest Law* 3: 106.

Lesher, M., and Neustein, A. (2005). *From Madness to Mutiny: Why Mothers Are Running from the Family Courts—and What Can Be Done about It*. Boston: Northeastern University Press.

Morris, A. (2004). "The Story of Naming Maternal Alienation: New Research Enters Policy and Practice." http://www.thelizlibrary.org/liz/maternal-alienation.doc.

Ragland, E. R., and Field, H. (2003). "Parental Alienation Syndrome: What Professionals Need to Know." *National Center for Prosecution of Child Abuse (NCPCA) Update Newsletter* 16, no. 6.

Trocam, N., and Bala, N. (2005). "False Allegations of Abuse and Neglect When Parents Separate." *Child Abuse & Neglect* 29, no. 12: 1333–45.

Wood, C. (1994). "The Parental Alienation Syndrome: A Dangerous Aura of Reliability." *Loyola of Los Angeles Law Review* 27:1367–415.

Fatherhood in the Public Eye

Associated Press. (2006). "A Girl Taken to Canada … by Her Mother … Will Now Live with Her Father." *Philadelphia Inquirer*, September 2, B06.

Barr, C. W. (2006). "For Fathers, a Chance to Improve, Become Mentors to Their Sons at Pr. George's Conference, about 100 Gather to Be Better Role Models." *Washington Post*, June 11, C09.

Boorstein, M. (2006). "Fatherhood Program Offers a Fresh Start to D.C. Dads: Goal Is to Strengthen Families, Renew Bonds." *Washington Post*, T.1.

Fathers & Families. (N.d.). *Who We Are.* http://www.fathersandfamilies.org/site/about/php (retrieved May 29, 2007).

Harris, H. R. (2006). *"Men Discuss Finding Time for Fatherhood Communication with Children Stressed." Washington Post*, T.3.

Leving, J. M., and Sacks, G. (2007). "New Column: Equal Rights Amendment Yes, 'Women's Equality Amendment' No." *(Louisville, KY) Courier-Journal*, http://glennsacks.com/blog/?p=691.

Montes, S. A. P. (2006). "Md. Man Gets to Say, 'Daddy Does Love You.'" *Washington Post*, April 18, B01.

"Nation in Brief." (2006). *Washington Post,* February 5, A08 (Lillington, N.C., archive excerpt—two girls reunited with their father after being abducted more than six years ago by their mother).

Tanfer, K., and Mott, F. (1997). "The Meaning of Fatherhood." http://fatherhood.hhs.gov/CFSForum/apenc.htm.

Thompson, D., and Sacks, G. (2002). "Fathers Bear the Brunt of Gender Bias in Family Courts." *Insight,* http://www.glennsacks.com/fathers_bear_the.htm.

"USA TODAY Snapshots." (2007). In *The Importance of Fatherhood*. National Fatherhood Initiative, January 12, A1.

Parental Alienation (not "Syndrome")

Drozd, L., and Olesen, N. (2004). "Is It Abuse, Alienation, and/or Estrangement? A Decision Tree." *Journal of Child Custody* 1, no. 3: 65–106.

Gould, J. W. (2006). *Conducting Scientifically Crafted Child Custody Evaluations*, 2nd ed. Sarasota, FL: Professional Resource Press.

Johnston, J. R. (1994). "High-Conflict Divorce." *Future of Children* 4:165–82.

Johnston, J. R., and Campbell, L. E. G. (1988). *Impasses of Divorce: The Dynamics and Resolution of Family Conflict*. New York: Free Press.

Johnston, J. R., Walters, M. G., and Olesen, N. W. (2005). "Is It Alienating Parenting, Role Reversal or Child Abuse? A Study of Children's Rejection of a Parent in Child Custody Disputes." *Journal of Child Custody* 5, no. 4:191–218.

Kelly, J. B., and Johnston, J. R. (2001). "The Alienated Child: A Reformulation of Parental Alienation Syndrome." *Family Court Review* 39, no. 3: 249–66.

Steinberger, C. (2006). "Father? What Father? Parental Alienation and Its Effect on Children." *Law Guardian Reporter* 22, no. 3, Appellate Divisions of the Supreme Court of the State of New York, http://www.drhavlicek. com.

Gardner

Gardner, R. A. (1987). *The Parental Alienation Syndrome and the Differentiation between Fabricated and Genuine Child Sex Abuse.* Cresskill, NJ: Creative Therapeutics.

Gardner, R. A. (1991). *Sex Abuse Hysteria: Salem Witch Trials Revisited.* Cresskill, NJ: Creative Therapeutics.

Gardner, R. A. (1992a). *The Parental Alienation Syndrome: A Guide for Mental Health and Legal Professionals.* Cresskill, NJ: Creative Therapeutics.

Gardner, R. A. (1992b). *True and False Accusations of Child Sex Abuse.* Cresskill, NJ: Creative Therapeutics.

Licata v. Licata. (2003). Brief and Appendix for Defendant-Respondent, Docket No. A-00660-02T3, Superior Court of New Jersey Appellate Division, June 1.

Custody and Abuse Litigation

Alford, N. M. (2003). Report of Court-Ordered Observations, dated June 16, 2003, in *Wilkins v. Ferguson*, DR-757-01 (on file with author).

Anderson, C. (2005). Report in *Wilkins v. Ferguson*, DR-757-01 (on file with author).

Finkelhor, D. (1986). *A Sourcebook on Child Sexual Abuse.* Thousand Oaks, CA: Sage.

Jaffe, P. G., Crooks, C. V., and Poisson, S. E. (2003). "Common Misconceptions in Addressing Domestic Violence in Child Custody Disputes." *Juvenile & Family Court Journal* 54, no. 4: 57–67.

Myers, Berliner, Briere, Hendrix, Jenny and Reid, eds. (2002). *The APSAC Handbook on Child Maltreatment*, 2nd ed. Thousand Oaks, CA: Sage.

Neustein, A., and Goetting, A. (1999). "Judicial Responses to the Protective Parent's Complaint of Child Sexual Abuse." *Journal of Child Sexual Abuse* 8, no. 4: 103–22.

Pearson, J. (1993). "Ten Myths about Family Law." *Family Law Quarterly* 27, no. 2: 279–99.

Petition in Accordance with Inter-American Commission on Human Rights. (N.d.). www.stopfamilyviolence.org/media/web%20Petition-B.pdf.

Chapter 8

An Introduction to the Fathers' Rights Movement

Joan Dawson

I didn't go looking for the fathers' rights (FR) groups—they came looking for me.

A few years ago, while I was living in South Korea editing textbooks, I began writing online about women's issues. Particularly in light of all the publicity about the "economic miracles" taking place in India, China, and Korea, I was astonished to find that women in these countries were often still confined to the home, that employers typically sought women younger than 35 years old, and that trafficking and prostitution were common trades. Males still dominated public life, and sex-selective abortions had left a gender imbalance that deeply affected private lives. Newspaper stories rarely included women, nor did the textbooks I was editing.

It didn't take long to receive replies to the articles I posted about women's issues from angry men. They hurled insults, attacked my credentials, disputed my data, and called me a "feminist mythmaker" (one of the kinder terms), even when I cited credible sources.

Despite reassurances that the insults were coming from a handful of young men "letting off steam," the attacks had an eerie similarity. Curious, I visited the Web sites they mentioned. *Wow*. Only those living in an ideological bunker could come up with such statistics. And I was the mythmaker? What I read on these sites about women in general and feminists in particular was jaw-dropping. I decided to write about what I found starting at Wikipedia, the open, online encyclopedia. I learned that men, mostly divorced men, had formed groups in various Western countries to fight for "fathers' rights." These fathers' rights groups were angry about getting a "raw deal" in family court with respect to custody and child support, among other concerns. In one of my first pieces, "Where Is the Love in Wikipedia?" I described how the FR groups had taken it upon themselves to rewrite Wikipedia's entries related to marriage and divorce.[1] They had replaced any references to love or other positive features of a partnership with references to "marriage strikes," malicious mothers, false allegations of domestic violence and rape, and similar issues. In other pieces, I wrote about the FR agenda and interviewed Australian sociologist Dr. Michael Flood, an expert in fathering and gender.[2] The response was predictable: one of my articles was reposted on Dads on the Air, an FR Web site. Like ravenous dogs being taunted by a juicy steak, they came prowling to my online site and went on the attack. I was glad to be returning to the United States. I left no forwarding address.

I even write this chapter with trepidation (and have been forewarned). Although I realize readers of these volumes are likely to be temperate, I also know that any challenge to the menace posed by FR groups has repercussions. Of course, it is precisely their propensity to try to intimidate critics that makes attempts to raise awareness about how they function so important. This chapter maps the terrain occupied by FR groups, putting their message in a historical and political context. I look at how and why they formed, how they are funded, what they stand for, and what their present and potential impact is on families seeking divorce.

IN THE BEGINNING

A movement to redefine manhood began in the 1970s, instigated in no small part by the unprecedented gains won by the march toward women's liberation in the 1960s. One wing of this movement was inspired by feminism to challenge ingrained ideas of male gender roles that could be limiting and destructive. Some of these men became aligned with women's causes, working with abusive men, advocating against rape or pornography, or simply embracing notions of masculinity that were not predicated on male power over women. But other men—the main subjects of this chapter—had a much more negative reaction to women's gains. For these groups, feminism is to blame for everything that had gone wrong in their personal lives as well as in the larger world. They set out to counter the perceived threat equality posed to the "natural" order of things.

Whatever their inspiration, all of the movements for social justice spawned in the turbulent 1960s reflected a broader emphasis on reexamining personal life choices. This could mean "dropping out" and joining a "counterculture" of alternative institutions, such as food co-ops, alternative schools, clinics, and the like. For those who pursued more conventional paths, an important influence was the human potential movement. Founded by two American psychologists, Carl Rogers and Abraham Maslow, the movement encouraged people to fulfill their untapped capacity for creativity and happiness through self-reflection, which often included taking a critical look at their assumptions on gender roles.

Subsequently, in the 1970s, a number of authors called on men to free themselves from traditional gender constructs and argued that the identification of masculinity with competing with others, dominating women, and masking human emotions could only lead to personal misery. These philosophies extended from popular books like Marc Feigen Fasteau's *The Male Machine* (1974; which used the upbringing of the Kennedys as a negative case in point) to more self-consciously political works like Jack Sawyer's *On Male Liberation* (1971).[3,4] Another important influence on the newly emerging awareness of masculinity was Warren Farrell's *The Liberated Man* (1974), a book *Ms.* founder Gloria Steinem endorsed as "an insightful guide" for men and women.[5] Years later, Farrell, who served as a board member for a local chapter of the National Organization of Women (NOW), would break away from pro-feminist groups and become an outspoken critic of feminism.

In hundreds of communities, men formed support groups and adapted the small-group consciousness-raising format popularized by women's liberation. Drawing on members' personal experience and the growing literature on masculinity, such groups expressed their new understanding of gender in a variety of ways. Many men simply expanded their personal priorities, taking up a larger share of housework, cooking, child care, or other facets of roles that had been assigned to women by default. Others explicitly embraced antisexist politics by forming men's centers. Early examples included the Berkeley Men's Center (1970), the Los Angeles Men's Collective (1974), the Men's Resource Center of Philadelphia (1979), and the New York Center for Men (1981).

This constellation of efforts to reform manhood was identified as the men's movement. By the 1980s, books about men and men's groups were growing in number and not just in the United States. In Australia, the Sydney Men's Festival, which still exists, held workshops on health, love, fear, anger, and meditation. A major concern of these groups was men's health and the extent to which the dominant model of manhood as risk taking and aggressive, obsessive, and possessive behavior contributed to premature death, high levels of injury, and widespread depression.

Particularly after the publication of Robert Bly's book, *Iron John: A Book about Men* in 1990, gatherings and festivals celebrating the positive features of masculinity with myths and poetry (mythopoetic) sprung up throughout the United States, attracting a large number of men who had no previous experience with the political wing of the men's movement.[6] With little understanding of sexism, these men often approached male archetypes such as the "warrior," "provider," and "brother" withour considering the effect of this imagery on women, releasing their "inner manhood" with ceremonies replete with drum beating and war paint.

PRIDE AND PRIVILEGE

Throughout the same decades, critics of feminism within the men's movement attracted a growing number of men whose bitterness and resentment toward women were the by-products of painful breakups, divorces, or custody battles. One of the earliest documented groups was known as Divorce Racket Busters, founded by Ruben Kidd and George Partis. It later became the United States Divorce Reform.

After going through a divorce himself in 1957, Richard F. Doyle became an advocate for divorce reform and formed the Men's Right Association (now the Men's Defense Association) in 1972 and MEN (Men's Equality Now) International in 1977. Free Men, Inc., also started in the 1970s and quickly folded, but spawned other groups like the National Coalition of Free Men.

The literature on men's gender roles that emerged from these groups emphasized that males were victims or were unaccountable for their behavior. In *The Hazards of Being Male: Surviving the Myth of Masculine Privilege* (1976), Herb Goldberg argued that men had paid a heavy price for their "privileges" and power, that price being that they were out of touch with their emotions and so couldn't be responsible when these emotions overwhelmed them.[7] In *The Rape of the Male* (1976), Richard Doyle angrily argued that men were the real victims in life, especially after divorce.[8] In *The Inevitability of Patriarchy* (1977), Steven Goldberg explained how male dominance was natural and unavoidable.[9]

By the 1980s, the National Congress for Men was formed and James Cook, an FR activist from the Joint Custody Association in Los Angeles, was selected as its head. It held conventions and spurred the formation of hundreds of smaller groups.

The first Equal Rights for Men rally was convened on Father's Day in 1982. Three years later, the National Council for Children's Rights was founded. In 1992 they changed their name to Children's Rights Council. Although the council claims its main mission is to advocate on behalf of children in divorce, its political agenda consists almost entirely of FR issues. The council remains one of the most influential organizations of its kind and has attracted many right-wing women, as well as prominent FR activists.

FR activism became increasingly militant by the 1990s. John Abbott formed the Blackshirts in Australia in 1992. Blaming women for skyrocketing divorce rates, he and his followers have "crusaded" to protect marriage by actually going to the homes of and harassing newly separated women and showing up at family court proceedings. Dressed entirely in black, these masked vigilantes have used megaphones to shame and terrorize women. In 1995, the Fathers Manifesto (American Institute for Men) was founded by John Knight in California. Like some other well-known FR activists, Knight had been jailed for refusing to pay child support.

The Fathers Manifesto seeks to exile blacks; repeal the Nineteenth Amendment, which gives women the right to vote; and reinstate patriarchy. The American Coalition for Fathers and Children was founded in 1998. Among other agenda items, the coalition calls for shifting custody from poor mothers who apply for food stamps or Medicaid to fathers if the dads are more financially fit. Like so many other FR groups, this organization seeks to punish women in some fashion for gaining custody or support or some other perceived injustice.

FR GROUPS: ORGANIZED AND DANGEROUS

Like the activists and groups of the past several decades that flanked the women's movement as allies and antagonists, the current advocates and organizations that comprise the parenting movement are just as divergent.

A variety of healthy and positive groups have formed to help support fathers during times of crises. These groups are often referred to as "positive" or "responsible" parenting groups. In the United States, Dads and Daughters is a national nonprofit that advocates healthy relationships between fathers and daughters. The National Compadres Network promotes positive involvement of Latino males in their families, communities, and societies. For men concerned with family violence, the Men's Network Against Domestic Violence offers positive, constructive means to combat it. Fathers Direct in the UK, according to their Web site (http://www.fathersdirect.com), encourages strong and positive relationships between children and their fathers and other male caregivers.

It can often be difficult, however, to distinguish positive fathering groups from groups whose focus on fathering is merely a cover for misogynist claims and threats (often called antifeminist or backlash FR groups). This is because many groups have learned to tone down their language so as to appear legitimate. Two examples of this are Media RADAR (Respecting Accuracy in Domestic Abuse Reporting) and This Is a War (http://www.thisisawar.com). Whereas RADAR initially denied the reality of abuse, downplayed its severity and duration, and dismissed abuse as *just* "marital discord," often with patronizing or smug language, it now presents similar sentiments but in less transparent ways. The change in presentation was motivated, in part, by the desire to align with an emerging group of academic researchers who are similarly opposed to feminism but would not openly identify with a group that held extreme views. This Is a War has also completely revamped its Web site to appear more reasonable and friendly, though it has retained its name—a dead giveaway.

Sociologist Michael Flood suggests another motive that has led FR activists to present a more moderate face: the desire to reform family law, usually in the name of children, an effort whose success depends on persuading a range of actors who may not share their extreme beliefs. Nevertheless, he warns that "their perspectives are still misguided, and their influence is dangerous. FR groups have successfully shifted family laws in some jurisdictions so that fathers' contact with children is privileged over children's safety."[10] Typically, fathers' rights mean exactly that, protecting the interests of fathers over all others, the same goal as traditional patriarchy. Some in the positive parenting movement believe these "angry dads" harm the legitimate interests of fathers. Others find their antics entertaining, even amusing, and don't mind the publicity they attract for fathers' plights. But Flood's take-home message is that such groups can be quite dangerous, especially to women and children.

THE ABUSERS' LOBBY

Hundreds of FR groups exist in the world today, most in Western industrial countries, including the United Kingdom, Ireland, Italy, the United States, New Zealand, Australia, and India. These groups vary in size and durability; appear in different organizational forms, including charities, self-help centers, help lines, membership groups, and Web sites; and operate in ways that extend from lobbying to civil disobedience. New groups pop up as others disappear, and membership appears to be fluid. The high turnover in FR groups has been attributed to leaders having big egos, clients joining in the midst of a bitter divorce and leaving once their needs have been met or they enter a new relationship, and the lack of awareness that men are being discriminated against. One group claims, "Every man is just one 911 call away from having everything he loves and has worked for to be stolen away."[11]

Men who are currently or recently divorced search the Internet looking for support, and when they stumble upon the FR sites, they can identify with the normal pain and confusion common to divorce that FR groups use to discuss and exploit. One recruitment ad asked, "Bitterness and pain. Alone in the dark? Hurt and confused? Feeling vulnerable? Get help. Get a voice. Get active."[12] Men are invited to express their hurt or anger on forums. But sympathy and statements of support gradually give way to recrimination, blaming all parties to the divorce *except the victimized fathers* and normalizing the anger as a legitimate response to the "discrimination" suffered by men at the hands of wives, feminists, and the family court. Instead of dispelling hostility and helping men to constructively move forward, a man's anger is given targets. Since divorce is widespread and is one of the most stressful events in our lives even when it is amicable, the market for this sort of emotional exploitation is huge.

Most men joining FR groups are white collar or lower middle class, white, heterosexual, and between the ages of 30 and 50. Whatever the various motives that bring men to FR groups, one thing is clear: they emerge with similar ideas. They blame women or feminism for the problems men face, deny men's power or privilege, and claim that men are the victims in today's society.

Although FR groups consistently deny they are trying to reverse women's gains or are seeking to reinstall patriarchy, the evidence suggests otherwise. Well-ensconced FR activists openly express vehement antifeminist views, claiming feminism only cares about women and that the world depicted by feminists masks the reality that women are now privileged while men are oppressed. Others insist that family court has been hijacked by feminism. While most couples negotiate custody decisions without going to family court, the minority who go to court with what they perceive as irreconcilable differences with respect to children and finances comprise the pool from which FR draws its recruits and supporters. Many of these men have been abusive. For this reason, some call them the "abusers' lobby."

Men, however, are not the only members of FR groups. Second wives, significant others, and family members also join. Still, trust is not readily handed over. FR activists remain suspect even of second wives. As one FR site warns,

> **Be warned** these second wives are also ex wives who screwed their other husbands. **Be warned** that while the Second Wives groups are currently helping men, they are only doing it for themselves. Do not trust them or count on them. If they get into a snit over their new husbands, they will revert to their true vindictive, vicious greedy nature. Quislings and collaborators are useful, but dangerous and never to be trusted.[13]

The tone of this warning is representative of many of the FR Web sites. Women and feminists are simply too vindictive and conniving to be trusted. Women are out to get men, to take them "to the cleaners," and to make men look evil and women appear innocent.

Some of the FR groups are openly hostile against gays, lesbians, abortions, and other progressive causes and may be linked to conservative or right-wing Christian organizations.

A number of other actors play a role in the FR movement, including legislators, judges, lawyers, psychologists, and researchers. Some share the FR agenda; for others, interest is largely mercenary. A number of law firms, for instance, now identify themselves as FR experts and promise to "teach her a lesson."

THE FUNDING FATHERS

FR groups are thought of as "well organized and funded with strong lobbying skills."[14] Many FR groups start with seed money from their founder. While many groups exist with only a Web site, others are more formally organized with offices in major cities of Western countries. To remain in business, FR groups lobby for federal funding, seek donations, charge membership dues, and sell various types of kits.

In the 1980s, American FR groups were able to receive federal funding designated to help meet the needs of noncustodial parents. And in the late 1990s, Congress appropriated US$10 million to states to develop programs associated with access and visitation for noncustodial parents. Some states also provided employment and training to low-income noncustodial parents through the Personal Responsibility and Work Opportunity Reconciliation Act of 1996.

The Children's Rights Council (CRC), a US nonprofit, also urged Congress to increase access and visitation grants from US$10 to $40 million. While CRC touts itself as a child's rights organization, it is listed on GuideStar under "single parent agencies/services," which aptly describes it as most of its services are for fathers rather than children. According to its Web site (http://www.crckids.org), its mission is to "help reduce divorce and strengthen families through custody reform; parental mediation and training; conciliation and access; parental financial and educational support systems; legislative revision and court briefs."[15] CRC charges an annual membership fee of $50.00 and has partnered with MBNA America Bank. MBNA makes a contribution every time a CRC member opens a credit card account or whenever members use their card.

The United States is not the only country where fatherhood has become a government priority. Fatherhood programs in Australia receive $59 million a year under the Family Relationships Services program. This money is used to provide courses on how to be better fathers when dads live apart from their children. More funding is being sought.

Most FR groups appear to charge membership dues that start at $25 but, on average, charge about $50. On the high end of the spectrum is the National Brotherhood of Father's Rights. For $875, members get a one-year membership, which includes "valuable insights" and unlimited consultation, when these are available:

> The **National Brotherhood Of Fathers Rights** is a membership organization which steps you through every phase of your court case. **We Are Almost Always Available** ... this can make the difference in your case. **Tell your friends about us—but not the wives!**[16]

Many FR groups sell books and kits on their Web sites. A custody and divorce kit advertises for $49, marked down from $75. Others sell "How to Minimize Child Support" ($25, plus shipping and handling) or "How to Stop a Divorce" (video, $40). Lastly, a Parental Alienation Syndrome (PAS) Packet can be bought for $34.95. PAS is a claim that one parent uses lies to manipulate children into hating the other parent. It has been used almost exclusively by men in disputed custody cases. (See further discussion below and in chapter 7 about PAS by Meier in this volume.)

FR MENU: SERVE CHILLED

While FR advocates are primarily interested in family law issues such as divorce, custody, and child support, they are also vocal about domestic violence and rape. FR men, then, claim to be victims with respect to all of these issues: unfair divorce proceedings, high child support payments, and false allegations of violence. FR groups claim that domestic violence accusations are largely fabricated and malicious and that, if abuse does exist, it is provoked, it is mutual, or the men were the *real* victims, claims they support by citing some research.

A number of population surveys have found that women report using force during conflicts as often as men, findings that have led Canadian psychologist Donald Dutton and a handful of others to insist there is sexual parity in violence and that any belief to the contrary reflects a "feminist bias." I deal with this issue later in the chapter. It suffices to say here that the methods used to generate these findings have been widely criticized for failing to consider the context, meaning, or consequence of this "violence" by women and that even the researchers who compiled the original evidence of female partner violence insist it would be an "injustice" to equate this with the sort of battering that has been the focus of widespread public concern.[17] The FR groups, however, have embraced the limited and highly controversial evidence of female violence as proof that men are the real victims of abuse in families, not women, and have used these findings to challenge domestic violence claims in hundreds of cases, perhaps thousands.

This is no small matter. Up to 50 percent of disputed custody cases involve allegations of domestic violence, so addressing these claims is important. Contrary to FR advocates' assertions, false allegations are no more common in divorce or custody proceedings than in any other court cases. Because of its private nature, however, domestic violence is hard to prove unless there are serious injuries, an arrest, or credible witnesses to the abuse. Moreover, family court evaluators and other professionals involved in divorce proceedings rarely have the training or willingness to properly assess abuse in these cases. The result is that FR arguments have had a chilling effect throughout the family court system, leaving tens of thousands of women and children at continued risk after a divorce.

Indeed, this chilling effect appears to be a conscious aim of many of the groups advancing the FR agenda. They use various methods to achieve these goals. Some FR groups, for example, have gained attention with zany publicity stunts. Fathers 4 Justice is well-known for these antics. In 2004, members dressed as Batman and Robin and scaled the walls of Buckingham Palace, where they perched themselves on a ledge for five hours to protest for fathers' custody rights. They also threw purple flour-filled condoms at then-Prime Minister Tony Blair. And, in Israel, Batman and 50 "civil rights activists" protested outside of family court. Such publicity-seeking actions have recently occurred in the United States and Canada.

Other groups resort to acts of aggression or public forms of harassment that mirror criminal acts, such as the Blackshirts mentioned earlier. In Canada, FR supporters have been accused of following feminists around at a conference and spitting on them. FR advocates also leveled death threats at Canadian activists seeking to create a memorial to women killed by men. Certainly, FR activists have displayed another form of aggression in their zeal to punish women. Fathers 4 Justice and other FR groups believe women should get jail time for denying fathers access to their children. In Florida and other states, FR groups have proposed legislation to harshly punish persons believed to make false claims of wife or child abuse. The threat of prosecution would undoubtedly make many mothers reluctant to press these claims, even when they believe it is in a child's best interest to do so. Finally, some members of FR groups have taken "justice" into their own hands with an even more devastating effect: they have committed murder-suicides; killed ex-partners, ex-wives, children, and court personnel, including judges; and threatened to bomb or actually bombed family courts and judges' homes.

DIVORCE FR STYLE

No-fault divorce was introduced in the 1960s and was adopted by every state by the mid-1980s. Since this made it possible to exit a loveless or abusive marriage more easily than proving a spouse's adultery, abandonment, or other charge, divorce rates doubled between the late 1960s and 1980, until one in two marriages was affected. This trend continues.

FR groups rightfully claim that women initiate divorce more often than men. They believe that women's main incentives for divorce, however, are driven by a "winner-take-all" mentality and that women do get it all: money, possessions, and child custody. Some research supports the view that women are more likely to divorce if they believe they will be awarded custody. Of course, having custody also limits a woman's options in the labor and remarriage markets. Another claim made by some FR groups is that women's decisions to divorce are typically "frivolous." This claim finds no support in research. To the contrary, most divorcing women make their decisions after extensive contemplation and rarely regret their decisions.

Exactly why FR groups seek to make divorces harder to obtain is not clear. Certainly, many FR advocates are religious or political conservatives who have strong traditional values. Protecting their income from alimony and child support is another major motive. Moreover, the frequency of abuse in disputed family cases suggests that divorce represents a significant loss of control for these men and loss of personal service from their wives that many men took for granted. While there is no evidence that husbands are significantly disadvantaged compared to wives by custody decisions, even in cases where abuse is alleged, the men who make up the core of the FR movement may be different in this respect. Finally, appearing to support marriage over divorce adds legitimacy to FR claims that *women* are the problem, not *them*. This particular FR site even goes so far as to advertise a self-help book for those seeking to prevent spouses from getting a divorce:

> How to Stop a Divorce (book or download) This book is written for those who DO NOT WANT their spouse divorcing them.... Christian-oriented but usable by all religions.[18]

IN THE NAME OF CHILDREN

Like divorce, child custody has also changed over the years. For much of the nineteenth century, fathers automatically received sole custody following divorce. Since most Americans lived on farms, this arrangement gave them a consistent source of labor and income. As families migrated to urban centers, men found work in factories that largely excluded married women, and the value of children as farm labor was replaced by the cost of preparing them for independence. Against this background, the same mothers who had been men's partners on farms were redefined as caregivers, and men as breadwinners.

This new arrangement was reflected in custody decisions. Mothers got custody of children during their "tender years" and then returned them to fathers at age six. By the 1920s, mothers were routinely identified as primary caregivers throughout the child's life, and the tender years doctrine was put aside. Beginning in the 1960s, which marked women's growing influence in the workforce, the focus shifted to emphasize the economic responsibilities of the noncustodial parent, usually the father, for child support and alimony, and the standard for custodial decisions shifted to "the best interest of the child." Because children are rarely involved directly in family court, the best interest of the child invited judges and evaluators to examine a range of character traits and behaviors assumed necessary to parenting, an approach termed "therapeutic jurisprudence."

Mothers end up as primary caretakers in the majority of divorces but largely by default or because judges assign primary physical custody to the person who has been the primary caretaker during the marriage, almost always the wife. Some men are undoubtedly discouraged from seeking custody because they assume it will automatically be given to their wives. Because women often receive custody, FR supporters claim the family court has been "hijacked by feminists."

FATHER'S RIGHTS OVER CHILDREN'S SAFETY

The proportion of men receiving sole or joint custody in disputed cases has risen dramatically in recent years, and it may be women, particularly those who have been abused, who receive the "raw deal." This is suggested by research like the Massachusetts Supreme Judicial Court Gender Bias Study (1990). The study utilized statistical data, expert testimony, and firsthand accounts to report that "the family law system consistently, and negatively, affects women." (Massachusetts is one of approximately 45 states to establish a gender bias task force.) The women studied, the report concluded, often lacked legal representation, didn't have access to free services, and found it difficult to navigate the system. They were not "on equal footing with men," particularly when they were abused. The study did conclude that mothers more frequently got primary physical custody of children following divorce. But, it added, "this practice does not reflect bias but rather the agreement of the parties and the fact that, in most families, mothers have been the primary [sic] caretakers of children. Fathers who actively seek custody obtain either primary or joint physical custody over 70% of the time."[19] Indeed, the courts hold higher standards for mothers than for fathers in custody determinations.

The bias against women in family court is particularly damaging to battered mothers and their children. Even though the risks posed by abusers to their former wives and children are well documented, evidence of abuse is rarely considered in family court cases and the judges commonly disbelieve women or give abuse little weight. In a Seattle study of all couples with minor children petitioning for a divorce in one year, researchers found that mothers with a history of being abused were no more likely to be granted child custody than the nonabused mothers. In fact, the vast majority (83 percent) of abusive fathers had *no restrictions at all* placed on their visitation. The outcomes for fathers whose documented history of abuse was not included in the family files or was only included as an allegation by their wives were no different than the outcomes for nonabusive fathers, evidence that the wives were not believed, even when police records of abuse existed. Not only is there no support for the FR claim that women are always believed in court (even when allegations are false), but also fathers are not even denied visitation when there *is* documented evidence of abuse.[20] This situation has been recognized by the American Psychological Association (APA). An APA report concludes that "many battered women find themselves in dangerous positions because the courts often do not give credence or sufficient weight to a history of partner abuse in making decisions about child custody and visitation."[21]

FR supporters have been successful at exploiting this situation. Fathers Rights Foundation founder Ronald L. Isaacs, JD, wrote,

> As militant feminists become more and more powerful and well funded, we see a dramatic increase in the use of false allegations of domestic abuse to gain an advantage in contested divorce and child custody cases. Learn how to make this backfire and cause a false accuser to lose custody!! One father went from being falsely accused to winning custody and having the false accuser arrested. Recently an attorney was disbarred for using the despicable practice of making false allegations to gain an advantage in a custody proceeding.[22]

Time magazine (December 2007) recently published a story about moms who would rather go to jail than allow their children to be handed over to batterers. In one case, the woman claimed the father (called the "alleged father" on FR blogs) beat her throughout her pregnancy. The judge referred to the dad as a "good catch" and wanted to force her to share custody. Defiantly, she, as others before her have done, went to jail.[23]

FALSE ALLEGATIONS—BUT *WHOSE?*

False memory, false sexual abuse claims, vengeance, are all the diseases of women.[24]

FR groups employ various tactics to discredit women in family court. These tactics portray women as vindictive, malicious, and just plain crazy and use a variety of "syndromes" to further "prove" women are unfit to parent.

As we've seen, FR men complain that women make false allegations of child abuse against them in court in order to gain custody. A number of FR Web sites (http://www.abuse-excuse.com, http://www.falseallegations.com, http://www.a-team.org, etc.) are devoted entirely to beating false allegations. The reality exposes this FR claim as transparently ideological.

Research shows men and women make false allegations at equal rates, and, in fact, some research shows fathers make more intentionally false allegations in family court than mothers. Child abuse allegations are rare in family court, and, when made, the majority can be substantiated. Domestic violence may or may not have taken place during the marriage, but it is well known that separation poses the greatest risk for women. Thus, charges may surface for the first time in the courtroom.

As we have seen, allegations of abuse in family court rarely have negative consequences for the accused. Many women are advised not to make charges as they may harm their case rather than help it. Strategically, then, allegations are not as powerful as FR activists make them out to be.

FR groups have cited the following "syndromes" on their Web sites: malicious mother syndrome (MMS), sexual allegations in divorce (SAID), hostile aggressive parenting (HAP), and lying litigant syndrome (LLS). All serve to discredit women.

MALICIOUS MOTHER SYNDROME

One father went from being arrested for child abuse to winning custody from a malicious mother.[25]

In a 1995 article, psychologist Ira Turkat described what he termed, "Divorce-related Malicious Mother Syndrome (MMS)." This syndrome allegedly dovetails with a form of borderline personality disorder (BPD) and, according to Dr. Turkat, is typically presented by "delusional accusers, usually mothers" and accompanied by "Pseudologia Fantastica" or pathological lying, another facet of BPD, Munchausen syndrome by proxy, or factitious disorder ("fantastic liars").[26] Dr. Turkat believes MMS is akin to a "campaign" initiated by a mother to hurt a father. No reliable statistics or peer-reviewed articles support this so-called syndrome.

PARENTAL ALIENATION SYNDROME

Some compare parental alienation to Stockholm syndrome, the process by which captives, especially children, form a bond with their captors.

Stephen Baskerville, PhD, president of the American Coalition for
Fathers and Children

The term "parental alienation syndrome" (PAS) was coined by American psychiatrist Richard Gardner in 1985 to refer to a pattern of behaviors through which one parent (typically the mother) poisons the minds of her children against the other parent. PAS has been widely adapted by fathers to counter claims that child abuse, sexual abuse, or domestic violence explains the child's fear of him or refusal to visit.

The American Psychological Association (APA) has no official position on the purported syndrome. But in 1996, an APA Presidential Task Force on Violence and the Family noted the lack of data to support parental alienation syndrome and raised concern about the term's use, particularly as an alternative to investigating reports of domestic violence in custody cases. Many other professional organizations, including the National Council of Juvenile and Family Court Judges, have urged their members to reject PAS as a legitimate diagnostic category.

Obviously, some parents involved in divorce deliberately or inadvertently influence their children's attitudes toward the other parent. The problems arise when so-called syndromes mask the realities of abuse as a source of fear, stigmatize protective parents, and reward abusive ones. In essence, this is exactly what FR groups want to happen.

FATHER ABSENCE

Another tactic for garnering sympathy for father's rights is to repeatedly cite the need for a father in the child's life. FR Web sites attribute endless social ills to "father absence," including child poverty, child suicide, teen pregnancy, school dropout rates, teen crime, and the use of drugs and alcohol by youth. All of this results when children are left with a single parent (read: mother). Of course, one is likely to agree that the presence of two loving parents is better than one. But the FR activists who wax nostalgic about the importance of Dad discredit the importance of parenting by single women, parents who are gay or lesbian, and stepfathers.

FR groups constantly remind us that mothers, more so than fathers, have higher rates of physically abusing their children. Indeed, the U.S. Department of Health and Human Services (HHS) reports that 57.8 percent of perpetrators of child maltreatment in 2005 were women and 42.2 percent were men. The majority (60 percent) of the maltreatment cases involved neglect.[27] A few things should be noted about these data. For one, men comprise the majority of perpetrators in cases where child abuse results in serious injury or death. For another, when we consider the relative proportion of children living with single mothers, we find that much higher rates of abuse and neglect are committed by men than women in families where *men are present*. In other words, it is the absence of men from so many families that explains why they are less likely to commit child abuse than women, not the greater propensity for mothers to abuse children. Moreover, neglect (i.e., lack of food or medical care), in some cases, can be explained by poverty rather than parenting skills.

There is some evidence that children who grow up in two-parent families do better, on average, than those who do not. Researchers, however, point out that the differences are small, certainly too small to blame single mothers for our country's most serious social problems, and note that most children who are raised by a single parent do quite well.

The question that bears most directly on the FR concerns is whether children are better off continuing to live amidst turmoil and possible violence than with a single parent or whether the effects of continued contact with their father outweigh the potential harms of being exposed to violence, manipulation, and/or control. FR proponents believe any contact with a father should be promoted, no matter his past "mistakes." Here, even those who favor joint custody agree: children are better off with the nonabusive parent.

Curiously, the same FR activists who stress the importance of men as a role model for children discredit the mother's boyfriend or second husband as a caretaker. They cite statistics showing that boyfriends or stepfathers abuse their children more often than biological fathers. FR groups interpret this as further proof that fathers can offer a safer home and are the "better parent" in the lot.

JOINT CUSTODY

Joint custody is high on the FR agenda, and FR groups have taken the lead in proposing and lobbying for legislation that would mandate joint custody in all divorce cases. While some form of joint decision making or shared custody may sound fair in principle, its function in the lexicon of FR is anything but. In an interview, Judith Stadtman Tucker of the Mothers Movement shared her thoughts on this issue:

> While many marriage and family experts believe that shared custody is ideal for children in post-divorce families, they emphasize that shared or split custody is only in the children's best interests when parents have a low-conflict relationship and are able to communicate well—which is normally not the case in the 10 to 15 percent of parental breakups that result in custody litigation. It is important to note that in nearly all states, *there are no legal standards that prevent family courts from granting equal or shared custody if both parties request it, as long as it's deemed to be in the best interest of the couple's children.*[28] (Emphasis mine)

In other words, there are no barriers to shared custody if both parents are in agreement. But in cases where conflict, control, or coercion have taken place in the home—almost certainly a majority of disputed custody cases—shared decision making or joint custody are little more than a pretext to continue abuse.

The consensus among experts is that joint custody should not replace the "best interest of the child" as a standard, particularly because of the level of conflict in some divorcing couples. This has not dissuaded FR groups in the least, however. In fact, Warren Farrell, American author and FR advocate, believes the greater the conflict, the greater the need to see both parents equally.

JOINT CUSTODY AS A RUSE?

Some believe FR proponents advocate for joint custody as a ruse to seek lower child support payments or to reach a more favorable financial settlement. In this argument, many fathers are seen as less interested in actually playing a primary role in their child's life than in using joint custody as a bargaining chip.

Undeniably, child support is a major topic on the FR agenda. Web sites are loaded with information and advertisements on lowering payments:

Just imagine yourself six months from today ... spending meaningful time with your children and paying a fair amount of child support, if at all. Completely equal in every way as a parent. No more pinching pennies to support your "X"'s lifestyle, no more wondering if you'll see your kids this weekend. **No more begging your "X" for time with your kids and no more catering to the "whims"** of the Mother, taking all the "guff" she's used to throwing at you."—National Brotherhood of Father's Rights advertisement for the "Father's Rights Protection System" (cost: $295.54)[29]

http://www.fathershelphotline.com

http://www.stopchildsupportnow.com

The name says it all.

Protecting Fathers' Rights and Victims of Child Support Laws For Over 10 Years

We will show you the totally legal techniques to lower your child support payment that your ex doesn't want you to know about. Are you tired of being portrayed as a deadbeat just because you want to make sure your support is actually being spent on your child.[30]

LOWER CHILD SUPPORT

FREE STEPS TO MODIFY AND LOWER CHILD SUPPORT PAYMENTS, AVOID IMPROPER COLLECTION EFFORTS & PROTECT YOUR NEW SPOUSES' ASSETS[31]

"Child support encourages greed and adversarial relationships due to this 'take 'em to the cleaners' approach, enforced by government policies."—Alliance for Non-custodial Parents Rights[32]

Typically, child support guidelines are set by each state and are based on several factors. They are reviewed periodically and they can be modified by a judge. According to the U.S. Bureau of the Census, of the 13.6 million custodial parents in 2006, 7.8 million or 57.3 percent had some type of agreement or court award to receive financial support. On average, the award amounted to $5,600.00 per year or $465.00 per month. In 2005, 77.2 percent of those due support received either full (46.2 percent) or partial payments.[33]

When a parent is not in compliance with their child support payments, there are arrearages. Fathers that don't pay their support are often called "deadbeat dads." FR proponents, understandably, are not happy about that term. But mothers can be called "deadbeat moms," too.

In 2005, mothers received $22.4 billion of the $34.7 billion due, which is 64.7 percent. Fathers received $2.4 billion of the $3.3 billion due, more than 70 percent. Parents also provide noncash support, such as health insurance, groceries, gifts, and so on.

FR groups insist that so many men fail to meet their support commitments to their children because they don't have the money, they spend what they do make supporting their second families, or their ex-wives have remarried a wealthy man and don't need the money. They also claim their ex-wives are not using the money as intended and are spending it on themselves rather than their children. Such claims find widespread endorsement and sympathy on FR sites.

Nothing I am saying is meant to impugn the legitimate interests that fathers have in maintaining a close, loving relationship with their children after a divorce. Nor do I dismiss the fact that paying child support can cause a financial strain. What concerns me are the ways in which these legitimate concerns are exploited by FR groups, redirected in ways that increase conflict rather than work to resolve it, and linked to anger against women in general and feminists in particular.

ADAMANT AND EVIL

If it isn't true, they make it up and convince themselves it is true and men end up in jail or executed as a result.[34]

If divorce and custody are the bread-and-butter issues of the FR agenda, then violence is the rancid red jam that adds the flavor to these staples. FR groups adamantly blame women for initiating half of all cases of domestic violence, make justifications for men's use of violence, accuse women of making false rape accusations, and attack services and policies for female victims of violence.

FR groups adamantly accuse women of initiating or causing half the cases of violent episodes in interpersonal relationships. Some research supports this claim. Community-based surveys, for example, can be used to detect moderate levels of violence that can be exhibited by both sexes. This form of violence stems from frustration and anger and occasionally erupts into physical aggression. Following researcher Michael Johnson's designation, the World Health Organization calls this "common couple violence." Violence that gets worse over time, becomes severe, has several forms of threats and abuse, and involves a high level of control is referred to as "battering." Battering is predominantly used by men. In addition, while community-based surveys may be better able to detect common couple violence, many fail to distinguish between the use of violence that is initiated and violence that is used in self-defense. Nor does it address the under- or overestimation of a partner's use of violence in a verbal account or take into consideration the overall picture. Women, undeniably, are more likely to be injured, suffer more forms of violence, need medical attention, and fear for their lives. Men who suffer from domestic violence rarely experience violence after leaving the relationship; whereas for women, leaving the relationship presents the greatest risk of danger.

Aside from explaining violence away as a mutual process, FR groups often rationalize or justify violent acts or offer sympathy for the perpetrators. Typically, they blame the acts on outside forces, such as saying men were pushed too far by the courts. On one FR message board a poster said, in referring to a woman who tried (and failed) to commit suicide after her husband killed her alleged 18-year-old lover, she should have done "a better job." Other messages further suggested adultery was a "crime against society," it was the adulteress' fault the victim died, and it was an "accidental shooting." The male perpetrator was, therefore, exonerated of the crime.

As with false allegations of abuse in divorce proceedings, FR proponents believe women who make unsubstantiated claims of violence should be subject to prosecution. They are particularly harsh with rape accusers: "American women who LIE must be punished, whether they lie about statistics, or about rape!"[35] These misogynist claims that state women lie about rape are deeply rooted in history and still affect women in court proceedings today. While courts treat accused rapists as innocent until proven guilty, they often treat rape accusers as "liars" until proven honest. Only 5.7 percent of rape charges in the United Kingdom and 13 percent in the United States end in conviction. As one British mother of a raped daughter asked, do they think 95 percent of women lie? Angry Harry believes they do. On his site (http://www.angryharry.com), under "rape baloney," he writes, "These 'rapes' are simply manufactured out of very thin air by various groups that, in essence, promote male hatred in order to reap some kind of benefit for themselves." FR advocates and other "angry Harries" believe claims of male violence are "misandry" rather than reality.

I have repeatedly come across comments online about women who've been the victims of violence that resemble the type of hatred and distrust of women displayed by Angry Harry—though, not as far as I could tell, from FR supporters—that referred to females as sluts, golddiggers, liars, and other derogatory names. Little was said about the perpetrators, and, in fact, when the perpetrators were serial killers they often received superhero titles (Spokane Killer, Green River Killer, etc.). It would seem (and my interview with Michael Flood confirmed this) that FR groups take the level of misogyny that already exists in our culture and maximize it in order to further their agenda.

Not surprisingly, then, FR groups attack services, policies, and laws that help female victims of violence. In 2003, a man sued nine of the 10 domestic violence shelters in Los Angeles County. While these shelters could provide assistance and referrals, they could not provide him with a bed. So he sued them for discrimination. There is, in fact, a shelter for men—the one he didn't call. And, of course, women are also turned away from shelters due to space limitations or for other reasons. Nonetheless, recently, a high court in California found in favor of the fathers rights' lawsuit. These combatant approaches are preferred to cooperating with shelters and helping to secure funds to open more. What effect the court decision will have on domestic violence services is not yet clear.

FR advocates also attack the Violence Against Women Act (VAWA), claiming it is sexist and provides the domestic violence "industry" with tons of money and imprisons "innocent men." First authorized in 1994, VAWA provided funding for domestic violence and sexual assault programs. It was reauthorized in 2000 and 2005. It has expanded over the years to include stalking, dating violence, and prevention and outreach activities. In 2005, $3.935 billion was allocated to VAWA for a five-year period (subject to annual appropriations). Since FR groups claim violence is mutual, some say they should share the grant monies. Certainly, they believe feminists profit from this "industry." They claim feminists inflate data and create "hysteria" to give a false sense of an epidemic of domestic violence. Media RADAR says VAWA allows for "loose definitions" of domestic violence that weaken "family tradition." David Usher, president of the American Coalition for Fathers and Children, calls VAWA an "anti-family tragedy" that is used as a "divorce weapon." He advocates fixing the disagreement (domestic violence) rather than seeking a divorce, claiming VAWA escalates "common minor family disagreements" into divorce and jail time.

CONCLUSION

Thus far, FR groups have made some inroads in pushing their own agenda, particularly in changing family court practice. They've also influenced policies, laws, and public perceptions on issues like divorce, custody, and violence.

Certainly, divorce is a major issue for FR groups and holds the key to their recruitment efforts. But not all of their members are divorced men fighting against what they deem unjust Family Court decisions. Other components of the movement need to be addressed, as well, particularly in regard to the opposition to women's rights and achievements.

So, what should we do to counter the threat posed by the FR groups?

With respect to divorce, I believe we must promote active involvement of parents in a child's life but continue to maintain the best interest of the child in custody decisions. I also favor promoting shared parenting *during* marriage as well as after divorce. Currently, women do twice the amount of housework and five times the amount of child care as men in two-parent households. And while couples should have the option of shared parenting during divorce, it cannot be mandated as FR supporters would like. To date, FR advocates have been largely unsuccessful in nearly a dozen states in mandating presumptive joint custody. This does not mean that states do not favor joint custody, however, but simply that the legislation to *presume* joint custody over the best interest of the child has not yet been enacted. Experts concur: joint custody works in low- or no-conflict relationships and cannot be mandated for all couples.

As we've seen, one of the most disturbing outcomes of advancing FR arguments in Family Court is that batterers are gaining custody and visitation rights and put into positions where they can continue and even extend control over their ex-wives in ways that threaten them and their children. In a number of well-publicized cases, FR activists have been successful not merely in gaining sole or primary custody, but in persuading judges (and even legislatures in some states) to impose penalties, including jail, on ex-wives who allege abuse to themselves or their children but fail to convince a court such abuse occurred or who fail to comply with an order mandating visitation with an abusive parent. Moreover, even when evidence of abuse does exist, it is rarely given any weight when it comes to making custody decisions. The current thinking is it's better to be with a violent father than not to be with one at all. This runs contrary to expert opinion, as well.

The FR advocates, therefore, have been successful in turning the tables on women, particularly where allegations of domestic violence are concerned. Batterers routinely get unsupervised visitation or even custody in these cases and women are portrayed as liars. Parental alienation syndrome, despite the complete lack of supporting evidence, is being widely used in courtrooms. Even the mainstream media have quoted FR members and referred to them as "experts." The most insidious consequence of PAS claims, an outcome that so-called experts fail to acknowledge, is that it can mask child abuse. Syndrome arguments provide a ready way to explain why children may share their mother's fear of an abusive father in cases where documentation is weak or absent. Only when this situation changes will allegations of spousal abuse and child abuse be given the serious consideration they deserve in custody decisions.

Lastly, we must protect the services that help victims of violence and create an environment that is respectful and sensitive to the needs of the victims as well as to the accused parties. We must foster an environment that condemns violence. One place to start is to protest when the media glamorizes violent images of women. While it is clearly easier (and undoubtedly safer) to ignore references to female victims as sluts, gold diggers, (vindictive) liars, and the like, the "culture of silence" that accepts and even normalizes this violence contributes to its durability. Attacking female victims of a serial killer rather than the perpetrator, for instance, provides a rationalization for violence in the same way that people credited Jack the Ripper for ridding society of its "dregs" in Victorian England. And when we discredit women, whether with derogatory terms or with disbelief, it serves a purpose: it provides impunity to the perpetrators. Impunity is one of the greatest obstacles to overcoming violence against women.

We must also view men as victims, not just perpetrators, and include them not only in services but also in our goal of eradicating violence from our families and communities. A cry of pain, masked in anger, is coming from these FR men. Although the anger is disconcerting, the pain needs to be addressed. But acknowledging the very real pain many men feel in divorce or custody cases can in no way be at the expense of attacking women or dissolving services for female victims of violence.

Above all, we must offer support and counseling to mothers and fathers that allow couples to separate amicably, survive as single parents, and continue active participation in their children's lives and welfare. Shared parenting should be encouraged for couples with low or no conflict. By contrast, abusive and controlling violence is incompatible with healthy co-parenting. Still, in the context of full accountability and help, recognizing abuse and holding perpetrators accountable can be consistent with the eventual reinvolvement of a father in his child's life.

It is this issue—men's responsibility for abuse and the full accountability for this abuse as a critical first step in a man's rehabilitation—that excites the FR groups the most. Their propensity to dismiss it or rationalize men's abusive behavior is not wholly surprising, particularly since many FR leaders have had domestic violence records or restraining orders against them. Given the high recidivism rates in battering, it may seem naïve to expect any change in these attitudes. Nevertheless, the credibility of FR groups could be greatly enhanced if they embraced accountability for abusive behavior and supported widespread and early intervention as well as preventive steps in schools, communities, or other institutions.

If we can begin with healthy relationships, perhaps when it is time to end them, which so often occurs, we can do so more effectively. One thing is certain: if we do not offer the right tools and road map to building healthy relationships, the FR groups will continue on their destructive path, recruiting angry, distressed men among their ranks.

NOTES

1. J. Dawson, "Where is the love in Wikipedia?" *Ohmynews* (Seoul), January 15, 2007, http://english.ohmynews.com/articleview/article_view.asp?menu=c10400&no=340058&rel_no=1.

2. J. Dawson, "Responsible Parenting and Fathers' Rights: Sociologist Michael Flood Promotes Healthy Family," *OhmyNews*, (Seoul) March 27, 2007, http://english.ohmynews.com/articleview/article_view.asp?menu=c10400&no=352644&rel_no=1&back_url.

3. Marc Feigen Fasteau, *The Male Machine* (NY: Dell Publishing Company, 1974).

4. Jack Sawyer, *On Male Liberation* (PA: KNOW, Inc., 1971).

5. Warren Farrell, *The Liberated Man* (NY: Bantam, 1974).

6. Robert Bly, *Iron John: A Book About Men* (NY: Perseus Books, 1990).

7. Herb Goldberg, *The Hazards of Being Male: Surviving the Myth of Masculine Privilege* (NY: Signet, 1976), http://www.amazon.com/Hazards-Being-Male-Surviving-Masculine/dp/1587410133 (Retrieved January 5, 2008).

8. Richard Doyle, *The Rape of the Male* (St. Paul: Poor Richard's Press, 1976).

9. Steven Goldberg, *Inevitability of Patriarchy* (London: Temple Smith, 1977).

10. J. Dawson, "Responsible Parenting ... Michael Flood."

11. J. Mulder, "20 Questions with Tony Taylor of the Mens Custody Shelter Network," Fathers Rights Forum, http://fathersrightsforum.blogspot.com/2006/02/20-questions-with-tony-taylor-of-mens.html (retrieved January 1, 2008).

12. Fathers for Justice, http://www.f4joz.com (retrieved January 4, 2008).

13. J. K. Inwood, "Fathers Rights," Canlaw, http://www.canlaw.com/rights/fathers.htm (retrieved May 31, 2008).

14. "Summary of Online Discussion Three Fatherhood Programs and Domestic Violence Prevention," Family Violence Prevention Fund, 2, http://endabuse.org/bpi/discussion3/Summary.pdf (retrieved March 30, 2007).

15. Children's Rights Council, "About CRCkids.org/Mission Statement," http://crckids.org/about-crc.htm (retrieved January 1, 2008).

16. Dennis M. Gac, "NBFR Membership," National Brotherhood of Father's Rights, http://www.fathershelphotline.com/a_membership_info.htm (retrieved on January 1, 2008).

17. Cited in M.S. Kimmel, "'Gender Symmetry' in Domestic Violence: A Substantive and Methodological Review" in *Violence Against Women* 8 (November, 2002): 1332–1363.

18. R. L. Isaacs, "Fathers and Dads for Equal Custody Rights," Fathers Rights Foundation, http://www.fathersrights.org, http://www.fathers-rights.com, and http://www.courttips.com/shopsite_sc/page10.html (retrieved January 1, 2008).

19. Massachusetts Gender Bias Study Committee, "Gender Bias Study," *New England Law Review* 24 (Spring 1990): "Executive Summary," p. 748. http://www.amptoons.com/blog/files/Massachusetts_Gender_Bias_Study.htm.

20. M. A. Kernic, D. J. Monary-Ernsdorff, J. K. Koespell, and V. L. Holt, "Children in the Crossfire: Child Custody Determinations among Couples with a History of Intimate Partner Violence," *Violence against Women* 11, no. 8 (2005): 991–1021.

21. American Psychological Association, "Violence and the Family: Report of the APA Presidential Task Force on Violence and the Family—Executive Summary," http://www.apa.org/pi/viol&fam.html (retrieved January 5, 2008).

22. Fathers Rights Foundation, http://www.fathersrights.org.

23. M. A. Lindenberger, "When Motherhood Gets You Jail Time," *Time*, http://www.time.com/time/nation/article/0,8599,1696718,00.html (retrieved January 5, 2008).

24. Canlaw, www.canlaw.com/rights/fathers.htm.

25. R. L. Isaacs, "Lower Child Support," Fathers Rights Foundation, http://www.lowersupport.com (retrieved May 31, 2008).

26. I. D. Turkat, "Divorce Related Malicious Mother Syndrome," *Journal of Family Violence* 10, no. 3 (1995): 253–64, http://fact.on.ca/Info/pas/turkat95.htm (retrieved November 2007).

27. U.S. Department of Health and Human Services, *Child Maltreatment 2005*, 17.

28. J. S. Tucker, e-mail interview, November 18, 2007.

29. National Brotherhood of Fathers Rights, http://www.fathershelphotline.com/a_membership_info.htm.

30. Child Support Savings, "Fathers for Equal Rights," http://www.childsupportsavings.com (retrieved May 31, 2008).

31. Fathers Rights Foundation, http://www.lowersupport.com.

32. Alliance for Non-custodial Parents Rights, "What Is Wrong with the Child Support System?" http://www.ancpr.org/wrong2.html (retrieved May 31, 2008).

33. T. S. Grall, *Custodial Mothers and Fathers and Their Child Support: 2005*, Current Population Reports prepared for the U.S. Department of Commerce, August, Washington, D.C.: US Census Bureau, 2007, 5, http://www.census.gov/prod/2007pubs/p60-234.pdf (retrieved January 6, 2008).

34. Canlaw.

35. Fathers Manifesto and Christian Party, "Damages from False Accusations," http://www.christianparty.net/r.htm (retrieved May 31, 2008).

BIBLIOGRAPHY

American Psychological Association. "Violence and the Family: Report of the APA Presidential Task Force on Violence and the Family—Executive Summary," http://www.apa.org/pi/viol&fam.html (retrieved January 5, 2008).

Dawson, J. "Responsible Parenting and Fathers' Rights: Sociologist Michael Flood Promotes Healthy Family." *OhmyNews* (Seoul), March 27, 2007, http://english.ohmynews.com/articleview/article_view.asp?menu=c10400 &no=352644&rel_no=1&back_url.

Goldberg, H. *The Hazards of Being Male: Surviving the Myth of Masculine Privilege.* Wellness Institute, 1982, http://www.amazon.com/Hazards-Being-Male-Surviving-Masculine/dp/1587410133 (retrieved January 5, 2008).

Lindenberger, M. A. "When Motherhood Gets You Jail Time." *Time,* http://www.time.com/time/nation/article/0,8599,1696718,00.html (retrieved January 5, 2008).

Massachusetts Gender Bias Study Committee. "Gender Bias Study." *New England Law Review* 24 (Spring 1990): "Executive Summary," http://www.amptoons.com/blog/files/Massachusetts_Gender_Bias_Study.htm.

Turkat, I. D. "Divorce Related Malicious Mother Syndrome." *Journal of Family Violence* 10, no. 3 (1995): http://fact.on.ca/Info/pas/turkat95.htm.

U.S. Department of Commerce. *Custodial Mothers and Fathers and Their Child Support: 2005,* report prepared by T. Grall. Washington, D.C.: U.S. Department of Commerce, 2007.

U.S. Department of Health and Human Services, Administration on Children, Youth and Families. *Child Maltreatment 2005.* Washington, D.C.: U.S. Department of Health and Human Services, 2007, http://www.acf.hhs.gov/programs/cb/pubs/cm05/cm05.pdf (retrieved January 5, 2008).

Chapter 9

Divorce in the Context of Coercive Control

Cynthia Wilcox Lischick

A year after I completed my dissertation on coping with domestic violence, an attorney contacted me to testify as an expert witness on battering and its effects. The case involved her client's claim of duress. Her client, Kelly, had signed two binding separation agreements with her husband in the presence of his attorney. The first agreement deprived Kelly of assets to which she was legally entitled, and the second of access to her portion of his future earnings. When I asked whether there had been any domestic violence in the relationship, the attorney said she wasn't sure, since Kelly had reported only two episodes, both minor: a backhanded slap on their wedding night 12 years ago while Bill was drunk and a recent altercation at the point of separation where he pushed her against the car in order to take the family minivan keys from her hand. Three years prior to the separation and without Kelly's knowledge, Bill had registered the family van to his business, enabling him to demand its return legally while leaving her stranded with no transportation for herself or their four children, who were ten, nine, four, and two years of age, making it impossible to take them to their various activities or even to get to the grocery store. They lived on a farm, and the closest neighbor was a mile away. Kelly had no independent access to income since she was an "at-home mom." A few weeks prior to the separation, Kelly had the van serviced and discovered a tracking device that allowed her husband to monitor her trips from his office. She suddenly realized how he was able to show up at places for which she hadn't received "permission" to go.

The attorney wondered what additional facets of a relationship would cause an intelligent, educated woman to feel so much fear that she chose to sign away her legal rights to marital assets and future financial security for herself and her children. The attorney asked pensively, "Do you have any theories about duress if there wasn't much in the way of physical violence during the marriage, no real domestic violence?"

This chapter summarizes coercive control, the model of abuse that framed my reply to the attorney's question. I describe the basic dimensions of coercive control, a widely prevalent and devastating strategy used primarily by men to frighten, exploit, isolate, control, and ultimately dominate female partners; summarize the findings of my own research to assess the importance of coercive control; and use Kelly's experience with Bill to illustrate the pattern. The redefinition of domestic violence as coercive control will be supported by empirical data as well as the forensic case. Taken together, the tactics that comprise the controller's strategy can fundamentally compromise a victim's autonomy, including her capacity to self-direct her life in key areas we associate with citizenship and personhood, as well as her physical integrity. And they can do this, as we will see, without severe or frequent physical violence, even when the coercive controller is not "on-site" in the relationship or in the home, and even in the absence of direct physical coercion of any kind.

Like so many who research or service offenders or victims of domestic violence, the attorney assumed that the level of abuse that occurred in this marriage could not have been serious enough to support a claim of duress because Bill had never been arrested for domestic violence, Kelly had never been injured, and the few minor incidents she described could have occurred even in a "good" relationship. As we will see, physical violence often plays a critical role in reinforcing the effects of other tactics deployed in coercive control. However, in many cases, the ends of coercive control are achieved with little or no violence. Bill ran a successful business that Kelly helped him develop and maintain. Three years prior to their separation, he had ended Kelly's connection to the business, moving the operation out of the home, and even forbidding her to pick up mail related to the business. These steps were complemented by the installation of the tracking device, following her, restricting her access to money, making rules about her behavior in and her movements outside the house, and other steps that typify how coercive controllers dominate their partners. I explained to the attorney that, when Kelly signed away her legal and financial rights, she may have been suffering from a level of fear that could easily paralyze her independent will, much in the same way hostages' level of fear might lead them to comply with demands that violated their basic sense of decency or principle. Although Kelly's physical integrity seemed to be intact, by eviscerating her rights as a free person, her husband had inflicted deep and abiding wounds to her psychological self, to her sense of personhood. How this could happen without the element of physical assault is the topic of this chapter.

BACKGROUND: IS SOMETHING MISSING?

Over the last 25 years, most of those involved with domestic violence have equated its occurrence with incidents of physical violence, assessed its severity by the means employed and their tangible outcomes such as injury, and linked its cause to intimate conflicts gone awry, where physically violent tactics were selected by one or both partners. In one version of this approach, if women suffer more often and more seriously than men in these encounters, this has less to do with the women's hesitancy to use violence than men's greater strength and physical prowess. This understanding dovetails with the justice system perspective, where domestic violence crimes differ from incidents of stranger-to-stranger assault largely because the self-identified victims are typically female intimate partners of their assailants rather than other men.

In this approach, the duration of abusive relationships is attributed to psychological deficits induced by violence (such as "learned helplessness") or to the confounding effects of "love" on women's decisions about their own or their children's safety.

Feminists offer an alternative view. They point out that the focus on discrete incidents among equal adults conceals the patterned and gendered nature of most domestic violence in which women are victimized as well as the patriarchal context of male privilege that continues to dominate heterosexual relationships. Persistent power differentials in society between men and women, including women's disadvantaged economic status, severely limit women's capacity to effectively resist or escape from abuse. Feminists also insist that reported levels of harm and fear are the cumulative by-products of an ongoing pattern of abuse rather than of discrete incidents.

Although I have long identified as a feminist, the inadequacy of the violence and incident-specific account only became apparent to me slowly. Two examples must suffice.

In the latter part of the 1980s, family courts were looking for ways to unclog their dockets while providing a more participatory, less expensive route for marital dissolution using the notion of "no fault" rather than sending all divorce cases to trial. As a graduate student in psychology at Rutgers University, I participated in a New Jersey, court-based pilot project of mediation as an alternative way to resolve custody and visitation disputes. Because New Jersey law prohibited the use of mediation in cases involving domestic violence, the mediator researchers on this pilot project felt assured that their sample would only involve "nonviolent" couples. Indeed, many of the participating couples preferred the mediation process to more formal dispute resolution by the courts and even became "friends for the day." However, mediation failed with a number of couples and their dispute over custody and visitation was sent back to court for trial. This was typically because one party was "stonewalling" and observed to be controlling the other party, answering for them and generally acting inappropriately while undermining any possible attempts to mediate. In these cases, it was almost always the dad who seemed unwilling to stay focused on the best interests of the children and was consequently labeled the "interpersonally dysfunctional parent," or IDP for short. His behavior in these cases was coercive, even though it was nonphysical. And, if this was how he responded in public and when his children's needs and wants were being negotiated, I tried to imagine what the mothers in these cases experienced behind closed doors. There was no further follow-up. But I always wondered what relationship, if any, there was between the literal physical violence excluded from mediation, the nature of the IDP's efforts at thwarting any resolution of conflict, and the IDP's *effectively suppressing their wives' expressions of disagreement* despite the presence of a highly trained mediator. The mediators felt challenged to remain "neutral" in these cases. But they completely missed the frankly abusive behavior they were witnessing.

More recently, I was consulting with the family court on how to assess the danger batterers posed to their children, when a judge's clerk asked about cases where a woman alleged abuse but there was no evidence of physical violence. In several cases that perplexed her, she sensed there was an abusive dynamic, but couldn't reconcile this with the absence of physical assault. New Jersey's domestic violence statute includes terroristic threats, criminal restraint, false imprisonment, harassment, and stalking, and the clerk was also aware that the absence of an arrest or a restraining order could simply mean the woman was hesitant or frightened to "go public" with claims of abuse. But the woman had described other acts that seemed to fall just outside the purview of the "criminal restraint" anticipated by the law, such as her husband's occasional "outbursts" of rage and his forbidding her to drive their jointly owned cars, have any visitors to the home, or access spending money. There was no mention of the husband using a gun or even raising his fist to stop her from taking the keys, getting money out of his wallet, or inviting friends to the house. These events were seen as disconnected, making it impossible to appreciate their cumulative effect. And there were not even minor bruises. The woman's level of fear suggested that either she was crazy or something terrible had gone on. "What am I missing?" she asked me.

The clerk's law school experience and belief in sexual equality made her acutely aware that something was inherently wrong when men were allowed to place these sorts of constraints on their wives. But she could not reconcile her intuition with statutory definitions of domestic violence. Nor did the patterned nature of the coercive course of conduct described in her case files match her image of adultery or other acts of "extreme cruelty" so often alleged in divorces over the years.

CHANGING THE PARADIGM: DEFINING DOMESTIC VIOLENCE AS A PATTERN OF COERCIVE CONTROL

The limits I was discovering in the traditional domestic violence model were also surfacing in other contexts. For example, battered women utilizing health services had been shown to suffer disproportionately from a range of medical, behavioral, and mental health problems found among no other population of assault victims. Although these problems only became widespread after the onset of their being battered and so could not be the cause of their being abused, nor could their emergence be explained by the relatively minor violence to which these women had typically been subjected. Nor could violence alone explain women's "entrapment" with abusive men that appeared to be as great where little or no violence occurred as when it was severe. Nor could it be explained by "intimacy" or women's alleged ambivalence about "leaving." For one thing, women did leave in droves, often multiple times in the course of a relationship. But when they did so, the abuse rarely ended, though it might change its form. For another thing, survey after survey showed that women who were single, separated, or divorced were actually at a higher risk of injury or death at the hands of a batterer than married women or women in intact relationships, a clear indication that it was something the perpetrator did that explained the duration of battering, not only the victim's behavior or the couple's physical or emotional proximity. Population surveys showed that women were as or almost as likely to use force against their partners as to be victims of male or female partners. But if women were as violent as men, why was there virtually no evidence that any substantial number of "battered men" sought help because of partner abuse from hospitals, courts, police departments, or other points of service? In each instance, the presence or absence of assault appeared to be a poor indicator of whether a victim suffered the consequences of being "battered" and required assistance and protection as a result. And yet, this was the common indicator on which courts, police, hospitals, and even many shelters relied.

To respond to these dilemmas, sociologist Evan Stark built a new model of domestic violence from older work and his own forensic experience, the model of domestic violence as "coercive control."[1] Many individuals continue to conceptualize domestic violence in terms of discrete acts of physical violence or as the tactical use of physical force to solve a particular disagreement or express a strongly held feeling. The new model acknowledges that domestic violence can certainly take this form and that abuse may be limited to physical assault and psychological abuse in a minority of cases. It reflects a growing conviction, increasingly supported by empirical research, that a majority of partner abuse cases involve a pattern of coercive and controlling tactics woven together over time and used instrumentally to exploit and dominate a victim.

In his pathbreaking account of coercive control, Stark subdivides the tactical elements typically found in coercive control into four groups: physical violence, intimidation (ranging from threats to various forms of degradation and insult), isolation, and control. In any given case, these tactics may coexist to any degree and in any combination. Also pathbreaking is Stark's reconceptualization of the harms caused by coercive control. Although physical and psychological injury remain important, he highlights what he terms "liberty harms" by which he means the degree to which coercive control compromises the victim's rights to social connection, autonomous decision making, and basic freedoms such as the freedom of speech, movement, and access to money and other necessities. It is the abrogation of a victim's rights that eviscerates her personhood in this model, not physical or psychological abuse alone or even primarily. Stark does not contest the claim that women and men may be equally prone to use violence to address their differences in relationships. But he argues that coercive control is a strategy used almost exclusively by males against female partners, is rooted in sexual inequality rather than the fact that men are physically "stronger" than women, and largely explains why abused women—but rarely abused men—seek help in such large numbers and suffer the dramatic health profile identified with "battering." Other writers have also distinguished the types of violence that couples use in "fights" or to resolve differences from the combination of violence and control that comprises true battering. Sociologist Michael Johnson, for instance, terms the former "common couple violence" and the latter "intimate terrorism," adding another type, "violent resistance," typically when women violently resist a male partner's control.[2] As I will illustrate in the case of Kelly, the proximate consequence of being subjected to coercive control is a sense of fear and vulnerability that can paralyze resistance or even independent action of any sort.

THE SURVIVAL SELF AND PSEUDO-CONTROL

The goal of the coercive controller is to stop a partner from doing or acting as she chooses, or to coerce her into doing things she does not want to do. The pattern of coercive strategies can involve overt and covert threats to the victim or persons in her family or social network; actual or threatened physical, sexual, or psychological harm; as well as tactics such as haranguing, wheedling, cajoling, coaxing, bribing, seducing, withholding love, harassing, or threatening to hurt or abandon the victim. The coercive controller's partner, most often female, responds by constructing what I term a "survival self" as a functional response to the coercive context. This may include the belief that if she changes her behavior to reflect his concerns and demands, then this will placate him or, at least, prevent him from escalating his coercive behavior. I label this belief "pseudo-control." Pseudo-control is a normal human response to being threatened that offers the victim a feeling of being able to control the batterer in a context of coerced powerlessness and constrained options. Often pseudo-control is reinforced by the batterer's statement such as "if you would just do what I tell you I wouldn't have to [follow/degrade/hurt] you." However, because the coercive controller's demands are designed as much as displays of power as because he requires a specific behavior from the victim, the victim's accommodation actually reinforces his control rather than shifts it to her. Other exposed individuals (e.g., children, extended family, and caregivers) in or around the home may be forced to construct a survival self that includes pseudo-control—believing they too can change the coercive controller by placating him. Often, along with outsiders, they reinforce the victim's pseudo-control by attributing to her the power to stop or change her partner's behavior and by blaming her for not "taking charge" or being decisive. When friends or helping professionals ask, "Why don't you just leave him?" to someone caught in the web of coercive control, they are reflecting the pseudo-control. These conjectures, so common among those charged with helping, protecting, or otherwise supporting battered women, miss the structural elements of coercive control, the extent to which the victim's disempowerment is enforced through a range of objective constraints on basic resources and relationships, much as a hostage's dependence on his or her captor might be. In reality, the coercive controller is the only person who can stop inflicting harm.

THE COERCIVE CONTROLLING PARTNER

Coercive controllers come from all social strata; their credo is "my way or the highway," though they may panic at any thought of a "real" separation that deprives them of their control.

To resolve this dilemma, they restrict or close off their partner's options for independent action and lay down standards, "rules," or "understandings" that prescribe how their partner *should* or *must* behave. These rules may be quite specific, referring for instance to exactly how long they may talk on the phone or take in the bathroom, or quite general ("you will not make me jealous").

They key here is that the controller is judge and jury of when a standard is violated and interprets disagreement or an abrogation of his rules as a sign of disloyalty and as an occasion for discipline, punishment, or other forms of what was once euphemistically termed "correction."

Punishment may extend from physical harm or the deprivation of vital resources (such as her car keys or credit card) to passive-aggressive responses, like staying away from home for days at a time or the "silent treatment."

Intimidation tactics are a constant, whether through open insults and overt threats of harm or more subtle warnings such as "forgetting" to pick up the children from day care or leaving a pornography Web site open so she will see how he regards women. Isolation tactics also run the gamut from literal prohibitions against seeing or talking with certain family members, friends, or coworkers to making it so uncomfortable or embarrassing when they are around that isolation and disconnection from one another become preferable choices. If unquestioned obedience is the only acceptable option, it is also difficult to achieve because the controller is continually modifying his rules to reflect his changing moods or the needs of the moment. The more irrational, arbitrary, or petty the standards embodied in his rules are, the more transparent it is that raw power and authority are at work and the more degraded is the woman who tries to comply.

Over time, as the partner becomes well aware of the pain the controller is capable of inflicting, fear and terror can be instilled simply by a threatening look or gesture. With every command or expectation, the implicit message is "or else." But even when a partner threatens to "lose it" or actually does so by flying into what appears to be an uncontrollable rage, these behaviors are no less chosen or instrumental vis-à-vis specific effects desired than when he installs a tracking device or carefully regulates or withholds affection. Thus, losing control is a tactic to *take control*. Some small proportion of controllers are mentally ill or substance abusers, and these persons should be considered more dangerous. As a general rule, however, coercive control is incompatible with high levels of mental or behavioral dysfunction because it requires attention to detail and calculation, an experimental attitude (since tactics that work are repeated and those that fail to achieve their ends replaced), as well as a capacity to read and predict a partner's reaction. Thus, coercive control must be considered rational, instrumental behavior organized strategically to achieve specific and self-interested ends.

Once we grasp the instrumental nature of coercive control with respect to achieving dominance and privilege, the controller's use of violence as a means of coercion can be reframed as a tactical choice with specific benefits and costs rather than as an imperative of control.

Nonviolent coercive tactics may achieve similar ends at lower personal risk than assault. While he may physically prevent her from leaving the house, for instance, he can also keep her from moving about freely in the world by taking her car keys, removing her distributor cap, or depriving her of access to money. When she is moving about in the world, he may stalk her or have others keep her under surveillance, check her mileage, monitor her cell phone, time her sojourns, and have her report "out" and "in." Under these constraints, she may voluntarily decide to limit her social connections rather than continually look over her shoulder and travel in fear. Or, knowing the risks she is taking, friends and family may feel so uncomfortable that they choose not to stay connected. In either case, as she becomes more isolated, with time she becomes more dependent and may even appear to her friends to be obsessed. She is forced to apply a calculus of relative fear to her options—to stay at home or to venture out and fail to comply with his standards—but whatever her choice, however much she maintains the illusion of choice, her fundamental freedom and autonomy are compromised.

Continued interrogation typically accompanies other intimidation tactics and often elicits confession and contrition. Questioning may focus on her daily activities, "why she acts so crazy," her "real" feelings about other men in her life, as well as contacts, the content of her conversations, or her expenditures. These sessions may occur at regular times, after dinner for instance, or may be initiated spontaneously. Often his inquires into the time she takes to get from one place to another, the content of her conversations, or her expenditures take the form of an interrogator questioning a prisoner of war. Indeed, in many cases, male partners awaken their wives in the middle of the night (or don't let them fall asleep), force them to stand, and lecture or question them, insisting, "The conversation is only over when I say it's over." The "right" to interrogate a female partner is linked to other seemingly innate male privileges tied to definitions of manhood such as the right to sex on demand, a clean house, dinner on the table, uninterrupted football games, and care for his children and their delivery when he is ready to play with them.

When he doesn't like his dinner, he can throw it on the floor and then rage at her while she tries to calm the children and get it cleaned up. She may argue with him about the mess he just made. However, he will skillfully blame her and degrade her in the process while the children look on, internalizing these explanations. He tells her that if she would just take more time and care, he wouldn't have to treat her this way. He tells her that she obviously doesn't care about her family because if she did, she wouldn't cook such lousy food. When this behavior is repeated over and over again, the victim may eventually internalize the controller's explanation, that it is her behavior that explains why she is treated in this fashion. Fear that he will be abusive in the same way again gradually becomes all-consuming. Note that few of these behaviors even approach criminal conduct: throwing the dinner on the floor is not against the law. Neither is verbal degradation. Suddenly, her decision making is circumscribed by fear of violating his wishes or rules or trying to conceal any thoughts or actions that might elicit punishment.

Weapons may play a role either directly because the controller uses or threatens her with a weapon or, as often, indirectly because one is available for use and she imagines the worst whenever he is angry. He may leave it on the table but forbid her to touch it, making her fear for her children's safety as well as her own. He may torture or kill her pet, or a pet may simply "disappear." Since avoiding punishment is her motive, implied threats are the most effective because she imagines the worst, a projection he feeds by remaining calm or explaining frightening events (such a gun going off or running over a pet) as "accidents." Over time, she may come to believe she no longer knows or recognizes herself, that she is no longer the person she was. A common plaint of controllers is, "Relax. What are you getting so excited about?" Keeping up appearances and excusing her partner's behavior feed the illusion that things are not as bad as they seem help her to survive.

UNDERSTANDING THE WOMAN'S RESPONSE TO THE COERCIVE CONTROL CONTEXT

In coercive control, the combination of threats and constrained options can render women helpless, even without physical assault. However when coercive control was missed, the resulting dependence was attributed to the victimized woman, masking her strength and resiliency. Society's belief in *pseudo-control* coupled with early images of black eyes and theories about battered women as dysfunctional or even pathological suggested they were helpless, pitiable souls rather than persons dealing with a pathological reality. Absent black eyes, she would never have been considered battered, at least officially. If and when she fought back, resisting her partner's control and domination, society labeled her an Amazon—particularly if she responded violently to isolation, intimidation, and control tactics—or suggested the couple was engaged in mutual combat and each gave as good as they got. As a result, assistance that reestablished her rights and freedoms was not offered and she remained entrapped. Had these same constraints on speech, movement, or access to resources been imposed at work or in any other public sphere, the pattern might quickly have been identified as a violation of basic rights to which legal redress or even violent resistance would be deemed appropriate. Because the pattern of non-violent tactics remained invisible, however, the coercive controller was not identified or held accountable.

Once we reframe our understanding of domestic violence as a dynamic pattern of coercive control, we are better able to evaluate a woman's choices and her choice of responses. If she selects "compliance," this is because this appears the best choice in the context of the constraints the coercive controller has constructed. The victim must continuously consider and attempt to predict the controller's response in every daily activity, never knowing whether he will "go off" or how he will respond if she says the wrong thing on the phone, inadvertently "stares" at another man, makes the wrong purchase, or exhibits other behavior with which he takes issue. Since avoiding pain is her aim, she must always assume the worst may happen.

When the victim does not comply with his demands, rules, or control (e.g., refusing to answer the phone when he calls for the 10th time in an hour, or refusing to have sex when he demands it) or when she fights back, he may increase his resolve and expand or intensify his coercive strategies. Although resistance may provide a modicum of dignity that she requires to stay psychologically intact, she also risks being harmed and having further constraints levied if she resists.

Over time, as a response to this type of coercion and control, the victim's "survival self" emerges and her behavior can no longer be viewed separately from the coercive control context to which it responds. So long as fear of reprisal is omnipresent, free choice is impossible. At times, behavior shaped to accommodate the coercion and constraints on her fits the "traditional" subservient female role, making her performance appear to be a slightly exaggerated version of "the good wife." At other times, accommodating his demands leads to actions that are completely opposite to her values and beliefs: she may lie to herself or others, commit a crime (e.g., murder, prostitution, child abuse, and child neglect), or, as in the duress case sketched earlier, agree to a settlement that is harmful to her own future financial stability and not in the best interest of her children. Again, however, she can appear to be criminal, crazy, or self-destructive unless these antithetical acts are traced to the duress emanating from the coercive context. In these circumstances, where victims compromise their values and beliefs, perhaps by harming others, they may come to loathe themselves.

To the outsider, the choices prompted by a woman's survival self may appear quite irrational, unethical, or self-destructive, particularly when the batterer has successfully manipulated public perceptions as well as concealed his control tactics. Physical violence may be inconsequential, decidedly infrequent and minor, or completely absent. The coercive controller need only select physical tactics when other coercive strategies do not produce the desired result.

As Evan Stark has emphasized, coercive control involves control over women's personhood, including their autonomy as adults fully entitled to make decisions in key areas of their lives (as well as in seemingly trivial arenas), to have or express opinions, or to be self-directed. Through his coercion and control, the batterer aims to impose women's culturally dictated subservient role as wife, mother, or sexual partner, facilitating the culturally endowed privileges once equated with manhood. However, coercive control does more than this, since his exploitation of her resources and the regulation of trivial aspects of daily living (such as how long she spends in the bathroom or to whom she can talk) serve a range of secondary aims, both real and symbolic.

EMERGING EMPIRICAL SUPPORT FOR COERCIVE CONTROL

For my PhD research in psychology, I set out to study which of the two models, domestic violence or coercive control, could best distinguish battered women from women who had experienced dating relationships that were difficult or hurtful.[3] Since I was testing how useful a violence-based model was in detecting abuse, I needed to identify my subjects on some basis other than their experience of violence. For this purpose, I separated the women based on the scores on their Women's Experiences of Battering (WEB) Scale, rather than on dimensions of physical violence tactics. The WEB was chosen because it reliably captures women's entrapment experiences in domestic violence relationships independent of the frequency of abusive episodes or the number of assaults. In other words, it can distinguish the profile associated with battering from other profiles regardless of whether a person has been assaulted.

My aim was to identify the factor or combination of factors best able to explain the differences between battered women (as identified by the WEB) and women in other types of difficult, hurtful relationships. In addition to asking about any physical aggression to which they had been subjected, I also asked about a range of coercive and controlling behaviors, such as threats, isolation, intimidation, and control, as well as about their own attachment style, general ways of coping, and attitudes toward women. Finally, I considered what I termed a "self-effects profile" that assessed the extent to which they had lost confidence, experienced self-doubt, and experienced a loss of rights, and the extent to which their behavior and coping response had changed to survive in the coercive context. Although I relied on earlier research to design my study, the principal impetus was the countless stories I heard from working with battered women in an urban mental health clinic and a residential domestic violence shelter program. Over and over again, these strong determined women confirmed that the physical violence was not the worst part of their experience, if it was present at all. They would tell me, in effect, that "the bruises heal with no trace but the terror lingers on along with the degrading diatribes that play over and over in my head and the realization that I was treated like a prisoner in my own home."

Their debilitation and low self-worth emanated from unique forms of degradation and devaluation as "no good" or "worthless," particularly if they were perceived to deviate from their culturally defined subservient gender role as sex partner, girlfriend/wife, and mother, or as "disloyal" because they were perceived to differ in their views or feelings from their partner, express themselves independently, or show an interest in others or in activities that fell outside their partner's sphere of need. These women were not only shut up, but also shut down, with any expressed conflict quickly quashed.

In my research, I conceptualized the effects of coercive control in terms of the subjective costs of entrapment (e.g., damaged self-identity), using a process of risk assessment. Rather than exclusively equate the self in abusive relationships with physical life and body integrity, the study included women's psychological functioning, their attribution processes, and dimensions of the experience that provided meaning and value to their physical existence. I conceived of their self-identity as constructed over time in response to the threat posed to its independent functioning by coercive control. Insofar as coercive control constrained these interactive or social aspects of the self, cutting the victim off from the outside world as a basis for reality testing and validation, the levels of fear it elicited were different from those experienced in other types of distressed dating relationships. A rational strategy of defensive coping was also expected, as a way both to manage the heightened fear excited by coercive control and to preserve a sense of her self-identity. Thus, women's aggressive acts were alternately framed as resistance to the suppression of rights and resources and as a means to reestablish self-functioning. To ward off fear and terror caused by the controller's tactics and the resulting entrapment, I hypothesized, victimized women would develop a survival self, whose dynamic I discussed earlier.

My research was also based on the belief that the meaning, motive, and outcome of events matter. At the time I conducted the study, the dominant research paradigm offered no framework to examine the nonviolent dynamics of coercive control that women repeatedly told me were most destructive. A related concern was that the focus on discrete episodes and the classification of domestic violence based on the calculus of harms identified with the tactics deployed in these episodes missed the well-known reality that serious and minor violence typically occurred in the same relationship. More important for my purposes was that women's experience reflected the cumulative effects of these multiple episodes as well as the combination of these effects with the consequences of the multiple nonviolent tactics women reported. Third, once we shifted the focus from discrete episodes of violence to multiple tactics deployed over time, a new range of harms came into view other than physical injury, exposing the serious limits of assessments or interventions predicated on the conflict tactics model of violence. These harms are summarized in the term "entrapment."

I needed a different research paradigm and new scales that took all of this into account.

Because it focused on the experiential consequences of being battered for women rather than on the tactics that elicited these consequences, the WEB scale allowed me to theorize that coercive control existed as a separate type of domestic violence and that other factors not previously identified may distinguish it from the type that involves unconnected physical tactics used in episodic abuse. I correlated women's WEB scores (as an indication of whether women showed the experiential effects of battering) with their reported histories of violence and other forms of abuse, and then compared how well these women could be identified by the Conflict Tactics Scale, the prevailing measure used in domestic violence research, with a Coercive Partner Profile (CPP) that highlighted questions about isolation, intimidation, and control, but not physical violence. The findings were dramatic. Looking at physical tactics of aggression helped distinguish a subgroup of women who evidenced high WEB scores from women in other types of difficult, hurtful relationships. But this frame missed half of the women who were identified as entrapped by the WEB scale. In other words, the dominant domestic violence model was a relatively poor way to distinguish the battered group from other groups of women in distressed relationships. Indeed, none of the correlates that were shown to be significant predictors in previous domestic violence research studies could separate the groups: not length of relationship or attachment style, not escalation or the general ways in which women coped, and not the frequency or severity of physical tactics, minor or severe, used by her or her partner. In contrast to the violence-based Conflict Tactics Scale, the CPP and the Self-Effects Profile (SEP) were able to sharply differentiate battered women from all other women in distressed relationships.

The CPP not only considered *what* the abusive partner had done, whether he had objectified and degraded her sense of self, threatened or otherwise intimidated her, and/or controlled or monitored her movement or attempts to leave, for instance, but also how much time her partner spent doing this as well as avoiding responsibility while blaming her for his abusive and controlling behavior. Importantly, the coercive pattern captured in the CPP characterized his behavior for more than two-thirds of the time they spent together in the year prior to exiting the relationship, a direct counter to the incident-specific understanding. The resulting debilitating effects on women's sense of self were profound.

The SEP assessed how women experienced intimidation, suppression of opinion, loss of self-identity, loyalty to her partner, loss of perspective on her rights and her sanity, as well as her loss of self-confidence. The women identified in this study as battered reported a significant loss of agency as independent and free beings while constructing a survival identity in its place that caused them to focus on loyalty to their partner and suppress their opinions while losing perspective on their rights and confidence in themselves. The loss of self in particular had no parallel in the reported experience by the women in the other types of distressed relationships.

Even a slight increase in the use of coercive control produced a substantial effect in the experienced loss of self. The loss of self as a free and autonomous being was powerful evidence that the subjective costs of being entrapped by a batterer's coercive control required a new calculus of harms.

My doctoral research was limited to a multicultural sample of mostly younger women in relationships, targeted the experience of heterosexual women only, and drew a convenience rather than a random sample. Thus, although I have no reason to believe my sample is atypical of battered women generally, we cannot generalize from this sample to the nature of abuse in the larger population. Despite these limits, the research illustrates the key point in this chapter, that coercive and controlling behavior in relationships has a range of devastating effects on personhood and the psychological self, that this behavior is ongoing rather than episode specific, and that it can elicit these effects independently of physical violence. Remarkably, where 29 percent of the abusive men in battering relationships use both minor and severe violence and 15 percent used only minor violence, the *majority of abusive men used no violence at all*. Clearly, to comprehend the nature of abuse in relationships, appreciate the harms it elicits, and respond appropriately, it is necessary to shift the paradigm away from an exclusive focus on physical tactics and a calculus of physical harms to the multiple tactics identified by the model of coercive control. Clearly too, the core issue is not physical acts of violence per se, but the context in which a pattern of coercion is enacted as well as the way that women experience it. Gender is not the only context in which violence or abuse occurs. However, it would appear that gender—or, more specifically, sexual differences in power expressed through gender roles—is the critical context in which battering occurs.

KELLY'S STORY: A CASE EXAMPLE OF COERCIVE CONTROL

We will recall that, in her divorce agreement, Kelly had signed over to her husband assets to which she was legally entitled as well as her rights to future earnings. The attorney informed me that Kelly's signature would be binding for the terms of the divorce unless she could prove that duress existed. One possible explanation for why Kelly had consented to this arrangement was that she suffered from a mental illness or a related personality deficit. The competing hypothesis was that contextual factors explained Kelly's experience or duress. These might include coercive control as well as factors related to religious, ethnic, and gender-related belief systems. To assess the latter hypothesis required a thorough understanding of domestic violence dynamics.

I ruled out individual factors such as the presence of psychopathology or cognitive impairment, since Kelly was neither psychotic nor developmentally disabled. I ruled out full-blown posttraumatic stress disorder since several features including flashbacks and avoidance were not present in her clinical picture. Hypervigilance was another matter. Although she was several hundred miles away from her hometown and legally separated from her husband, Kelly sat on the edge of her chair as if something threatening her safety could occur at any moment. When a loud rumbling diesel truck passed my office, she almost jumped out of her skin. I characterized that response as *real fear* rather than an exaggerated startle response or generalized anxiety or an irrational fear because the "trigger" matched the experiences Kelly detailed in her interview. Bill drove a big diesel truck just like the one that passed by, and he often followed her and snuck up on her since he could find her by using the tracking device. In my opinion to the court, I identified the psychological profile I observed, being constantly on guard and scanning the environment, as the cumulative effect of her exposure to a pattern of coercion and threats where she had to always be prepared for the next assault. Thus, hers was a normal response resulting from chronic exposure to Bill, a terrorizing and unpredictable coercive controller. This response serves a protective function though it continues long after the victim has escaped her entrapment in the relationship.

Reaching these conclusions required taking a full history of the relationship, including identification of the extensive rules imposed by the coercive controller, interviewing collateral contacts who had observed the couple's behavior, and reviewing many records that documented Kelly's experiences.

With the exception of an isolated incident 12 years earlier, Bill never really "put his hands" on Kelly during the marriage and he had never injured her physically. Although his pushing her against the car door resulted in Kelly's obtaining a domestic order of protection, Bill acted in an intimidating fashion that included minimal minor violence only *after* both agreements were signed. Kelly's attorney could not connect the high level of fear observed when she initially interviewed her to either the isolated earlier episode or the minimal abuse after the separation.

My challenge was to identify the conditions during the marriage that produced Kelly's high level of fear, and explain her choice to stay all of these years and her seemingly irrational choice to sign away her lawful assets.

COERCIVE CONTROL BEGINS

Kelly had recently graduated from college and wanted to be married in order to have a big family. She loved children. She reported no mental health problems prior to her marriage and had no family history of psychiatric illness. She had close relationships with her parents and siblings despite Bill's efforts to separate her from them. Kelly met Bill while out clubbing with friends. During their courtship, he berated Kelly's friends and demanded she spend all of her time with him. At the time, Kelly really didn't worry about this because she was in love and Bill seemed to want all of the things she wanted, including marriage and a family. Bill was tall, dark, and handsome, and everyone in her family considered him quite a catch. Although isolating Kelly from her friends was an early sign of coercive control, at the time it felt like an extension of his love. In his demand for her love, Bill framed her choice as a test of her love, identifying being with friends as a signal that she was not devoted to him, at setting off his fear that she would not stay connected to him. He posed the choice as "give them up or lose me." But there was no "fight" about this issue. He explained calmly that her friends didn't have her best interests at heart and that she needed to be with him now that they were getting married. He told her he couldn't bear being without her.

On their wedding night, Bill had too much to drink and hit Kelly. He backhanded Kelly across the face in their hotel room after she tried to remove his coat, screaming, "No one tells me what to do, especially you!" Then, he passed out. As an omen of the coercion to come, this minor incident laid the foundation for Kelly's fear throughout the marriage. She had seen a side of him that she never wanted to see again. She was afraid to confront him about it and too ashamed to tell anyone. Perhaps, she thought, the alcohol made him do it.

INCREASING ISOLATION AND SURVEILLANCE

Kelly's isolation from family and friends as potential sources of help or validation was used to keep her dependent and alone, and to keep Bill's course of conduct a secret. Bill continued to limit her contact with friends. Apart from the explicit rules he set to govern Kelly's interactions with others, he made demands regarding secrecy and on her time that made it difficult to establish close relationships. When Kelly started to befriend a babysitter early in the marriage, Bill threatened the friend, telling her to stay away from Kelly. He also forbade Kelly from coming to the softball games where he and the babysitter's husband played, explaining to her that she had too much housework to do. Three years later, Bill threatened Kelly not to talk to a different babysitter about him "or else." When Kelly dropped the children off at this babysitter's house, she pointed out to Kelly that Bill was watching from the parking lot across the street during dropoff and pickup. Bill began to interrogate Kelly about conversations she had with this babysitter and then threatened her, "You'd better not be talking about me because I will find out and you will wish you hadn't." Bill began timing Kelly's trip from work to home and would interrogate Kelly about how long it took, even if she "hurried." Bill's threats, rules for behavior, and surveillance constrained her options by making it feel too costly to engage friends. It simply wasn't worth the continued interrogation. Besides, she now had two children and a home on which to focus. Bill made efforts to isolate Kelly from her family as well. Kelly's sister reported that Bill once allowed Kelly to invite her on a family camping vacation at the beach where she watched Kelly do all of the cooking, cleaning, and child care while Bill sat back and did nothing or took off for hours at a time. She reported confronting Bill and telling him that Kelly needed him to be there for the family. As a result, she was never allowed to go with them on a family vacation again and made to feel so uncomfortable when she visited from out of town that she didn't want to visit at all.

Isolation also had another insidious effect: by limiting the breadth of Kelly's interaction with the outside world, it made her increasingly dependent on Bill's version of reality, including his insistence that his coercion and control were appropriate responses to Kelly's failings.

Approximately three years prior to the separation, Kelly met the one close friend she was able to keep. She had a car accident, and Sandy and her son came out to assist while they waited for a tow truck. Their sons befriended one another. Bill favored his oldest son and would allow him to have friends. Connections with Sandy for play dates provided Kelly a "legitimate" excuse to be around them. This friendship provided an important source of resiliency for Kelly and her oldest son, and Sandy and her husband remained friends with Kelly despite the uncomfortable feelings they had when Bill demeaned her in their presence. In similar situations, many people flee, embrace the myth of pseudo-control referred to earlier, or simply keep their distance because they believe interfering will make things worse or that a couple's problems are not their business. The coercive controller perceives this lack of confrontation as an unspoken authorization to continue his behavior, while the victim gets the message that she deserves this kind of treatment or that she is crazy to feel so fearful or upset.

Bill's surveillance extended to monitoring Kelly's movements to the store and the bank, as well as her conversations. Bill demanded continuous access to Kelly by buying her a cellular phone that he called many times a day to "check up." On occasion, Sandy would go with Kelly on errands and stay in the car with the baby while she ran inside to pay bills or pick up dry cleaning. After Kelly's phone rang endlessly one day, Sandy finally answered and told Bill to give Kelly some space to get something done. When Kelly returned to the car and Sandy told her what she said to Bill, Kelly's face went white as a ghost and her jaw dropped. That was when Sandy knew that something was "really" wrong because Kelly told her that she didn't have Bill's "permission" to drive with her in the car. Bill would rant and rage at Kelly when she resisted his control by breaking his "rules," and his rules extended to everything from her dress, to how the house should look ("perfect"), to working outside the home.

Bill also used menacing and stalking behaviors on a regular basis during the marriage and throughout the separation to keep her afraid and isolated. When Kelly did not get permission to go to a particular store (e.g., to Wal-Mart), Bill would "find" Kelly wherever she was; make menacing and contorted faces at her from his truck; scream, yell, and swear; point toward home; and tell her to "Get home NOW!" since he wanted her there doing housework. This ritual caused Kelly to constantly check her rearview mirror so that she could see him coming, particularly if she was at a place he had not authorized, and prepare the children by saying, "Get ready, here comes daddy the terrorist." From the insider's vantage, this parenting strategy appears to be a creative way to manage the coercive controller's efforts to surprise and frighten her and the children. Even the label "terrorist" both exaggerates the threat he poses in a somewhat humorous way and captures the discomfort of never being truly alone that she and the children share. To an outsider with no knowledge of the coercive context, however, she might easily appear to be a parent alienator set out to turn the children against their "loving" dad.

DEGRADATION

People often envision emotional abuse as name-calling during an argument. The pattern of emotional abuse in coercive control includes chronic insults, but extends to humiliation and degradation in public and private. Moreover, because accompanying threats or other forms of coercion make it dangerous for a partner to simply walk away or respond to insults in kind, even name-calling can be much more damaging in the context of coercive control. Bill engaged in regular diatribes directed toward Kelly's speech and at her identity as wife, mother, housekeeper, and woman. She was verbally attacked and demeaned about her appearance, particularly her weight; the way she dressed; the way she managed money; the way she kept house; the friends she had; and the jobs and hobbies she pursued. Bill humiliated Kelly by criticizing her in the home, when they were with friends or family members, at parties, at church, and on vacations.

In the home and in front of the children, Bill called Kelly fat, ugly, bitch, whore, slut, fucking bitch, and asshole. What made this so egregious was that he regularly involved the children in the degradation. For example, he would sing songs with them about their mother's weight (e.g., "She's so fat, she slipped on dog poop and broke her back"). The children would laugh because of the words "dog poop." One repeated form of degradation was that Bill took the children out for dinner while leaving Kelly at home, announcing that she was "too fat" and that she needed to stay home to diet. Kelly's oldest son told me he would beg his father to order something for his mother, but that his father would only allow the children to scrape what was left on their plates at the end of the meal into a doggie bag. Over time, the children began to stop eating their entire meal in order to bring their Mom a larger uneaten portion rather than their scraps.

This situation illustrates how coercive control extends to the children. They adapted to Bill's degradation of their mother by repressing their anger and rage at their father and compensating for their mother's deprivation by saving her food. However, they also felt shame for treating their mother like a dog. There were no bruises, no broken bones, and no imminent danger of a child being killed. Yet my interview with the oldest son suggested that the memory in the children's minds remains fresh about the type of values that they learned with respect to treating women in general and a partner specifically. This internalized thought process increases the probability of their being victimized in later life if they identify with their mom or of becoming a perpetrator if they identify with their dad. There may be also less obvious lessons learned from the mode of accommodating their father's abuse of their mother, such as "making do" rather than confronting a perpetrator.

Both the singing example and the restaurant ritual illustrate child abuse as tangential spouse abuse, where the abuser uses the children as instruments of his coercion and control of their mother. Caught in the middle of his abuse, the children tried to take care of their mother (by saving her food) and to simultaneously placate their father (by scraping food into the doggie bag). While the food-saving strategy might be thought about as a form of resistance to their father's abuse, what has been termed "control in the context of no control," it also placed the children in the untenable position of treating their mother like a dog, forcing them to collude in their mother's degradation. When the family returned, the doggie bag of scraps was thrown on the table, and Bill would say, "Here, we brought you something." Adding insult to injury, this degrading and humiliating display occurred in front of the housekeeper, who reported that when she witnessed the children bringing the doggie bag, she told Kelly she would break her arm if she dared to eat it, perhaps not the most sensitive way to express support. At the same time, the housekeeper was able to bear witness and so lend credibility to Kelly's claims. Unfortunately, little of this came out in the divorce case, where, absent physical injury or a criminal case against the controller, custody evaluators rarely assess for abuse, usually lack training or knowledge to assess for coercive control even when they do, and rarely interview potential witnesses outside the immediate family. When I asked Kelly if she had talked about this experience with the evaluator, she quietly replied, "I was never asked." Public humiliation often occurred whenever Kelly threw a party. Kelly's friend Sandy described how Kelly would go to great lengths to decorate and prepare food for the guests and recalled that Bill criticized her in front of everyone by saying loudly, "Look at all of the grease on this food. You ruined it." In response to criticism, humiliation, and degradation, Kelly felt incompetent, stupid, and weak. In addition, Bill blamed her for every problem, including those over which she had not even minimal control. The housekeeper witnessed Bill screaming at Kelly about the tidiness of the house (e.g., magazines, toys, and clothes not put away, etc.). As in the film *Sleeping with the Enemy*, Bill had a rule that everything had to be in its place. The problem was there were not enough dressers to put all of the children's clothes away because Bill used much of their space for his own clothes. Bill gave Kelly permission to buy a new dresser, then screamed at and berated her for choosing the wrong one, though he never communicated what dresser he thought was the right one. Thus, complying with his wishes was no guarantee that Kelly would escape his verbal assaults. The experience of being fearful, but never knowing how to placate Bill, was debilitating.

PSEUDO-CONTROL

Bill's pattern of blaming Kelly when things went wrong actually increased her risk by feeding her belief that she could control things that were never within her control, an example of *pseudo-control*. While pseudo-control is a survival strategy used to ward off feelings of utter powerlessness, it increased Kelly's dependence on Bill and, indirectly, further eroded her sense of self. Kelly was held responsible for Bill's verbal attacks because she had broken his rules. Bill had a rule that she should be thin, for example, and that she could avoid attacks (hence control *his* behavior) by complying. Since she was pregnant and/or lactating eight out of twelve years of their marriage, however, it was impossible for her to keep her premarriage figure. Kelly recalled that after her second son's birth, Bill didn't kiss or hug her. If Kelly attempted to hug Bill, he would tell her not to crush him, referring to her "excessive" weight. Thus, Bill's withdrawal of affection was reframed as Kelly's failure to obey Bill's rule. In response to Bill's perceptions, Kelly felt depressed, fat, abandoned, worthless, and a failure. Still, she worked hard at improving herself. Kelly believed she had the ability to reduce Bill's degrading statements by getting thin. She tried to be the perfect mother, kept up the house the way Bill liked it, and vowed to get herself back in shape. Upon losing weight, Bill and Kelly attended a wedding. Instead of complimenting her on her weight loss, Bill publicly humiliated Kelly in front of a group of his friends by saying, "What are you doing prancing around like a doe in heat?" In an effort to look nice for Bill, Kelly bought a new dress. However, he not only refused to dance with her but also shoved her into the bride's uncle, who had Down's syndrome, saying for all to hear, "Why don't you dance with my wife? No one else will." Kelly felt demeaned, ashamed, and confused at the way Bill treated her, convinced she could do nothing right. While Kelly was abused whether she capitulated with Bill's demands or refused, her diminished sense of self made the imagined risks associated with resistance unbearable. After all, resisting his domination by simply being her "natural" weight meant an even greater predictable level of degradation.

Sexual degradation can be the most devastating form. Bill frequently pressured Kelly to have sex in a way she did not like or want. Once in bed, Bill would only enter Kelly from behind after grabbing her breasts, thereby avoiding her face and her kiss. Again, the choice she faced was compliance or his hostility, in this instance expressed by his withdrawal from sexual affection. Kelly reported that Bill did not embrace her affectionately for almost eight years prior to the separation. If she initiated physical contact, he pulled away; yet he expected Kelly to accept on demand his sexual advances with no foreplay. The only time he willingly hugged her that she could recall was after she signed the first separation agreement depriving herself of her share of the marital assets. In response, Kelly felt humiliated, demeaned, and unloved. She was nothing more than a sex object for Bill's sexual gratification: no eye contact, no warmth, and no tenderness.

INCREASING THE DEPRIVATION, CONTROLLING ACCESS TO MONEY, AND "THE CAN"

At one point early in the marriage, Kelly tried to work outside of the home to bring in some extra money. Other women in my practice have used outside work to get "pin" money for themselves or the children, replace funds denied or appropriated by their husbands, or plan an escape. Bill made Kelly's effort to work outside the home unbearable by timing her to and from work, neglecting the children at home while she was away, and interrogating her about conversations or relationships at work. He needed no physical violence to obstruct her access to an independent income or her development of a work history that might translate into future employment. For example, Kelly found a house with a freestanding income-producing garage/ apartment that could defray the cost of the mortgage. She also took a job at a bedding store to help bring in some money. Kelly would rush home on her dinner break to make dinner for the family since Bill was in charge of the children while she was out. However, Bill refused to clean up after the dinner. Kelly would come home to a table full of dirty dishes, at least one toddler in a dirty diaper, nobody bathed or dressed for bed, and Bill asleep on the sofa. Again, Kelly faced a devil's choice. She could go without access to money while providing nurturing care for her children at home. Or, she could keep her job, get a little money, but watch her children neglected and endure regular interrogations about the imagined affairs she was having at work and the imaginary places she went while she was gone. That she would choose her children's welfare was a foregone conclusion.

To an outsider, both Kelly's decision to work and her decision to quit work might be explained by referencing traditional gender roles, the first as a rejection of her "proper" role as mother and the second as an example of her realization that her children and husband were the most important people in her life. Neither account would include the critical factors in her decision making, however: Bill's coercive behavior; his use of the children to control her; his manipulation of gender stereotypes to ground his demands that she stay home to cook, clean, care for the children, and provide sex on demand; and his belief that changing diapers, doing dishes, or cleaning up after the children was "women's work" in which he should play no part.

These stereotypes were incompatible with Kelly having access to an independent income, autonomous decision making, and a network of potentially supportive relationships. In other words, viewing Kelly as a traditional woman masked the constrained context in which she tried to "escape" to work or returned home. It was not work per se that Bill rejected for Kelly. Once she was back home, he enlisted her in working on building his home business, exploiting her social as well as her domestic labor for his own gain. Not only could he maintain much tighter control over her behavior at home, but also he benefited from having a captive but capable employee to whom he paid next to nothing.

Kelly's access to money was further constrained as Bill's coercion and control escalated.

Bill kept a can in their freezer containing money from the rent receipts on the apartment over their garage. He told Kelly that she was allowed to use this money for household expenditures and the children's' needs. Three years before the separation, he decided he no longer needed her in his business and cut her off completely from the business and personal bank accounts. At that time, Kelly recalled sewing the children's Halloween costumes and preparing for an annual Halloween party she held at the cabin. Bill began picking at her and telling her that she had no time for arts and crafts because there was cleaning she should be doing. Out of the blue, Bill demanded to see the checkbook. Kelly broke out in a cold sweat because she sensed he was about to engage in a raging diatribe about some displeasure she had caused him. After examining each entry, Bill shook his head, the common prelude to his demeaning her. Bill interrogated Kelly about each entry, date, amount, and exact list of goods purchased. He harangued her all day, making it impossible to finish the costumes. On Halloween, he announced, "That's it, I'm taking the checkbook; if you want to buy something like fabric, you need to ask." He also demanded that she account for the expenditures (i.e., diapers, groceries, children's shoes, and haircuts) she made using money from "the can" in the freezer. The interrogations about money became a ritual. Out of nowhere, he would decide it was time for an accounting and he'd yell, "Get the can!" Immediately, Kelly's heart would start to race and a feeling of dread would overcome her. She felt terrorized and debilitated, though he had never hurt her physically.

The interrogations about money were not an exchange between partners or even a fight about spending. They were unidirectional assaults on a field where one party had been systematically deprived of the equal footing she merited simply by virtue of being an autonomous adult. This was illustrated by the double standard at work: in contrast to Kelly, who required prior approval to take money, Bill was allowed to go into the can for whatever he wanted. Bill also forbade her to go to the mailbox, and told her that all mail had to go through him. She was forbidden to answer any more business calls or be involved in the business transactions. Bill also took all of the credit cards since they were in the name of the business. He also changed the ownership of Kelly's van to the business without Kelly's knowledge. Kelly thought about leaving Bill. But she had no idea how she would support three children and a household. To complicate the issue further, Kelly was pregnant again.

Needless to say, by depriving Kelly of money, Bill reinforced her complete financial dependence on him. Because she needed money to conduct the normal business of the household and provide for the children, asking for money was no more of a choice than leaving work had been. So she had no choice but to endure the verbal attacks that accompanied each request. On one occasion, the housekeeper witnessed Bill interrogate Kelly about her expenditures from the can. She was fully aware that Kelly had to record every expenditure on a piece of paper and keep it in the can for inspections. She also observed Bill take money without recording it and then ask Kelly where the money had gone, the kind of "gaslight" game that makes many battered women feel crazy. Since Kelly had not taken the money, she was at a loss in the interrogations, seemingly justifying his outbursts. In the face of the barrage of criticism, Kelly would insist she had dutifully recorded her expenditures. But this would rarely suffice. The housekeeper told me that even if the money was spent on diapers, "Bill would have a raging fit." In order to further frustrate and destabilize her, Bill set time limits on Kelly's shopping, making it impossible to get everything she needed in one trip. Not wanting to justify another trip and fearing the consequence of explaining why they were short, Kelly began to "sneak" to the store, making her feel scattered much of the time.

Occasionally, Bill would be nice, offering indulgences, like allowing Kelly to go out for a drink with her friend while on a vacation in the camper, or when he gave her diamond earrings one New Year's Eve. These occasional indulgences provided positive motivation for complying with Bill's rules and hindered Kelly's adjustment to deprivation. She loved their home and she loved her children and believed that if she just tried harder, love would prevail. She prayed he would change.

HIS PRIVILEGE TO MAKE THE RULES, RULES, RULES

Male privilege, as a driving force behind coercive control, includes the entitlement many men feel to be cared for and to have their needs, wishes, and desires put before those of their wife or children. Controllers take the belief in privilege one step further, setting down rules for how their demands and needs are to be met by their partner and monitoring her performance.

Moreover, privileges are the exclusive preserve of the man. Bill vacationed regularly without Kelly and the children throughout the marriage, but never offered her a similar luxury. He kept a large pleasure boat docked in another state that he regularly visited on weekends without Kelly or the children. Bill repeatedly ignored the needs of his family and retreated to his boat, even on occasions when Kelly or the children were ill and required his assistance. He did this once when Kelly was hemorrhaging from childbirth complications, once when she was caring for two of the children with croup, and once when she was too sick herself with the flu to care for the children alone. His departures often left her penniless: after he took her credit cards and checkbook, he would make sure the can was empty when he left, ensuring she would be unable to go anywhere or to obtain medicine. On several occasions, Sandy's husband silently watched Bill ordering Kelly around like a slave (e.g., change diapers, solve children's spats, and clean the basement) while he sat immobile on his chair shouting, "NOW!" Sandy's husband was fearful that if he confronted Bill, Sandy and their son would be forbidden to maintain their friendship with Kelly and her son. To this extent, the friends were confronted by the same constraints faced by Kelly: to say nothing and maintain a friendship while Kelly went downhill or to speak up and risk even further isolation for Kelly. Sandy's husband withdrew from the relationship, refusing to do any additional work for Bill, and stayed away whenever Bill was around. Bill devalued Sandy's husband and labeled him weak. Ironically, Bill's frequent exploitation of his privilege by leaving town whenever he wished merely strengthened Sandy's friendship with Kelly, reducing her isolation even when Bill was home.

INTIMIDATION AND RAGE AS ROUTINE

Bill used various forms of intimidation to maintain fear and control over Kelly's behavior throughout the marriage. Early in the marriage, Bill reminded Kelly that he could beat her, physically, if he wanted. Kelly recalled that on New Year's Eve, Kelly questioned Bill as to why he wouldn't kiss her after the ball dropped, and he told her, "You don't have it so bad; a lot of guys beat their wives. I could have beaten you and never did." Kelly felt afraid and trapped, believing she would just have to take him the way he was and be grateful he wasn't physically beating her. She also remembered the wedding night and knew that if she crossed him he could physically overpower and beat her if he chose to do so. Bill also recounted a history of bar fights in which he'd been victorious and confessed to beating up his brothers to control them. One sadistic form of intimidation used by Bill included killing Kelly's pet golden retriever puppy and then leaving it on the driveway for her to bury. This occurred approximately two years prior to the separation, when Kelly had planned a surprise birthday party after church at Safari World for her oldest son. Kelly took the children to the church where she taught Sunday school. Bill arrived at church and leaned over to callously whisper in Kelly's ear, "I ran over your dog. It's in the driveway; you might want to move it before the kids come home." This horrified Kelly. She reasoned that if Bill could hurt an innocent animal like the family puppy, he could also do this to her. When she tried to protect the children from this information, Bill took off with his oldest son. Kelly asked someone at church to watch the other three children, rushed home, and saw the puppy dead in the driveway. She quickly hid her dog in a box in the barn and returned to church to pick up her three children and get the balloons and a cake. Because they had to wait for the cake, they arrived at Safari World later than she planned. When they arrived, Bill went into a rage, screaming at Kelly, "What kind of mother are you, late for your own son's birthday party! What is your problem?" Bill knew Kelly would "choose" to stay silent. Bill gave Kelly the silent treatment for the next two days before leaving for Kentucky for a week on vacation without the family. Sandy's husband came over to bury the dog while Kelly sobbed in mourning for her pet. Unable to tell the children the truth about how the dog died, she told them a stranger ran over the dog. Kelly hated lying. However, she was more fearful of how Bill would react if she revealed the truth.

THE COERCIVE CONTROLLER ESCALATES HIS COURSE OF CONDUCT

One of the most terrorizing experiences with Bill occurred approximately one year prior to the separation. Bill arranged for the housekeeper to watch the children so that Kelly could drop him off to hunt. He loaded his gun and got into her car. When he demanded she drive him, Kelly felt a chill since this was a complete departure from Bill's usual routine of getting a ride or taking his truck when he hunted. Kelly agreed to drive to avoid an outburst. She thought it strange when Bill stood the hunting rifle in his hand next to her in the car as she drove him deeper into the woods under his direction. Kelly was shaking with fear. She could see him staring at her out of the corner of her eye. Kelly pulled her van up into a densely wooded area at the top of the hill where she saw a black cargo type van with blacked-out windows parked. Bill told Kelly to pull up over near the van. She refused, saying she would drop him off right where they were. Kelly tried not to show fear, but it must have been evident based on Bill's response.

'Do you think I hired a hit man to kill you?' he asked sarcastically. Kelly felt horrified, her mouth went dry, and she couldn't speak. Bill just laughed, looked at Kelly, and with a smirk said, "Keep your head down—you're not wearing orange." Kelly took that threat to mean that he or someone he hired could easily shoot her since she was in the hunting zone without the proper identifying colors and her murder would be deemed an accident. Kelly was so terrified that she has no memory of driving down the mountain. Where I come from, hunters put their unloaded guns in the rack behind them or in the trunk. An outsider might think this was a harmless incident to which Kelly overreacted. More likely, Bill knew exactly what he was doing when he alluded to a feasible, workable plan to kill her.

Several months prior to the separation, Bill gave permission for Kelly to take Sandy to get her car repaired because he needed her to run an errand. Kelly explained it might take them some time because they had to get money and there would be a Friday bank line. Bill arrived home first and sent the housekeeper home. When Kelly returned, he exploded because she had taken too long. She had broken his rule. He screamed, "I'm sick of your shit," then pounded his fist on the table and stormed out of the house, returning only much later in the afternoon. But his anger had not subsided. He backed the pickup truck under the second floor balcony and entered the house, raging, "I'm sick of you and all of your shit!" Bill went to the children's rooms and started throwing toy boxes and clothes off the balcony into his truck below. The children were running around, frantically hiding their precious belongings. Bill took his four-year-old son's play kitchen and threw the entire unit off the balcony into the truck below. Bill threw Kelly's sewing machine and her fabric off the balcony. Kelly was terrified, her heart was pounding, and she felt sick. She tried to calm the children. Kelly tried to confront Bill and told him he was scaring the children. He glared at Kelly using a menacing facial gesture and left, having never touched her or the children. Bill returned later, minimizing his behavior by explaining to the children he was "just cleaning up." He then made arrangements for the two older boys to stay with friends and left with the two younger children. Bill had never taken the children alone away from the house before. Kelly felt intimidated and punished for breaking Bill's rules: taking longer than he wanted her to return from the bank and not being there for him when he returned. When Bill returned later that evening, he gave Kelly the silent treatment. This lasted for two days. He then blamed Kelly for his rage, saying, "If you wouldn't have run off with Sandy, I wouldn't have gotten so pissed off with you." Bill extended his punishment by imposing an in-house separation from Kelly, locking her out of the bedroom so she had to sleep on the sofa. Kelly called Bill's father for help, but he didn't seem too concerned. All he said was "Yes, but did he put his hands on you?" Kelly felt terrorized and completely trapped.

SEPARATION

Kelly never contemplated divorcing Bill because she was too fearful of his reaction and of how she would support herself and the children. So it was Bill who decided to initiate a divorce, a move she mistook for yet another control tactic. He used a variety of tactics to coerce her to sign the first of two separation agreements, including misrepresentation, intimidation and threats, and moral coercion. He told her not to discuss the settlement with her mother, implying it would give her a heart attack. When Bill gave Kelly the 27-page separation agreement with 127 pages of attachments, he offered a $1,000 incentive if she signed quickly. Kelly felt nervous about signing the papers because she had registered for school for the first time in 20 years. She felt that something wasn't right. So she decided to secretly ask an attorney to look at the papers. Two weeks later, Bill told her sign the agreement when she returned from school that day. Kelly noted that Bill became very angry and irritated when she did not do what he told her within his timeframe. Kelly's fear began to mount.

Kelly's first attorney focused on the monetary portion of the agreement and identified the assets as undervalued. She advised Kelly that the agreement was "crazy and not to sign it." Although the attorney did not tell Kelly about her options for a different custody arrangement or her entitlement to a protection order from harassment and abuse, Kelly left the attorney's office determined not to sign. She returned home with the unsigned papers and Bill became very irate, again telling her that he had given her time. Kelly could feel the tension building as it had so many times before. Her mind was telling her not to sign, but as her fears of what he might do mounted, she became more terrified of not signing than agreeing to something that would hurt her financially.

The next morning, Bill was still furious, demanding that she give a reason for not signing. Although she felt threatened, she tried to stall by telling him she still needed more time. Seething with rage, he yelled, "I gave you time!" Then Bill offered Kelly money if she would sign, knowing that she needed money to go back to school. Kelly resisted and Bill shook his head in disapproval as he had done so often in the past before launching into a tirade of demeaning slurs.

He told her he needed to move on and that she was just making things worse for herself. When Kelly asked how she was making things worse, Bill exploded. In what seemed like an instant, he gathered the children on the porch and without any warning, announced that they were divorcing.

Bill glared at her with his intimidating look while Kelly stood in shock that he'd broken this news without any preparation or warning. The second oldest started to cry. Bill put his arm around him and asked Kelly, "Do you have anything to add?" Kelly said, "No," fearful of what Bill would do if she contradicted him. Then, Bill suggested she was not empathic to her son's emotions: "How can you just stand there and not even comfort your own child?" Kelly realized that it didn't matter who Bill hurt as long as he got his way. She could not bear to see the children suffer or to imagine what he might do if she did not sign. So she capitulated, signing an agreement that she would get the house, carriage apartment, and a portion of the business and that he would move out. After she signed, he told her he didn't have the $1,000 for her school he had promised. As before, Kelly believed that her concession would at least free her from Bill's physical intimidation.

But one week later, Bill was still in the house. Bill began staying up all night, alternately pacing the floor and standing over her bed. Kelly was too afraid to sleep, though she pretended to be asleep when he was staring down at her. She moved to the sofa, sleeping there with their two-year-old daughter, believing she was safe because Bill would not hurt or kill her with the child present.

One evening, Bill got his guns out from under their bed and the gun cabinet. He rattled the cabinet loudly as he did this, so his action was unmistakable, and carried the guns outside near the sofa where she feigned sleep. He came back inside, stood over Kelly on the couch and ordered her outside (4:00 a.m.) on the porch swing. Kelly thought that he was going to kill her. She was terrified. She believed he wanted revenge for all the misdeeds for which he held her responsible and that this could involve killing her, hurting her, or financially ruining her and the children. She looked outside on the porch for the guns. He yelled, "I can't believe you can sleep at a time when we are going through this." Kelly's heart was racing, but she followed his instructions because she didn't want her daughter to see him hurt her. She felt sick to her stomach. Her arms and legs were numb, almost paralyzed, as she walked outside. Bill started a degrading diatribe, red-faced: "How can you live with yourself after you've done this to your family? After all I've done, how could you be so ungrateful? After I let you sit in this house and let you watch those kids and gave you everything?" She started to reply, but Bill silenced her. "I don't want to hear a word from you," he said, "I'm not through with you yet." Kelly recalled little of what he said next. The next thing she remembered was that Bill left and she went into the bathroom and threw up. She thought this was the way she would die, even if she had escaped this time. Two days later, Bill admitted to Kelly that he would awaken in a rage, go looking for her to discharge his anger, feel better when he had, and that, then, "it" starts again. The similarity of his description of himself and the guns he owned was chilling. Bill told Kelly that he loved her and asked her for a hug. Kelly felt confused by his confession and his gesture. Bill was being nice?

He agreed to take three of the four children to his mother's so that Kelly could take their eldest son camping nearby because it was his wish to spend some special time with his mom before school started. Kelly wasn't sure of what to make of Bill's indulgence. She wanted to spend time with their son because this was a request he made specifically to be with her. Kelly didn't trust Bill's "nice" behavior. Two days into the camping trip at the crack of dawn, Kelly heard Bill's diesel pickup truck come barreling toward the camper, reawakening the fears she had felt on the porch.

Bill jumped out of the truck in a full-blown rage. His face was red and contorted, and the veins were bulging in his neck as he screamed,

"You are so busted!" Bill headed straight for Kelly's vehicle and forcefully began ripping out the engine wires. Kelly was terrified. The 11-year-old child heard his Dad screaming at his mom and he told me it wasn't the first time he'd seen his father in a rage. The child reported feeling both confused and afraid. Bill screamed at Kelly and threatened her. "I found out everything! You are going to lose the kids and your house, and all you might be able to live in is this camper when I am through with you!" Bill ordered the child into his truck. He barreled away, leaving Kelly, crying. Then, he turned around and drove back toward her. She was terrified. He jumped out of his truck, walked to her vehicle, and reattached the wires. Bill told Kelly, "I don't give a shit what happens to you!"

Three days later Bill moved out of the marital residence and into his mother's home. During the next two weeks, he alternated between terrorizing Kelly and complying with her requests to help with the children. On a daily basis, he would storm into the house without knocking like he still lived there and drive up and down the driveway, revving his engine while peering in the kitchen window, glaring at her with his intimidating "look." If Kelly was on the phone, he would shake his head and grimace. Kelly felt vulnerable, afraid, and debilitated. When he was nearby, he would call the house repeatedly, demanding personal property that had been assigned to her in the initial separation agreement.

When Kelly approached her attorney with the agreement, he told her she would be "crazy" to sign away her assets. However, to her, surviving by complying with his demands seemed the least dangerous way to survive the fear, entrapment, and debilitation she felt. While the myth of pseudo-control reinforced the belief that complying would end his abuse, the alternative, to confront his continual rage, seemed unendurable, particularly in combination with her objective situation–four children, no money, no job, and continued life with a husband who knew how to demean, deprive, and terrorize her and her children.

Kelly believed Bill when he told her he would move on and felt very afraid when he said she was the one holding him back. While his promise of money for her school was an added bonus of signing, the financial situation that framed her poverty was the direct by-product of his coercive control. While her first attorney gave sensible advice—not to sign—she did so without appreciating that, without some insulation from Bill, this was not an option. Indeed, by suggesting Kelly was crazy rather than empathizing with the dangerous and irrational reality with which she had to cope and offering no remedies, such as a protective order, the attorney actually reinforced Bill's message rather than steeled her courage and fed the myth of pseudo-control to which Kelly clung for survival. Bill too told her she was crazy.

Most people think coercion and control end with separation, but it does not. Several days before the second agreement was signed, Bill held Kelly in hostage-like conditions in his mother's basement using the sick children as a lure. It benefited him to have her come to the house to care for the sick children so his sleep would not be interrupted. The conditions of coercion and abuse in the basement mimicked the conditions she endured in her marriage. Bill offered her scraps off his half-eaten plate like she was an animal and humiliated her by forcing her to sleep on the basement floor with the two sick children while he slept upstairs on a comfortable bed with the two healthy children. He continued to harass, berate, and control her, timing her going and coming for instance while yelling when she did not arrive exactly on his schedule. He prohibited her from going into certain parts of the home, and repeatedly blamed her for destroying their marriage, all with the children present. He made statements indicating that he could hear what she was saying on the phone in her own home, behavior referred to in the advocacy literature as "demonstrating omnipotence." While his claims might appear absurd to an outsider, to Kelly, given his unrestricted access to her life and her isolation from supports, the idea that he knew what she was saying and doing while alone seemed credible. Two weeks later, Bill again shamed and threatened Kelly should she go against his newly devised separation agreement. Bill dictated to Kelly what she would do at an appointment he set with his attorney: sign over the alimony and remaining assets or else experience more of his wrath including a long court battle and his efforts to obtain sole custody. Bill called Kelly every day to ensure she was coming to his attorney's office and to make her recite her promise to sign.

Throughout this process, Kelly calculated her risk of harm from Bill daily and sometimes from moment to moment, when he was close enough or had access to a weapon. Kelly chose her actions based on the information she had in the moment, including her gut feelings about the level of fear she faced, and the lessons she had learned from how Bill had responded to her behavior in the past, a process of prediction in which battered women have a unique expertise or heightened reasonableness. Kelly was unaware of her legal remedies. When she met with his attorney, Bill paced back and forth outside the conference room, placing himself where he could still catch her eye, sending chills up her spine. Kelly capitulated because this seemed the safest option in that moment, particularly given Bill's predictable response if she refused to sign. Kelly bolted as soon as she signed, feeling weak, powerless, and unable to effectively resist Bill's control. Perhaps it is not surprising that her first attorney and Bill's lawyer, like the crisis worker at the counseling center, effectively colluded in her entrapment by mistaking what they saw as her naturally deferential and passive personality. Armed with even minimal knowledge of coercive control, they could have asked and learned why this otherwise intelligent, assertive, and competent woman was acting in ways that undermined her future and that of her children.

CONCLUSION

Like the domestic violence field generally, Kelly's husband Bill equated abuse with physical violence and injury. However, the mantra that followed from this equation, "After all, I didn't hit you," was small comfort to Kelly, though it confused her for a time, convincing her she should count her blessings. Taking violence as a common denominator for abuse allowed the helpers whom she encountered (e.g., counselors, mediators, judges, lawyers, police, clergy, custody evaluators, and so on) to unknowingly collude with Bill's pattern of coercive power and control while simultaneously masking the significance of his nonviolent deprivation of her rights and resources. Kelly's entrapment, like the entrapment experienced by millions like her, was the by-product of this institutional collusion as well as of Bill's coercive and controlling behavior.

Bill never used physical violence with Kelly because he could get what he needed to preserve his privileges though nonviolent forms of coercion and control. Bill's coercive control was mediated by cultural prescripts that saw nothing strange about a competent, fully able woman withdrawing from school, giving up credit cards, being ordered around like a slave during her daily rounds of housework, becoming ever more impoverished psychologically, and then signing a divorce agreement that denied her the range of family assets to which she was entitled. No one asked any questions about why her personhood seemed so damaged since much of this was merely a somewhat exaggerated enactment of what women were supposed to be or do. If anything, outsiders reinforced the myth of pseudo-control, that Kelly was the one who had "chosen" the life she was leading and so she should be the one to get out of it. Bill was nowhere in this picture.

I hope that this chapter makes it clear that physical violence, and particularly injurious physical violence, is merely one of many tactics coercive controllers deploy to subordinate their partners, and injury is only one of many possible outcomes they elicit. As salient as injury are the deprivations of such basic rights as the right to move freely and engage in autonomous decision making or contribute to society in ways she deems valuable through paid employment. This is why, alongside Evan Stark, I consider coercive control a crime against women's liberty and autonomy, not merely their physical or psychological being.

NOTES

1. Evan Stark, *Coercive Control* (New York: Oxford University Press, 2007).

2. Michael P. Johnson, "Patriarchal Terrorism and Common Couple Violence: Two Forms of Violence against Women," *Journal of Marriage and the Family* 57 (1995): 283–94.

3. Cynthia Wilcox Lischick, "Coping and Related Characteristics Delineating Battered Women's Experiences in Self-Defined, Difficult/Hurtful Dating Relationships: A Multicultural Study," PhD diss., Rutgers University, 1999.

Index

abuse, VAWA definition, 99
abusive parent, impact on child, 80. *See also* intimate partner violence; violent parents
accountability for violence, 1, 6, 16, 46, 48, 63, 68, 93, 168, 186–87
Administration for Children's Services (ACS), 13
adolescent romantic relationships, 27, 28, 29, 30, 31, 34, 35
Adoption and Children Act 2002, 133, 136
Adoption and Safe Families Act, 20
Advocacy for Women and Kids in Emergencies (AWAKE), 17–18
advocates: for battered women, 1, 6, 11, 14–15, 17; for fathers' right, 179–74, 175, 181, 183, 184–85; for parent alienation, 156–57
agencies, 75; child protection agencies, 128; child welfare agencies, 11, 13; collaboration, 18–19
aggressive protection of children, 129
alienation. *See* parental aleination syndrome
American Coalition for Fathers and Children, 169
American Psychological Association (APA), 177, 179
Annie E. Casey Foundation, 16
antisocial behavior and genes, 32–33

Appeal Court, 142–43
attachment theory, 4, 27–30; insecure attachment, 28–30
attitudes, 27, 33–34, 91

battered men, 97, 105. *See also* fathers' right movement
battered mother's dilemma, 95–98, 113–15
battered women, 85–86, 202
Battered Women's Testimony Project, 97
batterers: attitude toward change, 69, 89–93; awareness, 90–93; bond between children and, 84–86; toward childbirth, 70–72; child abuse, 9; control over partner's fertility, 70–71; culutral impact, 71–72; double standards, 87–89; equality before the law, 86–87; interventions, 69–70; toward newborn and toddlers, 72–75; as parents, dilemmas and decisions, 82–84; toward school-age children, 75–80; toward teenagers, 80–82; using children as weapon against survivors, 71. *See also* perpetrator; violent parent
battering, 69, 70, 78, 86, 103, 105, 123, 183, 196, 202, 205
behavioral genetics, 32–33, 37; biological basis for antisocial behavior,

About the Editors and Contributors

Evan Stark is a professor at the Rutgers School of Public Affairs and Administration, Rutgers University–Newark; the Department of Women and Gender Studies, Rutgers University-New Brunswick; and the University of Medicine and Dentistry School of Public Health, where he chairs the Department of Urban Health Administration. His most recent book is *Coercive Control: How Men Entrap Women in Personal Life* (Oxford University Press, 2007).

Eve S. Buzawa is a professor and the chairperson of the Department of Criminal Justice at the University of Massachusetts–Lowell. She is the co-author of the best-selling *Domestic Violence: The Criminal Justice Response* (Sage, 2003) among other works.

Alison C. Cares is an assistant professor in the Department of Criminal Justice and Criminology at the University of Massachusetts–Lowell. Her primary research interests are intimate partner violence, the social-psychological impacts of victimization, and evaluating the impact of criminal justice policies. She is currently completing work on a grant studying intimate partner violence for Holocaust survivors in a large urban community and a project assessing crime, victimization, and services on a university campus.

Joan Dawson is a freelance editor and journalist who writes about health, human rights, and travel. She holds a master's degree in public health from Johns Hopkins University.

Marianne Hester (MA, Oxon; PhD, Leeds) is professor of gender, violence, and international policy and codirector of the Violence Against

Women Research Group in the School for Policy Studies, University of Bristol. She has directed groundbreaking research on many aspects of violence, abuse, and gender relations, including recent work on children and domestic violence, domestic violence perpetrators, abuse in same-sex relationships, and sexual exploitation. Much of her research is comparative, focusing on the United Kingdom, China, and Scandinavia.

Cynthia Wilcox Lischick is a cognitive developmental psychologist who has worked on behalf of battered women and their children as a director, service provider, researcher, forensic expert, trainer, and consultant for two decades. She received her PhD from Rutgers University, where she holds various adjunct faculty appointments; and served on the staff of the New Jersey Coalition for Battered Women.

David Mandel, MA, LPC, is the statewide service administrator for the Domestic Violence Consultation Initiative at Connecticut's Department of Children and Families. An expert in batterer accountability and change, he consults nationally to child welfare and other agencies on the Safe and Together model for intervening in domestic violence cases where children are involved.

Joan S. Meier is a professor of clinical law at the George Washington University Law School, where she founded two nationally recognized interdisciplinary domestic violence clinical programs. In 2003, she founded the Domestic Violence Legal Empowerment and Appeals Project (DVLEAP), whose mission is to provide legal advocacy for abuse survivors at the appellate level by conducting appellate litigation, national trainings, ongoing consultations, and judicial and legal education.

Judy L. Postmus, PhD, ACSW, is an assistant professor at the Rutgers University School of Social Work and director of the school's Center on Violence against Women and Children. She came to Rutgers after 20 years of social work practice with families in crisis in Florida, serving as executive director in a domestic violence shelter, and teaching at the University of Kansas School of Social Welfare.

Hilary Saunders is a training and research officer in the Hadley Center for Adoption and Foster Care Studies at the University of Bristol. She came to Bristol after working for eight years as the children's policy officer for the Women's Aid Federation of England.